Hara Hotel

Hara Hotel

A Tale of Syrian Refugees in Greece

Teresa Thornhill

VERSO

First published by Verso 2018
© Teresa Thornhill 2018

The moral rights of the author have been asserted

1 3 5 7 9 10 8 6 4 2

Verso
UK: 6 Meard Street, London W1F 0EG
US: 20 Jay Street, Suite 1010, Brooklyn, NY 11201
versobooks.com

Verso is the imprint of New Left Books

ISBN-13: 978-1-78663-519-8
ISBN-13: 978-1-78663-522-8 (US EBK)
ISBN-13: 978-1-78663-521-1 (UK EBK)

British Library Cataloguing in Publication Data
A catalogue record for this book is available from the British Library

Library of Congress Cataloging-in-Publication Data

Names: Thornhill, Teresa, author.
Title: Hara Hotel : a tale of Syrian refugees in Greece / Teresa Thornhill.
Description: London ; Brooklyn, NY : Verso, 2018. | Includes index.
Identifiers: LCCN 2017046461 | ISBN 9781786635228 (hardback)
Subjects: LCSH: Refugees – Syria. | Syrians – Greece – Social conditions. |
 Refugee camps – Greece. | Greece – Emigration and immigration – Social
 aspects. | Syria – Emigration and immigration.
Classification: LCC HV640.5.S97 T46 2018 | DDC 305.892/756910495 – dc23
LC record available at https://lccn.loc.gov/2017046461

Typeset in Fournier MT by Hewer Text Ltd, Edinburgh
Printed in the UK by CPI Mackays

To all the brave Syrians I met in Greece;
and to my beloved mum, who taught me compassion.

Contents

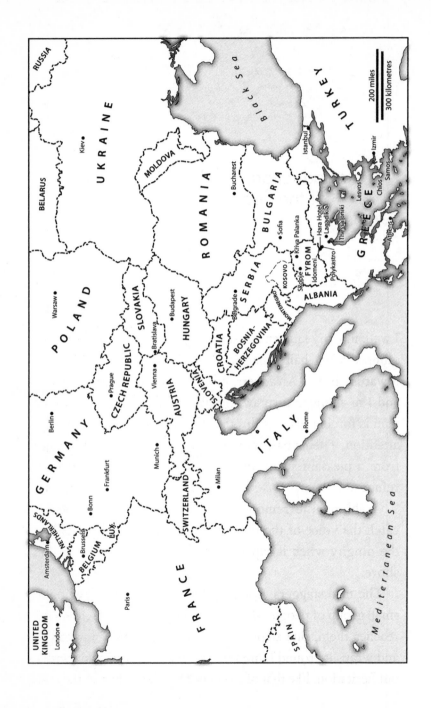

Introduction: A Man Wades out of the Sea, January 2016

I walk into my kitchen and stop in front of the TV in time to glimpse a big hairy man in shorts wading out of the sea towards a beach. An advert, I think, for a Caribbean holiday, and I'm about to turn away, but something in the way the man is forcing his legs through the shallow water holds my attention. Then it dawns on me that the man is not returning from a pleasant swim: the scene is Lesvos and the man a refugee.

Grabbing the remote and turning up the volume, I catch the voice of the reporter: '. . . thirty-four people in the dinghy when it capsized, and just one made it to the shore.'

The man staggers, dragging his legs, his eyes fixed on a small group of people who stand waiting on the beach. As he reaches them, one steps forward with a large stripy towel and wraps it around him. The gesture is tender, made without hesitation, like that of a parent meeting a child at the end of a swimming lesson. Seconds later, the man crumples onto the shingle, too exhausted to stand.

For the next two days, the big man and his narrow escape from death refuse to leave my thoughts. Whether I'm driving, working, hanging out with my teenage son or walking in the woods, my mind replays the sight of him emerging from the sea. Who is he, this sole survivor? Channel Four didn't give any details.

I imagine he's Syrian; and a man of means, judging by his well-covered frame. I push myself to imagine what it would be like to abandon the country where you've spent your entire life, cross a small stretch of water to a new continent, and at the same time lose everyone you love. Two questions plague me: *What is the man feeling now?* And, if the sea has swallowed his wife and children, *how does he go on?* Does he pick himself up, hitch a ride to the registration point and take a ferry to Athens? I picture him sitting on the beach staring at the waves, unable to go forwards or back. The scale of the psychological shock is beyond imagining.

But perhaps the man was travelling by himself, a lone figure in an overloaded dinghy surrounded by strangers. If so, when the vessel hit trouble, he could simply strike out for the shore. He must have been a strong swimmer and his thickset frame would have given him resistance against the cold. Yet even if he was alone, many of his fellow passengers must have been his compatriots. How does he feel, waking the next morning in a tent on Lesvos, reliving the horror of their shouts as they disappeared into the sea?

Ten weeks later, in April 2016, I set off for Greece. Since the previous August, hundreds of European volunteers had travelled there to help the scores of thousands of refugees arriving on the islands. They'd come from Norway, Sweden, Germany, Spain, the Czech Republic, Slovakia and many other countries, using Facebook to fundraise and to encourage others who couldn't join them to send material aid such as second-hand clothing, nappies and tents. On Lesvos, Chios, Samos and other islands they'd stationed themselves on the beaches throughout the winter, guiding the smugglers' dinghies to the safest landing spots and helping the refugees ashore. I'd been with them in spirit for many months, but it had taken time to free myself from the demands of work and family life. Now, at last, I was free to travel. It was the Easter holidays and my son was staying with his dad.

I'd had my doubts, of course. Wasn't it for UNHCR and the big NGOs to receive the refugees? Could a bunch of untrained volunteers really contribute something useful, or might they do more harm than good? From the safety of England it was hard to be sure, but the blogs I'd read suggested that the NGOs were hopelessly overstretched, and that much of the work done by volunteers was invaluable. On Lesvos, over the winter, it had fallen to volunteers to support distraught refugees who'd lost relatives in the course of their journey and to provide them with dry clothes, baby food and sleeping bags. Families had been driven across the island by volunteers in hire cars, to a camp where they were fed and hosted until they were able to register with the Greek authorities.

I'd had to think hard about what skills I could offer. My work as a family lawyer had given me endless experience of supporting people in distress, but it wasn't aid work. What I did have, however, was a working knowledge of Levantine

Arabic. I wasn't bound for the islands, but for northern Greece, where I'd arranged to work with a tiny Norwegian NGO called Northern Lights Aid (NLA). They were based at Hara Hotel, a small camp half a kilometre from the border with the Former Yugoslav Republic of Macedonia (otherwise known by the acronym FYROM).

As more and more refugees poured out of war-ravaged Syria, European governments were desperately looking for ways to stop them leaving the Middle East. On 9 March 2016, in response to border restrictions further north imposed by Austria and some of the Balkan states, FYROM had closed its border to refugees for an unspecified period of time. As a result, some 12,000 people were now marooned in makeshift camps at Idomeni on the Greek side of the border. Most were Syrians, but there were also Iraqis, Afghans, Iranians and Pakistanis. Like the big man on my TV screen, the vast majority had made the perilous sea crossing from Turkey to the Greek islands in inflatable dinghies supplied by smugglers. Greece had allowed them to land and shipped them to Athens on safe seagoing ferries, and from there they'd taken trains and buses to the border.

The refugees were united in the goal of reaching Germany, where they planned to claim asylum; but for the time being they were trapped. In late August 2015, Chancellor Angela Merkel had made a public commitment to receive Syrian refugees, regardless of whether they had passed through another 'safe country' en route. Many Syrians had fled their country heading for Germany, however, long before this commitment was given.

My motivation in volunteering was only in part humanitarian. I was sickened by the British government's refusal to take more than a handful of Syrians and wanted to do my bit to help them. But something else was driving me, too. In my thirties I'd spent a lot of time in Palestine, Lebanon and the Kurdish areas of northern Iraq. I'd loved the searing light, the ancient olive groves of the Levant and the high mountains of Iraqi Kurdistan. My encounters with ordinary people, both Kurds and Arabs, from children to young women to old men, had fascinated me and I'd often been received with great hospitality. I'd only spent a few days in Syria back in 1992, but the crushing of the revolution in 2011, the country's descent into war and the west's failure to support the opposition had left me deeply uneasy. I felt a sense of obligation to do something, however small, to help. And I badly wanted to gain an understanding of what was driving the war. Over the past winter I'd started to read everything I could find on the subject. Now that I thought I'd grasped the broad picture, I wanted to meet and talk with some people who had recent, first-hand experience of the conflict. The safest way to do that was to visit a refugee camp.

I spent two weeks at Hara Hotel in April 2016 and the narrative in Part I is based on my encounters there. One of the refugees I met at Hara, Juwan Azad, a young Syrian Kurd with fluent English, agreed to talk with me in some detail and his personal story runs as a thread throughout the book. Several months after leaving Hara I learned that Juwan had made it to Austria, and in August 2016 I arranged to meet him in a small town south of Vienna. Part II is about his clandestine walk through the mountains of Macedonia and his journey through Serbia and Hungary.

The informal refugee camps at Hara and Idomeni were dismantled in late May 2016 and the remaining inhabitants were moved to government-run camps, mainly in and around Thessaloniki. In January 2017, during a bout of exceptionally cold weather, I returned to Greece, hoping to discover how things had moved on – or not – for some of the Syrians I'd met at Hara. Part III covers that nine-day visit.

The other thread which runs through the book, crucial to making sense of the refugee crisis, is the history and politics of the Syria conflict. I am not a historian or an international relations specialist and did not do original research for this part of the book. I pieced the story together largely through reading and what I have produced is not a blow-by-blow account of the war. Rather, it is an attempt to get to the bottom of a number of questions.

Why and how did the spontaneous and non-violent uprising launched by Syrians in the spring of 2011 metamorphose by the winter of that year into an armed struggle?

How did what began as an internal conflict between the Syrian people and the regime become a major international one, in which a number of proxy wars were being fought on Syrian soil? Who were the main non-Syrian actors, and what was driving them?

What role did the actions (and inaction) of western countries – principally the US, Britain and France – play in the evolution of the conflict? And what was behind the major hands-on role played by Russia?

I also wanted to understand why both the Syrian political opposition and the Syrian fighting formations had come to be dominated by groups which espoused radical forms of Islam.

Then there was the question of Syria's Kurds, many of whom live in areas bordering Turkey. In 2014, Syrian Kurdish separatists declared a de facto autonomous region, Rojava, in north-eastern Syria and their fighters took on a major role in confronting ISIS. How had the Turkish state, generally so hostile to its own Kurdish population, reacted to this development on its border?

Finally, ISIS. Where did it come from? How did ordinary Syrians see it? What was the relationship between ISIS and the Syrian regime? And how did Syrians view the western-dominated air campaign to destroy it?

List of Abbreviations

AKP	Justice and Development Party (Turkey, led by Recip Tayyip Erdogan)
CDS	Council for Democratic Syria
ECHO	European Civil Protection and Humanitarian Aid Operations
FSA	Free Syrian Army
ISIS	Islamic State in Iraq and Syria (also known as Daesh)
KNC	Kurdish National Council
LCC	Local Coordination Committees
MB	Muslim Brotherhood
MC	Military Council
NC	National Coalition for Syrian Revolutionary and Opposition Forces
PKK	Kurdistan Workers' Party (Turkish Kurds)
PYD	Democratic Union Party (Syrian Kurds)
SDF	Syrian Democratic Forces
SMC	Supreme Military Council

SNC	Syrian National Council
UNHCR	United Nations High Commissioner for Refugees
UNSC	United Nations Security Council
YPG	People's Protection Units (men's militia of the PYD)
YPJ	People's Protection Units (women's militia of the PYD)

Part I
Greece, April 2016

1

Hara Hotel and the Family from Homs

My flight to Thessaloniki landed at midnight. After a night in a cheap hotel, I crossed the city on a series of buses. It was a Sunday morning and the sky was as grey as the concrete office blocks that lined the boulevards. Signs of Greece's economic plight were everywhere: litter blowing down the streets, peeling paintwork, shuttered shops. I stood in the aisle of the swaying bus with my backpack heavy on my shoulders, wondering whether my Arabic was going to prove as helpful as I'd hoped. I hadn't used it much in the last ten years, and was hoping the words would come back to me once I was immersed in life at the camp.

At last I reached the stained concrete dome which housed the central bus station. Here, after buying my ticket, I spent two hours sitting at an outdoor café table, surrounded by ashen-faced chain-smokers of all ages, conversing in Greek. I hadn't yet seen any obvious refugees and it bugged me that I didn't know Greek, beyond words of greeting. I would have so liked to start a conversation and steer it towards people's feelings about the arrival of tens of thousands of Syrians, Afghans and Pakistanis in their midst. Instead, I sent a text to my son, and wrote my journal.

My two o'clock bus took me in less than an hour through flat, featureless fields to Polykastro, a small town seventeen kilometres from the border with FYROM. At first the town appeared little more than a sprawl of shops strung along the main road. But the sun came out as I stepped off the bus and I saw that the pavements thronged with visitors, some eating at café tables, others hanging out on benches in the square: cool young people for the most part, average age twenty-five, in skinny jeans and T-shirts. Precious few of them looked Greek, so I assumed they were north Europeans working with the refugees.

My heart sank as I wondered whether I'd be the only middle-aged volunteer. After a few minutes of confusion I found Charly, the Norwegian with whom I'd been communicating by WhatsApp for the last ten days, in a nearby restaurant. She was tall, blonde and astonishingly casual in manner, exactly as she'd been in her messages. 'Hi Teresa, good to meet you, just sit with us while we finish our meal and then we'll give you a lift to Hara.' This seemed to be the policy among the volunteers: no questions asked, and the only expectation was a willingness to work. In terms of health and safety, it would have made a professional aid worker shudder, but I got the impression that Charly knew what she was doing. 'I've booked you a room in our motel, just over the border in FYROM,' she added with a smile. 'It's tacky but cheap, only twelve euros a night.' Charly had been in Greece six months, mainly in Lesvos, where she'd saved the lives of a dozen half-drowned refugees, using the CPR she'd learned as a security guard in Oslo.

Sitting with Charly at the table were her long-term volunteer, Sintra, a warm and bubbly British woman in her thirties; a pale, unassuming twenty-one-year-old American student called Ian; and a trio of men who lived in London: a sharp-boned Irish social worker who kept cracking jokes, a bearded Greek student who chuckled at them, and a French photographer who seemed relieved when I spoke with him in French. These latter three had pitched up the day before and spent just twenty-four hours helping at Hara. The conversation was upbeat and, to my surprise, the refugees didn't get a passing mention. I experienced a moment of doubt. Did these people appreciate the true depths of the situation they were dealing with? Or had they learned to put dark thoughts aside when taking breaks? But their appreciation or otherwise of the trauma which the Syrian refugees were living through was hardly my concern. The atmosphere was friendly and I decided there was no need to get hung up about my age – or theirs.

In the late afternoon we crammed into Charly's car, among boxes of second-hand clothing, tightly packed new tents and bottles of water, for a fifteen-minute high-speed drive to Hara. Charly, I was to learn, was incapable of driving slowly. She told me that about six hundred refugees were living at Hara. It was a satellite to the vast camp at Idomeni and lay just half a kilometre from the border, on a slip road that came off the main international highway. Following the shock of the border closure, refugees had gathered at Hara because, as well as being a petrol station, it was a hotel of sorts with rooms to rent and a restaurant to eat in.

We parked on a country road beside a large forecourt with petrol pumps on which blue, green and orange tents stood in closely packed groups. Some spilled over into the adjacent fields.

It was early evening by now, warm and sunny. Children and men milled about in the road. Women in headscarves sat in open tent doorways. Young men in jeans stood smoking and conversing, nodding and smiling at Charly and Sintra as we got out of the car. A woman perched on a log with her back to us, tending an open fire which burned in the carcass of an oil drum. The sweet smell of woodsmoke wafted towards us. I noticed that the tents on the forecourt were pitched without guy ropes, presumably because pegs couldn't be hammered into the tarmac.

Charly gave each of us a purple vest to wear, with the words 'Northern Lights Aid' printed in white. I felt a bit of a fraud as I put mine on, but perhaps it was best to be identifiable as belonging to an organization. I had no idea what work I'd be doing for Northern Lights; all Charly had said in our WhatsApp exchanges was that my Arabic would be useful.

At the back of the forecourt I saw a broad, single-storey building with a spacious verandah, the hotel-cum-restaurant which gave Hara its name. At the front, on the roof of a mini-supermarket, a giant sign bore a flamboyant, cut-out figure of a chef in Ottoman-style clothing and the words 'WELCOME TO GREECE'.

We hadn't been on the forecourt long when a middle-aged man and his son came up to me. The man looked about fifty, with thick black hair flecked with white. The son was slightly built, with the same luxuriant hair, cut to stand up in spikes,

Rod Stewart style. We exchanged greetings in Arabic and without more ado the man told me they needed a lamp.

'How many are you?' I asked.

The son pointed to some tents to one side of the hotel. 'There are twelve of us, come and see.' I followed them across the forecourt to a group of three tents set up facing each other. In the open doorway of the furthest one a handsome older woman sat cross-legged on a grey blanket, a cotton scarf draped loosely over her long, plaited hair. At the back of the tent another grey blanket was folded neatly, beside a canvas holdall. The woman regarded me with sharp, intelligent eyes, and when I greeted her she smiled.

'It's very dark at night,' the man explained. 'The kids wake up wanting water, and we can't see a thing.' The son stood beside his father, watching me in silence. I couldn't decide if his expression was one of suspicion or shyness.

'I've only just arrived,' I explained, 'so I don't know what Charly's got in her car. I can ask if she has lamps, or torches.'

'Thank you,' the man replied. 'And we need another tent, if possible. My other son and his three boys are sleeping in this one' – he gestured at the tent opposite the one the woman was in. 'It's too small, nobody gets to sleep properly.' As he spoke, two small boys with long hair hurtled past us in pursuit of a football, narrowly missing my ankles.

'It must be very cold at night,' I thought aloud. The tents were small and flimsy, designed for two adults at most in fair weather conditions.

'It's extremely cold!' The woman interjected.

I squatted down to hear her better. 'Is that what you're sleeping on? Just a blanket?'

She pulled a face. 'Just one blanket under us and one on top. And my back is terrible.' She reached her hand behind her and rubbed her lower back.

I frowned. 'That must be very uncomfortable.'

'So can you get us another tent?' the man persisted.

'I'll try,' I replied, wondering who the tents in the car were intended for. 'I'll go and ask Charly. What's your name?'

'Wisam.' The man gestured at the woman. 'This is Hiba, my wife; and my son's called Bassem.'

Hiba was watching me with approval. 'Where did you learn Arabic?' she asked.

'In Palestine.' I hesitated. 'Well, first in Palestine, then I went to Iraq, and then to Lebanon.' I stood up slowly. 'My accent's a bit of a muddle!'

'No, no, you speak well!' She smiled.

'You're from Syria?' Charly had told me there were Iraqis as well as Syrians at Hara, and I couldn't immediately tell from the accent who was who.

'*Eh*,' Wisam replied. In Levantine colloquial Arabic, '*eh*' means 'yes'.

'From which city?'

'From Homs.' Wisam raised his thick eyebrows, studying my face as if to see if I knew what had happened in Homs. One of the smaller cities between Damascus and Aleppo, Homs had risen up early in the revolution and had suffered a prolonged and devastating attack by the regime in response. I wondered at what point the family had left. 'The regime destroyed everything we had,' Wisam announced, as if reading my thoughts. 'Our house, the car, the whole neighbourhood was flattened.' He crossed his forearms and forced them apart, to represent total destruction.

'In 2012?'

'*Eh*. We fled to the border with Turkey. We spent four years there in a camp – me, my wife, our sons, the grandchildren' – he swept his arm in a wide gesture to embrace the inhabitants of all three tents – 'and then the Russians started to bomb.'

The full-scale Russian military engagement in the war had begun in September 2015. Claiming their intention was to weaken ISIS, the Russian air force had in fact targeted more moderate elements of the opposition, with a devastating impact on civilians. For the last few months, people had been fleeing north towards the Turkish border as the Russians hit hospitals and schools.

'It got to the point where we weren't safe even at the Turkish border,' Wisam went on, 'so we crossed to Greece and came here.'

'And now you're stuck?' I was expecting an expression of frustration and despair, but Wisam seemed philosophical. 'We're alive.' He shrugged his shoulders, took out a packet of cigarettes, gave one to Bassem and lit up.

At that moment Sintra walked past, so I left the Homsi family and went to ask her about the lamps. Sintra had thick dark hair, a long face with high-arching eyebrows and olive skin. From her looks, she could have passed as Middle Eastern, but she spoke with a South London accent. Yes, she said, there were small lamps in Charly's car that worked on solar power. But the tent problem was a different story. Charly's policy was to keep the few spare tents for newly arrived families who would otherwise be obliged to sleep under the stars. Around midnight every night she made a tour of the entire camp, checking for newcomers.

After I'd delivered the lamps and explained to Wisam that we couldn't help with the overcrowding, Sintra asked me to take a lamp to a family in the field on the far side of the perimeter fence. To get there I had to walk past the fifteen UNHCR portaloos which were shared by the entire camp, and follow a small, rubbish-strewn path of packed earth through the bushes and trees that formed the petrol station boundary. The smell in this part of the camp, although unpleasant, was not as evil as I'd expected.

Out in the field, shoots of wheat were starting to push their way up in tentative rows, their colour the sappy green of early spring. A fluffy white blossom, like cotton boll, drifted in the air and rolled about in clusters on the ground. I walked a little way along a track at the side of the field, trying to work out where the white blossom was coming from. It lay like clean fluff, in hollows in the roots of trees. Above my head the branches were bedecked with catkins, buds and whiskery blooms in different shades of grey, yellow and green.

Half a dozen tents stood in the corner of the field nearest the road, at the bottom of a small bank. They'd been cleverly pitched with their backs to the traffic, leaving a comfortable space between each tent and with the doorways opening onto the landscape. Two women and a handful of children were seated on the ground, drinking from plastic bottles, while at a little distance an old man poked at a fire which burned in another upturned oil drum. Despite the rubbish littered all over the bank, it was a calm, peaceful scene and I breathed a sigh of relief. In the distance, across the open fields, the land rose in a chain of low mountains.

'*As-salaamu alaikum*,' I called as I approached the women.

'*A leekum issalaam,*' they replied, looking up and smiling. I produced the light and demonstrated how it worked, before complimenting them on their choice of campsite. The women shrugged, seeming a little nonplussed, and I asked where they were from. 'We're Kurds from Syria,' the younger woman said.

Syria has almost two million Kurds, concentrated mainly in the north and north-east of the country. They form a distinct ethnic group with their own language and culture, part of the thirty to thirty-five million Kurds who live in the region. The Kurds are the world's largest group of people who have never had a nation state of their own. The lands which they have inhabited for millennia, now divided by modern state boundaries, are in south-eastern Turkey, north-eastern Syria, northern Iraq, north-western Iran and western Armenia.

I told the women that I'd spent time in Iraqi Kurdistan. The younger woman's face lit up. 'You've been to Iraqi Kurdistan?' She looked at the woman next to her with an expression of astonishment. 'Did you hear that, Mama?'

'In the 1990s,' I added. 'Quite a while ago!' In 1993 I'd spent possibly the most interesting seven weeks of my life travelling through the region to research my book *Sweet Tea with Cardamom*. I'd spent time in the great Kurdish cities and in mountain villages, listening to Kurdish women and men describe how they'd survived maltreatment at the hands of Saddam Hussein.

'In the 1990s?' The younger woman opened her eyes even wider. 'I wasn't even born till 1996!' She giggled. 'Whereabouts did you go?'

'D'hok, Howler, Sulaimani . . .' I'd been to Halabja, too, the town near the border with Iran where Saddam Hussein had gassed up to 5,000 Kurds with chemical warheads in 1988.

'We were in Howler,' the older woman said, 'we fled there for three months, at the beginning of the war. Then we came back to Hasakah, and now we're here.'

'Is Hasakah your home town?' Hasakah was the name of a province and a city in Syria's north-east, with a mixed Kurdish and Arab population.

'We're from a little village in the countryside.'

'In the mountains?'

'No, Hasakah is flat. But you can see the mountains across the border in Turkey.' The woman smiled.

In 1993, when the Kurds of northern Iraq rose up against Saddam Hussein at the end of the second Gulf War, the regime chased them across the mountains into Turkey. Many of the Kurds I'd met while I was there had told me how they'd fled their homes on foot, carrying babies, children and bundles of food, to escape the regime's vengeance. Turkey had opened its border to receive the refugees, but many had spent months in squalid outdoor camps in conditions of great hardship. They'd remained in Turkey until the British and French set up a 'Safe Haven' in the northern part of Iraqi Kurdistan, policing the skies with reconnaissance flights to prevent Saddam resuming his attacks.

The Safe Haven had made possible the establishment of an autonomous Kurdish region in northern Iraq. The Kurds had set up their own parliament and for a few heady months had operated an 'experiment in democracy' in which they governed themselves without interference by Baghdad. The experiment had ended when fighting broke out between the two principal Iraqi Kurdish political parties, but the region remains semi-autonomous to this day. It didn't surprise me to learn that Kurds from Syria had fled there for refuge from the civil war.

Later that evening, Charly drove me to FYROM and dropped me off, with my rucksack, at the Motel Vardar in Gevgelija. We volunteers could cross the border; the refugees could not. Mine was a dingy little room with a filthy floor, twin beds and a mattress that sank before I even lay on it. It was hardly appealing, but after spending a couple of hours at Hara, I appreciated that having a proper roof over my head was something to be grateful for.

Feeling a little claustrophobic, I walked to the window. I'd barely heard of FYROM a week ago, and now I was facing a fortnight living in this tiny, non-EU republic about which I knew nothing. I didn't even know what language they spoke, nor what currency they used. Was it okay for us volunteers to cross the border into Greece every morning and return every night, or would it make us the object of suspicion? And what did the people of FYROM, whose government had closed the border and whose border guards had a reputation for violence, feel and think about the refugees? I would have liked to ply Charly with questions, but she'd gone back to Hara to give out tents to new arrivals.

I had to thump the handle of the dusty casement window to get it open. As the wooden shutters swung out to reveal a neglected garden, a fresh smell of young shoots pushing up through soil drifted into the room and I breathed more easily. Over to the west, a high mountain ridge floated in the distance, a tempting white silhouette; and the bank above the road was studded with scarlet poppies.

I slipped on my shoes and walked out in the dusk to where, a hundred metres to the east, the wide, slow-moving river Vardar flowed past the motel. In certain places the river formed a natural barrier between Greece and FYROM.

I stood on the bank, remembering how, three weeks earlier, I'd watched news coverage of a group of refugees who'd formed a human chain across the river. Standing thigh-deep in the swirling water, they'd passed small, terrified children from person to person. It had been a shocking sight, which had brought home to me more than anything else the utter desperation created by the border closure. Three people had drowned in the course of this incident, which had become known as 'the river crossing'. Those refugees who'd made it to the FYROM bank of the river had been beaten by border guards and sent back to Greece.

2

'We didn't risk our lives for this'

The following afternoon I stood on the international highway a few hundred metres from the Greek border post, with Sintra, Ian and several Syrian boys and young men. It was hot in the sun and I rummaged in my bag for a scarf. Behind us, women and children had gathered on the grass, leaning against the barrier at the central reservation, watching and waiting with an air of anticipation. In front, a few feet away, thirty or so refugees sat cross-legged on the tarmac, staging an impromptu protest. Some had knotted T-shirts over their heads against the sun. Two small tents, one dark pink, one blue, marked the front of the demonstration. A woman sat in the doorway of the blue one, fanning herself with her hand.

The protest blocked the path of the freight lorries travelling from Greece to FYROM. A single line of Greek policemen stood between the demonstrators and the first, massive lorry in a queue which already extended as far as the eye could see. Resembling workmen more than police in their dark blue fatigues, the officers lounged on their plastic riot shields, lighting cigarettes and regarding the refugees with an air of bored benevolence.

I'd spent the morning with Charly, shopping in various supermarkets in Gevgelija, buying large quantities of shampoo, deodorant, hairbrushes and other items which the female refugees had requested. I was still unclear as to whether Charly had a particular role in mind for me, but for the time being I was happy to lend a hand with whatever she was doing. When we reached Hara she'd disappeared, leaving me free to attend the demonstration.

I felt tempted to go and sit among the demonstrators, but a young Syrian Kurd with good English said, 'Don't, it could compromise your position with the Greeks.' I'd noticed Sintra joking with him earlier, and now she introduced him as Juwan Azad. He was of middling height with a neatly trimmed beard and, true to my memory of Kurdish men, his cheekbones and chin were sharply defined and full of character. A long scar followed the line of his left eyebrow. '*I* should go and sit with the demonstrators,' he told me, 'but I'm not going to!' I glimpsed a playful quality in his eyes, mixed with a sharp intelligence.

I didn't want trouble with the Greek police and could see that, since I'd come to Hara as a humanitarian volunteer, I should stick to that role. So I stood quietly watching, drinking from my water bottle and taking photographs. A couple of lads near the front of the demonstration had written a slogan on a piece of cardboard. A tall, thin man in a baseball hat moved through the crowd with a restless, impatient energy. He had a brown, weather-beaten face and greying hair. '*Yalla*,' he cried in Arabic, 'come on all of you, *chant*: OPEN THE BORDER!' He used the English words.

The men got to their feet and the chant rose in a crescendo, while the tall man waved his arms like a musical conductor, urging them to keep in time by stamping his feet. His eyes burned with a passionate energy.

Journalists were beginning to appear, men in jeans with large cameras slung around their necks and runners with television microphones. The atmosphere became more tense when a Greek woman burst through the police line and screamed at the demonstrators. She was trying to drive to FYROM and the sit-in blocked her route.

I glanced at the lad standing beside me, who was somewhere in his mid-teens. He was swigging from a bottle of water and rubbing his head. 'A car hit me,' he explained in Arabic. 'I was out there on the tarmac with the men, when they first sat down, and a man drove his car at us.'

'What, just like that?'

'He wanted to get through and we were in his way.'

'Are you okay?'

'I'm alright, but my head's a bit sore.'

'Have you got a bump?' I reached out and touched the place he'd been rubbing. There was nothing obvious. 'Does it hurt?'

The boy nodded. He had a lovely face with a wide mouth and the beginnings of a moustache on his upper lip. It disgusted me that someone should have driven a vehicle at him. I reached in my bag for my Panadol supply. 'Do you want to take something?'

'*Eh.*'

'Try this, it works really well for headaches. Put it in your water and let it dissolve.'

He opened the bottle and I broke the tablets and dropped them in. 'What's your name?'

'Hasan.' He grinned at me.

'From Syria?'

'From Aleppo.'

'Welcome to Europe!' I smiled back. In the Arab world, when someone asks where you're from and you tell them, they say '*Ahlan wa Sahlan*' (Welcome), by way of welcoming you to their country. I was saying it now to all the Syrians I met. Greece wasn't my country, but it certainly wasn't theirs, and I felt it was important to tell them that, as far as I was concerned, they were welcome in Europe.

'How old are you, Hasan?'

'Sixteen.'

I smiled. 'Same as my boy.'

'Yeah?' His grin widened. 'Is he here?'

'No, he's at home with his dad. He's got exams coming up and he has to study.'

Hasan pursed his lips. 'Yeah,' he said. 'Exams. Of course.'

Behind us a group of young women had heard me speaking Arabic. 'Where's she from?' they asked Hasan.

I turned round to face them. 'I'm from Britain. And you?'

'From Syria!' The young spokeswoman wore a long dark green coat dress and a matching headscarf. She had prominent cheekbones, a high forehead and smooth, beautiful skin which glowed with health, despite her circumstances. 'Where did you learn Arabic?'

I gave my little speech about my funny confusion of accents.

The woman beamed at me. 'No, no, your Arabic's not funny,' she protested. 'We thank God that somebody speaks our language! We don't know Greek and we don't speak English!'

I asked the women how long they'd been at Hara.

'Forty days,' one replied. 'Some of us a bit less, but most of us forty days.'

'You must be exhausted!' Much as I love camping, I couldn't imagine sleeping on that unforgiving tarmac even for a week, with nowhere to cook and nowhere to wash. And for most of the previous forty days, it had rained.

'We *are* exhausted!' The women stared at me. 'But what can we do? We're waiting for the border to open!'

A short woman in a grey headscarf had taken out her phone and was scrolling through images. 'Look,' she said, thrusting the phone towards me. 'I took this video on the way here.' On the screen I saw a tightly packed cluster of men, women and children, their faces taut with fear, lurching this way and that as their rubber dinghy was tossed by the waves. 'We were so scared,' the woman added, 'we thought we were going to die. And when we reached the island, we had to wade to the beach through water which came up to here.' She held the palm of her hand against her midriff.

'Is that the smuggler at the back, holding the rudder?' I pointed to a thin figure at the back of the group.

'Smuggler? No, no!' She wagged her finger at me. 'The smuggler doesn't travel on the boat! All the smuggler does is take the money, supply the boat and tell the people where to find it on the beach.'

This was news to me. 'So who drives the boat?'

'The *people* do! On my boat, it was a boy, he wasn't more than fifteen, sixteen!'

I gulped. It was horrifying to imagine a child refugee from a near land-locked country like Syria, Afghanistan or Pakistan having to operate an over-crowded dinghy on the open sea.

'You see!' The woman in the long green coat dress leaned towards me again, her eyes wide with anger. 'We didn't risk our lives on those boats to then have to sit here in Greece, day after day, week after week.'

'Of course not.' Uncomfortable, I glanced back at the demonstration. The tall man was on his feet again, rousing the men to a new chant.

'When *will* they open the border?' another woman asked, looking at me sharply. She had a toddler in her arms and wisps of hair were escaping through the sides of her head-scarf. She was very pale, with dark shadows under her eyes.

I shrugged my shoulders. 'I wish I knew! I guess it's up to the Macedonians.' The FYROM parliament had passed a decree a few days earlier saying they would keep their border closed to refugees until the end of 2016; but I wasn't aware of that yet.

'My husband's in Germany,' the woman went on. 'He's been there eight months. I want to join him, but I can't if they don't open the border.'

'No,' I replied. 'And you've got a child with you.'

'I've got three!' She tossed her head in the direction of a pair of kids who were running about on the grass.

I looked at her again. To my eye she wasn't older than her early twenties. A second later, she started to cry. Tears coursed down her face and her friends bunched up close around her. 'I'm so sorry you're going through this,' I murmured. 'You've been through hell in Syria, hell on your journey to Greece, and now you're stuck.' I paused for breath. 'But it's good that your husband's in Germany. Has he applied for asylum?'

The woman blew her nose. 'He's applied, but they've not yet made a decision.'

'Once they do, I think he'll be able to bring you and your children to join him.' With a husband in Germany, I thought she should qualify for the Family Reunification programme, which required that you had a close family member already legally in a European state. 'I'm no expert,' I went on, 'but I think you've a good chance.'

The woman in the green dress spoke again. '*Inshallah!*' (God willing). She stared at me. 'But if they don't open the border, how is she going to get there?'

The afternoon shadows were lengthening when I scrambled down the embankment of the highway with Hasan and Ian and crossed the small side road to Hara Hotel. Small children wandered in the road, their parents apparently oblivious to the intermittent cars which swooped down off the main highway and passed the camp at thirty miles an hour. Young men stood on the roadside, smoking, chatting and occasionally turning aside to kick a stray football back onto the forecourt.

Petrol was no longer sold at Hara, but the yellow canopy roof under which the pumps had stood was still in place, with 'KA OIL' emblazoned in blue plastic letters. Twenty or so tents had been pitched beneath, crammed together as if for safety. Beyond the canopy, the mini-supermarket-cum-café still functioned, though it sold little more than ice creams, cigarettes and pricey plastic sandals. The Greek manager sat all day behind a massive desk, glowering at the refugees who occupied the café chairs and tables, chain smoking, conversing in languages he couldn't understand and rarely, if ever, buying a drink.

Three or four sleek white taxis had parked in front of the hotel, as if waiting to drive an invisible but affluent clientele to local amenities. The drivers stood about in the sunshine, smoking, chatting and – as I later discovered – observing the comings and goings of the refugees and volunteers, in order to report on them to the authorities. In front of this impromptu cab rank, in an area between the taxis and the road, boys of all ages played football.

As I followed Ian and Hassan, I was struck by the amount of rubbish on the ground. Plastic bottles, dirty wipes, cigarette butts and discarded food containers rolled around on the tarmac and accumulated into little mounds against any available wall, alongside the wedges of fluffy white blossom. Several large metal dustbins, filled to the brim, occupied a wall at the back of the supermarket, with black plastic bin bags stacked up beside them. A tap was fixed to the wall beyond the dustbins, the only free source of water for the refugees.

A white van, marked with the letters 'MSF' (Médecins Sans Frontières) was parked to one side of the forecourt, and a queue of people stood in line waiting to see the doctor. As we passed by I noticed, near the front, a very old woman seated in a wheelchair. She was small and brown and her cheeks were hollow. She sat upright in the chair, with a pale orange headscarf draped loosely over her head and shoulders, her eyes sharp little points of anxiety. For a moment my heart stood still. Something about those sunken cheeks reminded me of how my own mum had looked in the weeks before she died, just one short year ago.

When we reached the back of the forecourt, Hasan said goodbye, Ian went in search of Charly and I climbed the steps to the hotel verandah, none too sure what I was supposed to be doing. It was very tempting simply to move around the camp, observe the goings on and chat with anyone who felt like talking.

There were never less than fifty refugees sitting, standing or walking about on the verandah, and, at busy times of day, probably a hundred. It was a fine spot for meeting, smoking, conversing and being somewhere other than in the confines of your tent. The smell of cheap tobacco made me feel slightly sick.

At one end of the verandah, double doors opened into the hotel bar and restaurant. This must be an even better spot for meeting, smoking and conversing, especially in cold weather. The restaurant alone could seat 150 people. Perhaps in better days it had been a place where tourists newly arrived from FYROM would have a celebration meal, their first in Greece; but today the entire clientele consisted of refugees.

Seated behind a counter I spotted a character who I thought must be Hercules, the owner of Hotel Hara. Charly had told me about him. He was rummaging through a file while shouting into a telephone receiver which was hooked under his chin. A tall, bulky, middle-aged man, he had sagging shoulders, a paunch and a lined, rubbery face. His bottom lip jutted out beyond his top one, forming a curious

point at the centre. His hair was thick and curly in the
manner of a Greek god and he wore an expression of
enraged despair.

As the older brother of the supermarket manager, Hercules
was the patriarch of the family. The other volunteers would
later tell me they thought him a deeply unpleasant man; but
I was never sure. It can't be easy, having spent your life
building up a family business, to witness it suddenly overrun
with 'customers' who are mostly unable to pay and unwilling to leave. It was true that a small number of refugee families were renting Hercules' half-dozen hotel rooms, but the
vast majority were camping for free on the forecourt and in
the adjoining fields.

Hercules' right-hand man was a slightly younger character who went by the name of Stassos. Stassos was as tall as
Hercules and equally flabby. He spent most of his time shuf-
fling about in a pair of moccasins between the restaurant and
the kitchen, the smoke from a lit cigarette trailing from his
fingers, his belly bulging through his dirty white T-shirt.
When he wasn't at the counter conferring with Hercules, he
was snarling at refugees or firing orders at the mainly female
kitchen staff.

The small bar at the back of the restaurant had comfortable seats and a large television. I was on my way there now
for a cup of hot, sweet tea. The heavily made-up Greek
woman serving could not have been nicer to me. She smiled
when she saw me coming, laid her cigarette in the ashtray
and enacted an elaborate mime to establish exactly how
much sugar I wanted. Perhaps there was something a little
conspiratorial in her attitude – *hello love, you're middle-aged
like us, you're European and we know you're trying to help; you*

can see that we're going through hell with this crazy invasion of
refugees, but we won't take it out on you! I wasn't too sure
we'd agree on many things had we been able to have a proper
conversation in a language we both understood, but I made
a point of thanking her, in my minimal Greek, for her
kindness.

As I stepped away from the bar, my eye landed on Sintra,
who was sitting on one of the black plastic sofas with Juwan,
the young Kurd I'd seen her with at the demonstration. He
was giggling as he showed her something on his phone.
Sintra glanced up and waved. 'Hiya, Teresa!' she cried.
'Come and join us.'

I picked up my tea and sat down beside her on the arm of
the sofa.

'Juwan was just showing me a film of his cousin's baby,'
she explained. 'It's so sweet, you've got to see it.'

Still chuckling, Juwan held out the phone to me. 'Look,'
he cried, 'see this boy!'

I watched as a sturdy-looking baby in a white babygro,
lying on a rug, rolled from his back onto his side with an air
of determination. But each time he succeeded, a woman's
hand pushed him back. After a few seconds the little face
puckered up and he started to cry.

'Why won't she let him roll over?' I asked.

'He's trying to roll towards the TV, and she doesn't want
him to. She's so mean to him!' Juwan's expression was
indignant.

'Poor baby,' I smiled. 'Where are they?'

'Damascus.'

'Is that where you're from?'

'Yes.'

'But you're a Kurd?'

'Lots of Kurds live in Damascus.'

The Syrian Kurds intrigued me, so I asked if he'd mind telling me a bit about them.

'Sure, I love to talk about the Kurds. Where shall I begin?' The playful look I'd noticed at the demonstration returned to his eyes.

'Are you from a political family?' It was awkward talking across Sintra, so I picked up my tea and moved to a vacant armchair on Juwan's side of the sofa.

'Yes and no.' He jiggled his head from side to side as he weighed up the question and I was struck again by the strong, sharp lines of his forehead and chin. 'Yes, in that my family were very proud to be Kurdish. When I was growing up, we all had a strong emotional attachment to the idea of a Kurdish state.' He rested an elbow on the arm of the sofa. 'But no, my family was not directly involved in any political party.'

Juwan's father and uncles had all been to university and there were writers and poets in the extended family.

'They wrote in Kurdish?'

'Of course. My parents are fluent in Kurdish, Arabic and English.'

'Ah, that's why your English is so good!'

Juwan nodded. 'My parents started to teach me English when I was five or six. They used to show me things and say, "This is a tree" or, "This is a bird".' His eyes seemed to grow larger as he spoke and the scar above his left eyebrow shifted towards his hairline. 'I loved the sound of English words from the first moment I heard them, although in those days I couldn't pronounce them very well. Instead of "This is", for example, I used to say "*Chiẑ biẑ*".' . . . He caught my eye and laughed.

It wasn't hard to imagine a six-year-old version of Juwan, following his parents around a comfortable house and garden, picking up English words with the extraordinary absorbency of a young child's brain. Like most Kurds, Juwan's family were Sunni Muslims, but nowadays his siblings didn't practise their faith and some of his relatives were atheists.

'How about you?' I asked.

'Till I was in my teens, I was a believer. But then I read Descartes, and I lost my faith! His *cogito ergo sum* made me an atheist.' Juwan looked from Sintra to me, as if wondering what we would make of this. 'But much later, after I'd been through a lot of things, I came back to Islam.'

'And what about politics?'

'When I went to university, in Raqqa, I became a student activist. My activities were more cultural than overtly political. I was an independent, not attached to any political party. A few of us used to organize events with Kurdish music and poetry.'

After all the media coverage of Raqqa as the headquarters of ISIS and its 'caliphate', I found it hard to imagine it as a city where students had once lead a normal life. 'Was it safe to hold parties?' I asked. These days music was banned by ISIS; in the past, I thought the regime might have seen the celebration of Kurdish culture as a threat to national identity.

'Safe enough. We invited Arab friends along, people who had connections, to protect us. We held a few of those parties, and then we stopped.' He put his tea down on the table. 'The

PKK approached me around that time, wanting me to edit their newspaper. But I didn't want to, so I refused.'

The PKK, known in English as the Kurdistan Workers' Party, is the dominant Kurdish separatist organization in Turkey.[1] In the 1980s and 1990s its leader, Abdullah Ocalan, had spearheaded an all-out war against the Turkish state. Much to the chagrin of the Turkish government, Hafez al-Assad had allowed the PKK to run training camps for its fighters in both Syria and Syrian-occupied Lebanon. Due to this, in 1999, Turkey had threatened to invade Syria and in response Hafez had forced the PKK to leave; but the organization had retained a major influence in Kurdish areas of the country.

Juwan cleared his throat. 'The PKK asked me three times to edit their paper, and each time I refused. After my third refusal, I started to receive threats. That was in 2008.'

'So it was dangerous?' I glanced at Sintra, wondering if she was interested in what Juwan was saying. She was listening with rapt attention.

'In those days,' Juwan went on, 'if someone even heard you curse Abdullah Ocalan, just curse him, you might be killed by the PKK. So they didn't like my refusal. After that, I stopped holding the cultural parties. I went on studying, but the teaching was poor. After two years, I packed in my studies.'

'What d'you think of the PKK now?'

'I see the PKK as the Kurdish ISIS. Although they're atheists, they have the same intolerant mentality as ISIS, the same way of treating people – they're a bunch of tyrants.' He paused. 'And the PYD[2] are no better.' Juwan was perched now on the edge of the sofa, looking at me intently as he spoke, as if to make sure I was following. I listened in silence, nodding from time to time. So far, I liked everything about this young man. His command of idiomatic English astonished me.

'So, Juwan,' Sintra said after a pause, 'how did you become a refugee?'

Now he flashed Sintra a smile, joining the thumb of his right hand to the fingertips. 'I'll tell you,' he began, shaking his hand in a gesture which meant *be patient*, 'but first you have to understand the background.'

We looked at him expectantly.

'As you know, the crisis started in March 2011. After people saw the uprisings in Tunisia and Egypt and Libya, they wanted something to happen in Syria; but for the previous forty years, the mass of the Syrian people had not been politically organized. There were Syrians living *outside* Syria who were politically organized, but the people *inside* didn't know them. The Syrian Kurds were organized, of course; but when the revolution started, they held back.' Juwan looked from Sintra to me. 'D'you know how the revolution started?'

I did know, but I was interested to see how he would tell the story.

'The first big demonstration took place in February in Damascus.'

'Were you there?'

Juwan sucked his teeth. 'No, no, I was in Raqqa, at the other end of the country.'

I felt a curious blend of relief and disappointment. I'd naively imagined that everyone of student age would have been at the centre of the action, wherever that was.

'Then there was a "Day of Rage" on 15 March,' Juwan went on, 'when thousands of people demonstrated in lots of big cities.'

'Peacefully?' Sintra's eyes were on Juwan.

'Sure, totally peacefully, *selmiyyeh* (peaceful) was even one of the slogans. People were demanding the release of political prisoners and the lifting of the decades-old emergency law.' He caught his breath. 'But the thing that started the revolution so that there was no going back was the events in Deraa, right down in the far south of Syria.' Juwan looked from Sintra to me. 'It's a big irony that Deraa is in a very tribal area, where everyone used to support the regime. One day in March 2011, some kids wrote slogans on the wall of their school.' He cleared his throat. 'They were just young kids, thirteen, fourteen. You know what the regime did to these kids?'

I nodded in grim silence: the regime had detained and tortured the children, pulling out their fingernails.[3] In recording the history of the revolution, there is no way to avoid this stark and horrific fact.

'Initially the kids' families didn't want to challenge the regime, so they went to a tribal head to ask for their kids back. The guy was a head of political security. You know how Sunni tribesmen wear the traditional Arab headdress, the *keffiyah*, held in place with a black ring? The men of the families took off their black rings and put them on the guy's table and then they asked for their kids to be released. But the guy was an asshole. He swept the black rings onto the floor, saying, "If you need kids, go and make new kids." This was a huge insult to the honour of those families.'

'It's unbelievable,' Sintra whispered.

'Yes,' Juwan replied in a matter-of-fact tone, 'but it's true.' I observed his expression, grave but calm, and reflected that I didn't know how he'd spent the previous five years. To me he appeared young and empathic, but perhaps he'd seen so much horror as to numb his emotions.

'Were the children ever released?'

'No.' He took his phone out of his pocket and began to turn it over with his fingers. 'So then the demonstrations began. 18 March was the first Friday, "The Friday of honour". There were big protests in Deraa and in Homs, with the slogan "*hamiya haramiyya*" (The protector is a thief), directed against the governor of Deraa. And every Friday after that there were protests. Each town that demonstrated went out in support of other towns that were protesting.' Juwan looked up at us. 'When the protests started, many old men were crying with happiness. After forty years of repression, people had lost hope; and now they saw a chink of light.'

I knew that the regime had responded to the peaceful demonstrations with extreme violence. Demonstrators had been bludgeoned to death by the regime's *shabbiha* (organized thugs) or shot dead by snipers. In just the first three months of the uprising, nearly three thousand people were detained.[4] The regime made a point of returning the mutilated corpses of protesters who had died under torture to their families. Children were treated no better than adults:[5] on 25 May 2011 the body of a thirteen-year-old boy arrested a month earlier in a protest against the siege of Deraa was returned to his family with gunshot wounds, cigarette burns, broken bones and a severed penis.[6]

I had tried to read accounts of what went on in the regime's detention centres,[7] although I found the material unbearable. I felt I knew enough to understand the extraordinary courage it must have taken to go out onto the streets, even in a crowd of many thousands.

'So what about you?' I asked at last.

'Me, I was watching and waiting to see how things would develop. I was due to start my military service the following March, in 2012. By September 2011 the situation was so bad that I knew I couldn't go into the army and fight for the regime. If I had done, I would have been expected to shoot my own people. So in December 2011 I started to make plans to leave the country.'

'How old were you then?'

'Twenty two. A relative of my mother promised my family that he would put me up at his home in a coastal city in Turkey and help me get to Europe.' Juwan put away the phone, took his left hand in his right and cracked his knuckles, one by one. 'I was never happy about this plan. I'd not met the guy personally and I felt uncomfortable about throwing myself on his hospitality; but my parents insisted, saying they'd got it all arranged. I had to leave Syria as quickly as possible, and I didn't have a better option. So I packed a bag and got myself ready. It was difficult to say goodbye to my family and I couldn't take much with me: I had to leave all my books and my laptop behind.'

'That must have been hard.'

'It was all hard, of course.' As he spoke, a young man of about Juwan's age strode up, nodded at me and Sintra, and began to speak to Juwan very fast in Arabic. Within seconds Juwan rose to his feet. 'I'm sorry, you two, I've got to go and interpret for a patient at the MSF medical van.' He jerked his head in the direction of the forecourt. 'Their interpreter's gone home early and they're stuck.' He smiled at Sintra. 'Thanks for the tea.'

'Sure,' she replied. 'But we want to hear the rest of the story. Promise you'll tell us another time?'

After Juwan had gone, I joined Sintra on the sofa. After all my months reading about the Syrian revolution, it was a shock suddenly to come face to face with someone who had lived through it. I was glad that Juwan hadn't been a demonstrator; if he had, chances were he would not be at Hara now.

Sintra was shaken, too. 'We don't know we're born, do we? Our lives in the UK are *so* easy.'

I nodded.

'I mean, life doesn't always feel easy in the moment, but compared to what these people are living through . . .' She jutted her chin at the melee of people moving to and fro in the crowded bar.

Sintra was returning to the demonstration, so I got up and went to the back door, curious to see what lay behind the hotel. Yet more tents were arrayed along the wall of the building, their occupants young Pakistani men, the only group at Hara travelling without women and children.

Ducking under a washing line, I found myself once more at the front of the building. Tired and a little dazed, I stared at another confusion of tents pitched crazily close together. Here, on the far side of the forecourt from the taxis, a group of Afghan families had made their pitch. In front of them, closer to the road, I found more Syrian Arabs and a handful of Iraqis. And then, at the very front of the forecourt, and to the left, the ground sloped sharply down into another field. Here the campers were Syrian Kurds along one side and Afghans on the other.

I returned to the bar and asked the friendly Greek woman if I could use the hotel toilet, the door of which was locked. She told me to speak to Stassos, who I found sitting at the counter in Hercules' seat.

Stassos rummaged around with a surly air, then thrust a small bunch of keys in my direction. I unlocked the door expecting to have a single toilet to myself, and was surprised to find a little cloakroom in which two giggling young women were washing their hair in the sink and a third was brushing her teeth. All three were dressed in skinny jeans and loose tops. They were all Syrian and I wondered whether Stassos's rationale for allowing them access was the fact that they were young and pretty.

When I came out of the toilet, the woman who'd been brushing her teeth asked me how she could get permission to join her husband in Sweden. I would get a lot of requests for advice, as word got round that I spoke Arabic. The woman looked twenty at most.

'Has he got asylum?' I asked.

'Not yet, but he's made the application.'

I thought for a moment. 'Do you have your marriage certificate with you?'

'Yes, yes, I've got all my papers.' She gazed at me intently, urging me to give her an answer.

'Look, I'm not an immigration lawyer.' I smiled at the woman. 'But I think your husband should be able to bring you to join him, so long as he gets his asylum.'

She brightened. '*Inshallah*. But what do I have to *do*?'

'Are you in touch with him by phone?'

'Facebook.'

'Tell him to go and see a lawyer, and tell the lawyer that you've made it as far as Greece and he wants you to join him.' I smiled. 'I think you'll be alright. Where are you from?'

'Afrin.' This was a mainly Kurdish town to the north of Aleppo.

'Any children?'

The woman clicked her tongue, in that inimitable Middle Eastern gesture which simply means 'no', but which, to an English ear, contains a subtle implication that the question is a daft one.

'I'm so scared they'll send me back to Turkey,' she went on.

'We're all terrified of being sent back,' her friends at the basin chimed in. One girl was wrapping a towel round the wet head of the other. 'We'd rather die than go back to Turkey.'

I shook my head and stared at them. This was strong language for people who had almost certainly had close brushes with death in Syria. 'No, no,' I said quickly, 'they shouldn't send you back.'

'Are you *sure*?' Three pairs of eyes implored me to give categorical advice.

'Well, let's see.' I went to the free basin to wash my hands, and one of the girls passed me a cake of soap. 'What date did you all arrive in Greece?'

On 18 March 2016, the EU had struck a deal with Turkey aimed at stopping the flow of refugees into Europe. Under its terms, those who had reached Greece prior to midnight on 19 March were at liberty in Greece and free to move on northwards to their chosen country of asylum, should FYROM decide to open the border. Those who arrived *after* the deadline, by contrast, were detained on arrival and liable to deportation to Turkey. 'Did you arrive before or after the twentieth March deadline?'

'Before,' said the woman with the husband in Sweden. 'On the sixth.'

'Us too,' said one of the girls at the basin. 'I came on the eighth and Haifa here came on the thirteenth.'

'Then I don't think they should send you back, so long as you apply for asylum. It's people who came *after* the deadline who are at risk of being sent back.' As I spoke I realized how little I knew about the detail of the EU–Turkey Agreement. Given that the border with FYROM was closed, where and when were the refugees supposed to make asylum claims? And to whom?

When I returned the keys to Stassos, he glanced at my purple Northern Lights vest, jerked his chin in the direction of the verandah and said in English, 'Chairs! All broken! *You buy!*' I smiled politely and asked him which chairs he was talking about. He beckoned to me to follow him through the double doors, and picked up a dirty white plastic chair with a broken leg. 'All broken,' he repeated. 'New chairs. *You buy!*'

I had no idea what Charly's policy was on broken chairs, so I smiled again, said I would find out and let him know. Later I learned that Charly had already promised to buy thirty replacement plastic chairs for the verandah, but not until after the refugees had left – whenever that might be. When I passed this on to Stassos the next day, he seemed satisfied. But from then on, at least once a day, he would approach me in the restaurant with furrowed brow and put the same question. 'New chairs! When?'

Keen to remain in his good books, for the sake of being allowed to continue to use the indoor toilet, I invariably smiled as sweetly as I could and repeated Charly's promise.

3
The Assad Dynasty

By seven p.m. I was hungry and tired. The sit-in was still going on, making it impossible to cross the border by car, so I decided to walk back to the motel. It wasn't more than five kilometres and I love walking.

The line of stranded container lorries on the highway was now several kilometres long. The engines stood idle and the drivers had blended away into the soft spring evening, evidently accepting that they were not able to continue with their journeys north. I slipped past the line of seated refugees and set out across the tarmac no-man's land between the front of the demonstration and the Greek border post, enjoying that especially deep hush of a thoroughfare brought to a standstill. Yellow catkins and grey-green, whiskery buds dangled from the trees on the verges; a white haze was settling over the mountains to the west.

When I reached the Greek border post, I handed my passport to a frowning official who sat at a small window. He found the page with my photo and thrust the passport into the jaws of a scanner.

'Where you going?'

'Macedonia.' I thought this was obvious.

He shot me a look of fury. 'Skopje! There's no state called "Macedonia" – Macedonia is here in Greece!' He made a sweeping gesture with his arm, indicating the land to the south of the border.

'Okay,' I replied, 'Skopje. So sorry. But I'm only going to Motel Vardar.'

The man snapped my passport shut and thrust it through the window.

On either side of the border post, a ten-foot-high double-wire fence stretched in both directions as far as the eye could see. Sand covered the space of two or three metres between the two walls of wire. Beyond the FYROM side of the fence, another tarmac no-man's land filled half a kilometre, flanked to one side by a series of neon-lit casinos on a man-made hill. I set off slowly, half amused, half ashamed about my faux pas. I liked the Greeks and felt inclined to sympathize with the man's fury about the appropriation of a name by this new state which had emerged on his country's northern border.

Trudging over the tarmac in front of the casinos, I wondered if I was being watched or filmed. I hadn't expected to be crossing borders, certainly not alone and not on foot. But the evening air was pleasant on my cheeks and beneath a superficial sense of unease I felt quietly elated. It had taken some bottle to leave the safe familiarity of my home in England, but Hara was proving more fascinating than I'd dared imagine and my rusty Arabic was beginning to flow.

I was just starting to wonder if I'd reach the motel before dark, when a taxi pulled up beside me. A young man in the passenger seat leaned out of his open window. 'Good evening,' he said in German-accented English. 'I'm going to Gevgelija, would you like a ride?'

I glimpsed a rucksack wedged between his knees and asked if he was a volunteer.

'No, no, I'm a tourist,' he replied, 'just passing through. Like you, I had to walk across the border because of the demonstration, and then I found this taxi.'

Instinct told me he was genuine, so I thanked him and climbed into the back. Ten minutes later I waved goodbye, crossed the motel garden and mounted the steps to the entrance. I was ravenous.

The dining room was impossibly spacious, stretching beyond the motel into a glass extension where the light glowed green from the leafy trees that overhung it. Two hundred people could have dined at once, at dark wooden tables laid with pale pink cloths and excessive quantities of cutlery. But tonight the only customers were a couple of men in business suits who sat at a table against the back wall.

A screen hung from the ceiling in the centre of the room, on which a stream of jarring 1990s music videos played in unrelenting succession. I chose a table as far away as possible and watched the grey-haired head waiter hurry to my table, impeccably dressed in a faded pinstripe suit and pale pink bow tie. His hands shook as he removed the second place setting, smiled politely and asked in his limited English if I wanted to eat fish or meat. The fish, he said, was excellent, freshly caught that morning.

While I was waiting for my bream, I thought about the three or four hundred Syrian refugees who would be sleeping in tents at Hara tonight. They were only a tiny fraction of the almost five million who had fled the country since 2011, and the six million who had suffered internal displacement. If someone asked me to explain the chain of historic events that had led to this catastrophic uprooting of an entire people, I wondered where I would begin.

An obvious starting point would be the carving up of the Ottoman province of Greater Syria by Britain and France in 1920 in the wake of World War I. Ignoring Arab demands for independence, the Allies had drawn arbitrary boundaries for what would eventually become the modern states of Syria, Lebanon, Iraq and Jordan. The French were granted a mandate over the newly created state of Syria in 1920 and maintained their presence there by the use of force until 1946, exploiting the time-honoured colonialist policy of 'divide and rule' to inhibit the growth of nationalist sentiment among Syria's disparate ethnic groups and religious sects. From 1925 to 1927 they used air power against civilians to crush a major rebellion, in a move which foreshadowed the tactics adopted ninety years later by Bashar al-Assad.

But perhaps it wasn't necessary to delve so far into the past. In order to grasp the basic causes of the revolution and war, one needed a picture of the ethnic groups, sects and tribes that make up the Syrian population; an understanding of the character of the Assad dynasty, which has dominated the country from 1970; and a grasp of the enormous regional and international pressures with which it has had to contend.

The Syrian people are predominantly Arab, with a large Kurdish minority – just under 10 per cent of the pre-war Syrian population of twenty-two million – of which both Juwan Azad and the family I'd met in the field on my first night at Hara formed a part. There are also Turkomen, who are ethnic Turks, the descendants of families who found themselves on the 'wrong' side of the arbitrary border drawn between northern Syria and the new state of Turkey in 1920; Armenians, the descendants of families who fled to Syria from the massacre of their people in Turkey in the early twentieth century; and Circassians. In the north-east of the country, there are Bedouin tribes.

In terms of religious and sectarian affiliation, around two-thirds of Syrians are Sunni Muslims.[1] Syria has relatively small minority groups who follow various branches of Shi'a Islam.[2] The most significant in size is the Alawites, who form around 12 per cent of the population and from whom the al-Assad dynasty is drawn. Geographically, their heartland is the mountainous north-west corner of Syria, though the role played by Alawites in running the country from 1970, particularly in the army and security forces, has resulted in many moving to Damascus. Alawites are regarded by some Sunni Muslims as apostates (former Muslims who have abandoned their faith). Alawites with close links to the regime lived privileged lives in pre-revolution Syria; the majority, however, are poor.

The Druze are another minority within Shi'ism and form around 3 per cent of the Syrian population. They are a close-knit community, with a geographical concentration to the south of Damascus. They, too, are regarded as apostates by some Sunnis. The Ismailis are a third Shi'a minority and the

Twelvers a fourth. Each of these sects represents about 1 per cent of the population.

Syria also has a number of small Christian communities, some of which are Catholic, but many of which belong to the Eastern Orthodox churches. Christians make up 8 per cent of the population. In two villages close to Damascus, the inhabitants still speak Aramaic, the language of Christ (although many have fled in the course of the war). In the past, there was a Syrian Jewish community, but, by 2005, fewer than one hundred Jews remained in Syria.[3]

I wondered about the sectarian affiliations of the Hara Syrians. Were they mostly Sunni? And were there some Christians and Shi'a among them? Hara was a curious melting pot in that most of the people there, even within the Syrian group, had not known each other before arriving. They had made their journeys through Turkey and across the sea to Greece either alone or in family groups. Chance had thrown them together on the forecourt at Hara, and although some had bumped into people they knew from their home cities of Homs, Aleppo, Damascus and Afrin, most friendships struck at Hara were between people whose paths had never crossed before. In my day and a half at the camp, I'd formed the superficial impression that people were getting along with one another remarkably well; and I was clear it was not my place to go around asking which sects people belonged to.

When the French finally left Syria in 1946, the country was ill-equipped for democratic self-government. Organized political parties were in their infancy; wealth and power were in the hands of a relatively small number of 'notable' families and senior figures in the army, while the majority of Syrians lived in poverty on the land and in the cities. Broadly speaking, the people were conservative in their outlook and deeply attached to tradition and – for the most part – Islam. Over the next two decades the political parties that emerged included Communists, Islamists and nationalists of various hues, and power was transferred through a series of coups d'état. Gradually, the Ba'ath Party became by far the most influential force in Syrian politics. Developed by the Orthodox Syrian Christian Michel Aflaq, Ba'athism was a blend of Arab nationalism and socialism which aimed to bring about radical change to the power structures of Arab society. It was from within the Ba'ath Party that Hafez al-Assad rose to power, becoming president in a coup d'état in 1970.

Assad came from an Alawite peasant family and had grown up in a home with neither electricity nor running water. A cold but extremely clever man, after ten months training as a pilot in the USSR, he had made his way up through the ranks of the armed forces. Shortly after his accession to power, he amended the constitution to make the Ba'ath the leading party in the Syrian state, while simultaneously remoulding it to ensure that its main function was to support his role as leader. From now on the only route to success in Syria was via party membership. The power of the 'notable' families was finished, as was that of other political parties. Large numbers of Alawites were recruited into the armed forces and the security apparatus under Assad, although some Sunnis were also given positions of power. The *mukhabarat*, or security services, were exempted from judicial control, enabling them to torture and kill dissidents with legal impunity. At the head of the system, real control of the country was vested in Assad alone.

My clearest memory of my visit to Syria in 1992 is of the ubiquitous, life-size posters of Hafez al-Assad on display in public places. From high on the walls of every coffee shop and bank and on street hoardings, he stared down at his people, tall, stiff and square-shouldered in a grey business suit, his face pink and lined, his gaze expressionless. I had found those posters chilling, a stark reminder that the man had eyes and ears everywhere.

Although Assad turned Syria into a police state, he also developed the country in ways which benefited the mass of the Syrian people. He built many kilometres of roads and railways and extended the provision of electricity and water to the entire country. The availability of education was greatly extended and literacy rates increased dramatically. Land reform measures took land from the wealthy and redistributed it to peasant farmers. Infant mortality was reduced and life expectancy increased. The economy, however, did not thrive and both inflation and corruption became serious problems.

The Syrians I was meeting at Hara were mostly under thirty-five years of age. They would have been born well after the country was stabilized by Hafez al-Assad, and received their education in the schools he established. It wasn't an education aimed at encouraging critical thinking; but it provided literacy and numeracy and enabled many to go on to university.

Just two years after independence, the violent birth of the state of Israel in 1948 changed forever the regional environment in which modern Syria was to develop. Seven hundred thousand Palestinians fled their homes to Syria, Lebanon and Jordan, where they would remain for generations to come. A series of Arab–Israeli wars followed over the next twenty-five years, in most of which the US supported Israel, to which it provided enormous financial subsidies and military resources. One result was that Arabs and Arab regimes were left feeling humiliated and angry with Israel and the west. In the 1967 Six Day War, in addition to invading and occupying the Arab West Bank and Gaza, Israel occupied the Golan Heights, part of Syria's sovereign territory. This enabled the Israelis to line up tanks only thirty-five kilometres from Damascus, and to observe the city from Mount Hermon.

The geopolitical backdrop to the Arab–Israeli conflict was the Cold War, the dark shadow of which now fell across the Middle East as the two superpowers vied for influence over the newly independent Arab states.[4] The US would eventually persuade Egypt to make peace with Israel; Syria, by contrast, refused to compromise, proclaiming itself a 'frontline' state and leader of the Arab confrontation with Zionism. Rejecting overtures from the US which sought to tie aid and arms sales to neutrality towards the Jewish state, Syria began to purchase weapons from the USSR in the 1950s. Strong links were formed between the military establishments of the two countries. Trade and cultural ties also developed, with many young Syrians being sent to study in the USSR. Syria continued to purchase its weapons from the Soviets during the Lebanese civil war.

For the next sixty years, mutual suspicion would characterize relations between Syria and the west. Although the collapse of the USSR in 1991 brought the Cold War to an end, apart from a brief thaw that year, relations between the US and Syria remained shaky up to the outbreak of the revolution.

In 1975, Lebanon disintegrated into a civil war which would last for fifteen years. Hafez al-Assad played a major, though ambiguous, role in Lebanon. From 1976 the Syrian army occupied parts of its tiny neighbour, using its weight to influence the course of the war, indirectly confronting Israel and preventing it from pursuing its goals there. Despite his professed ardent support for the Palestinian cause, Hafez al-Assad abandoned the PLO in Lebanon, siding instead with the Maronite Christians. Much later, he would support the development of the PLO's Islamist rival, Hamas, despite his opposition to Islamism inside Syria. Hafez al-Assad was above all a pragmatist, bent on his own survival.

The security apparatus now held Syria in a tight grip, with all independent political activity proscribed; and yet opposition to Assad and his Ba'athist revolution began to develop. It was led by Islamist militants, who in 1976 assassinated a number of senior Alawites. The militants were Sunnis and took their inspiration from the ideas of the Egyptian thinker Sayyid Qutb.[5] They believed the Ba'ath Party was causing untold damage to Syrian society and accused it of atheism. Pointing to a fatwa which claimed that Alawism was inimical to Islam, it was easy for the militants to harness people's real grievances to their own sectarian ideology.

There were further disturbances in 1979, when some landowning families who felt they had been dispossessed by the Ba'athist revolution decided to fund the Syrian branch of the Muslim Brotherhood (MB). Intermittent bomb attacks were launched against the regime and, in 1982, the MB staged a major uprising in the city of Hama. The militants killed around seventy Ba'athists; but this is a tiny figure when compared to the number butchered by the regime in response, during a siege of the city which lasted a week. The dead are believed to have numbered somewhere between five and twenty-five thousand. A tight security blackout ensured that no western journalists were able to enter the city to report on the massacre.

I thought the older Syrians at Hara would definitely remember Hama.

In the wake of the Hama uprising, the security services took an even tighter grip on Syria. Some surviving Islamists took refuge in Iraq and other Arab countries, where a pan-Arab Islamist revival was well underway by the 1980s.

In Syria, over the coming years, many citizens became disillusioned with the Ba'athist regime, for a variety of reasons. In the domestic sphere, the economy was in a mess. The life of the country was choked by bureaucracy, yet those close to the regime were becoming wealthy, partly through ubiquitous corruption to which the president turned a blind eye. In the international sphere, Assad's support for the Maronite Christians in Lebanon in the second half of the 1970s had caused people to question the sincerity of his anti-Zionist rhetoric. They had also noted that the ferocity of his retribution against the people of Hama was at odds with his failure to confront Israel directly in Lebanon.

Assad's health began to fail in the early 1980s, although he managed to hold onto the presidency, fighting off an attempted challenge from his power-hungry younger brother Rifaat. In the early 1990s Assad began to prepare his older son, Basil, to succeed him as president. It was only after Basil's death in a road accident in 1994 that the younger son, Bashar al-Assad, was brought back from ophthalmology studies in London to prepare for power. In 2000, on his father's death, he became president at the young age of thirty-four.

When Bashar came to power there was optimism that he would usher in an era of positive change in Syria. Part-educated in the west, he soon married a British-born and educated Sunni Syrian, Asma al Akhras, who'd had her own career in the financial services industry. In the early days of his presidency, Bashar repeatedly spoke of the need for national dialogue and suggested that a process of democratization might be possible, although he was clear that Syrian democracy would not be modelled on the western variety. During his first few months in office he introduced a number of measures which seemed to move in the direction of reform: political prisoners were released, independent newspapers were granted licences and human rights groups were allowed to establish themselves. The Human Rights Association in Syria was established in 2001, followed by the re-establishment of the Committee for the Defence of Democratic Freedoms and Human Rights in Syria and, in 2004, the Syrian Center for Media and Freedom of Expression. These groups operated openly but were in effect illegal, as they did not have government permission to exist.

The period has been referred to as the 'Damascus Spring'; it was to be short-lived. The liberalization measures appear to have upset some of the senior regime figures and Bashar was warned by his security chiefs that, if he continued in this direction, his presidency might not survive.[6] The period of reform came to an end in September 2001 with the arrest of a number of activists. Whether Bashar capitulated to pressure from his elders, or whether his apparent interest in reform was never genuine, remains unclear.

In 2005, more than 250 opposition figures signed a document called the 'Damascus Declaration' which criticized the regime for being authoritarian and totalitarian and called for a peaceful process of national dialogue and reform. A handful of opposition groups, both secular and religious, Arab and Kurdish, also signed. Twelve members of a committee associated with the declaration were later sentenced to prison terms of two and a half years.

A series of crises in the Middle East from 2003 to 2006 may have served to distract Bashar from any intention to enact reforms. Following the collapse of the USSR, the US was now the only superpower and George W. Bush was attempting to impose his 'New World Order'. In 2003, the US and Britain invaded Iraq on the pretext of seeking to destroy weapons of mass destruction allegedly held by Saddam Hussein. One of the results for Syria was a major influx of Iraqi refugees, whose presence pushed up the price of accommodation and overwhelmed the job market, thereby making life harder for ordinary Syrians. Another result was the arrival in Syria of foreign Islamist fighters en route for Iraq, where they intended to help Sunni insurgents resist American troops. Despite his distaste for radical Islam, Bashar allowed these men to cross Syria, thereby incurring Bush's wrath. In 2003 Bush passed the Syria Accountability and Lebanese Sovereignty Reform Act, which banned the export of US goods other than food and medicine to Syria and outlawed US investment there. It also named Syria as a sponsor of 'terrorism' and demanded that it withdraw from Lebanon. When, less than two years later, in 2005, the Saudi-backed former Lebanese president and Sunni businessman Rafiq Hariri was assassinated in Beirut by a giant car bomb, the finger was pointed at Syria as the culprit. Within a couple of months, Syria was pressurized into withdrawing all its remaining troops from Lebanon, ending an occupation which had endured since 1976. A little over a year later, in July 2006, war erupted between Israel and Hizbullah, sending a fresh wave of refugees into Syria.

By now the economic situation in Syria was serious. Unemployment was on the increase, particularly in the cities. The young were unable to find jobs when they completed their degrees. Corruption was endemic, with those closest to the regime being the main beneficiaries. Some modest reform to the economy and antiquated banking system had been enacted during Bashar's early years as president, but progress was slow and growth of the economy lagged behind that of neighbouring countries such as Egypt and Turkey. One of the reasons for this was cultural: many civil servants had been in their jobs for a long time, and were doggedly wedded to the socialist values originally associated with Ba'athism. They were resistant to change and able to sabotage moves towards a market economy.[7]

Unlike his father, who had successfully dominated the country as a lone figure, Bashar surrounded himself with members of his family as advisers. He and those around him lived a life of wealth and comfort, with access to western consumer goods, and it is possible that he was unaware of just how difficult life had become for the poor. That difficulty was greatly increased in rural areas by a five-year period of drought, which began in 2006 and continued until 2010.

In December 2010, a brave young Tunisian street hawker set fire to himself in protest at state injustice and humiliation, sparking uprisings in Tunisia, Egypt, Libya and other Arab countries – the 'Arab Spring'. Initially, it was widely assumed that Syria would prove immune to a comparable disturbance. And so it might have, had the regime not reacted with unparalleled cruelty to the demonstrators who ventured onto the streets of Deraa and Homs and other Syrian cities in early 2011. The regime's tactics over the next weeks and months, in which Syrians seeking to demonstrate peacefully were punished by the use of lethal force, suggests a body politic in panic, for which survival was the only goal, and no price too high to pay.

It would be wrong, however, to suggest that the regime's brutality in the early months of 2011 was what caused the exodus of refugees. There were a number of stages in the transformation of the confrontation between angry citizens and the Syrian government into civil then international war.

4

The Engineer from Damascus

When we arrived at Hara late the following morning, many of the refugees were just getting up. This wasn't unusual, for Hara was a busy place at night, being the principal departure point for smugglers and their clients. For a hefty fee and under cover of darkness, smugglers would lead bands of refugees high up into the mountains, to remote places beyond the end of the border fence, from where it was possible to slip into FYROM undetected. Because of this, and perhaps also because of the sheer discomfort of sleeping on tarmac with inadequate bedding, noise and activity continued until late every night. Small children would keel over earlier with their exhausted mothers beside them, though I sometimes saw four- and five-year-olds trotting round the camp close to midnight. Meanwhile, their elders sat around small fires at the perimeter of the forecourt, smoking, talking and trying to plan their next moves. Hasan had told me that he rarely lay down before four a.m., and the dark shadows under his eyes attested to the truth of this.

It was another fine spring day and Charly, Sintra, Ian and I decided we should do something about the rubbish that lay in drifts against every wall and danced across the forecourt in the breeze. The refuse lorry had not paid a visit for several days and the bins behind the supermarket were overflowing. Charly produced a supply of black dustbin bags and rubber gloves from the back of her car and we spread out in different directions. I chose to work down by the road, because I could watch the comings and goings as the camp woke up. In the field, the old Syrian Kurd was bent over his oil drum, raking the ashes of last night's fire with a stick and coaxing it back to life. The distant line of mountains behind him, pale blue in the morning haze, brought me happy memories of Iraqi Kurdistan.

I held my black bag in one hand as I stooped to pick up cracked plastic bottles, cigarette packs and dirty wet wipes with the other. In the bushes beside the camp entrance, I found discarded nappies and toilet paper.

Now I took a few steps into the camp. The first tent was a large one, with a separate bedroom and a living area shaded by an awning. The woman I'd seen tending a fire when I first arrived was seated on her log, dressed in a long robe, chopping tomatoes into a plastic bowl. She called out a greeting and I called back. It was only then that I spotted, in the dull light beneath the awning, also seated on the ground, the very old woman I'd noticed in the queue for MSF. She still wore the orange headscarf draped over her head, but the look of fear had left her pale, watery eyes. Behind her the wheelchair stood neatly in a corner.

As I moved slowly on, children ran up to push used food containers into my black bag. A little girl of three or four clung to my arm. A man sitting outside his tent called out 'Thank you' and I replied 'You're welcome.' Over on the far side of the forecourt, a double queue had formed in anticipation of the arrival of the food van. Every morning and every evening, a dark blue transit brought a basic meal for the entire camp. I'd heard Charly and Ian refer to the people who made and delivered the food as Aid Delivery Mission (ADM) or 'the anarchists', another group of volunteers. I stopped to watch as the van appeared from nowhere and screeched to a halt in a cloud of dust. Two young European men dressed in shorts leapt out, flung open the back doors and began to hand out packets of food wrapped in paper.

I watched for a few moments as the refugees took their packets and dispersed, some beginning to eat before they reached their tents. Then I moved on past the portaloos, where the tarmac was surprisingly clean. Under the trees of the perimeter fence, a middle-aged couple sat on plastic chairs in front of a line of neatly zipped up dome tents. They were both a little overweight, with lined, weary faces, and their mood seemed sombre. I stopped to chat and the man told me they were Arabs from Tikrit in Iraq, the birthplace of Saddam Hussein. They'd fled to Iraqi Kurdistan after ISIS attacked Tikrit in 2014, but hadn't felt safe there.

'Good for you,' the man said, gesturing with approval at my black bag, 'but we just swept this whole area an hour ago and look, it's filthy again.' He clicked his tongue with an air of disgust and his wife wrinkled up her nose and shook her head. I understood their frustration: if everyone cleaned up in front of their tent, the problem would be solved; but most people, it seemed, were too preoccupied with survival even to notice the rubbish.

Beyond the Iraqi tents, a gap in the line of trees allowed me to see through into the field of the Syrian Kurds, where a barber's shop was in operation. A handsome young man sat in one of Stassos' plastic chairs with a towel round his shoulders, while his mate, the barber, gave him a stylish undercut, shaving sharp little points into the stubble in front of his ear.

A one o'clock I met Sintra by the overflowing dustbins. We tied up our rubbish bags, removed our gloves and cleaned our fingers with anti-bacterial gel. It was time to take orders for the second-hand clothing, shoes, bedding and nappies which had been donated by refugee action groups from all over Europe, and which were kept in the Czech store in Polykastro.

Among the volunteers, for many of whom English was a second language, the process of taking orders had mysteriously become known as 'registration', a literal translation of the Arabic word, *tasjeel*. Ian and Hasan appeared carrying a plastic table between them. Someone else brought chairs and we set ourselves up in a tiny patch of shade against the wall of the mini-supermarket. The sun was high in the sky and the breeze had dropped.

Within a couple of minutes, half a dozen women and as many children were crowding round the table. Most were Arabic speakers: Syrians and one or two Iraqis. It would be a few days before I began to reflect on why this was and what could be done to encourage members of the other language groups to make orders. For now I was fully absorbed trying to follow Sintra's instructions on how to use the order book and wondering if I had the vocabulary for every garment I was likely to be asked for. I needn't have worried, for Sintra had taken the trouble to draw on pieces of card the clothes which were most commonly requested and which she knew we would find at the store. She'd added some items such as deodorant, soap and shampoo which we'd buy in FYROM.

The first person I attended to was a tall woman I'd spoken with the day before, when she'd approached me to ask if I could get her a buggy. She looked about forty, wore dark-rimmed spectacles and dressed in a long grey velvet coat dress, which reached to the ankle. Her grey wool headscarf was folded closely around her face. She had a particularly likeable, humorous manner and I'd taken to her instantly. She had an injured leg and was finding it hard to carry her baby when chasing around the camp after her toddler. Buggies were in short supply, but I'd promised to check at the store.

I was happy to see her again this afternoon, with the baby tucked under her arm, so I greeted her warmly and asked how she was.

'*Alhamdulillah*, I'm well thank you, and you?' She returned my smile. 'Please, I need a T-shirt.'

I could see from the look on her lined, brown face that she was exhausted and still in pain, but I nodded and picked up my pen.

'For you?' Sometimes people ordered clothes for their children, but she nodded. 'Long sleeves or short? And I need your name.'

'Fatima Mohammed. Long sleeves.' The woman ran her free hand along the sleeve of the coat dress and stopped at her wrist. 'And long in the body, please, to cover my hips.' She held her hand against her thigh.

I checked the carbon paper was in the proper place in the order book and wrote *Fatima Mohammed, 1 × long-sleeved woman's T-shirt, long in the body*. 'What shall I put for size?'

'Large, *habibti* (my dear), of course!' The woman chuckled. A dozen women and girls were clustering round her, pressing against the table, but Fatima didn't seem to mind.

I smiled. 'Anything else?'

'A pair of trousers, also for me, also large.' She slid the baby onto her hip.

'Okay.' I wrote this down. 'Anything else?' Today we'd set a limit of four items per person.

'Nappies, please, size two.'

Nappies were in plentiful supply. 'Is that it?'

Fatima thought for a moment. 'Ah, you know what I could really do with?' She fingered the thick woollen fabric of her headscarf. 'A lighter scarf. Do you have any?'

Headscarves weren't among the items which Sintra had drawn, but I'd seen some at the store. 'I think so,' I replied. 'I'll have a look for you. Something for summer?'

'Thank you so much.'

'Any particular colour?'

Fatima sucked her teeth. 'Any colour. You choose! But nothing too bright . . .' She smiled again, and I liked her even more.

I completed the list, checked that it had gone through onto the next page, tore off the top copy and handed it to her. 'Come back tomorrow, around one o'clock, and we'll have a package ready for you.'

Fatima beamed at me. 'Thanks, *habibti*, thank you so much.' She lifted the baby a little higher and hobbled slowly away.

My next 'customer' was a girl of about fifteen and her younger sister. Neither wore a headscarf and their luxuriant brown hair fell in gleaming wedges down their backs. They were of that age where it is hard, if not impossible, to stand still. The younger one jiggled around then rested her head against the older one's shoulder, while staring at me with large, green eyes. I opened a fresh page in the order book, took their names and asked what they needed. 'T-shirts, please,' said the older girl, 'one for me and one for her.'

'Long sleeves?'

'Either. Short sleeves is okay.' She smiled, then dropped her voice. 'And do you have underwear? For girls?'

Female underwear was in short supply. I wanted to check with Sintra, but she was engrossed in taking an order from an Afghan woman.

'I'm not sure,' I said, also lowering my voice. 'I'll do my best. What size?'

The girl glanced at her sister. 'Medium,' she said, speaking in a whisper.

I nodded. 'Anything else?'

'Mm,' the girls glanced at Sintra's drawings, then pointed to the one of a cake of soap. 'Some soap!' The younger one cried. 'And a bottle of shampoo!'

I added these to the list. 'You girls have beautiful hair,' I couldn't resist saying.

The older one frowned. 'Thank you, but it's so hard to keep it clean in this place! We asked the man in the hotel if we could use his showers and he wanted ten euros each!'

I'd heard the same from Charly. She was hoping to negotiate a better deal, but had been too busy with everything else. I shook my head.

After the girls, it was the turn of a woman holding the hand of a small boy. 'Please,' she began, 'he needs a T-shirt and a pair of shorts. My name's Aziza Rashid,' she added with a smile.

When I asked the child's age, she replied that he was seven. I tried to hide my astonishment: I would have said four at most. I thought for a moment, then wrote on the order book *Aziza Rashid, 1 x boy's T-shirt, age 4–5; 1 × boys' shorts, ditto.* Thinking she might be able to read English, I hastily explained that a lot of the clothing at the store had been donated by Germans, and that their children were exceptionally tall. I was soon to discover that it wasn't just Aziza's son who was small for his age, by European standards. Nearly all the Syrian children were small and slim. Whether this was a natural phenomenon, or the result of food shortages, I had no way of knowing. The children of five and under had known nothing but war from birth.

And so it went on. By half past two we'd taken over forty orders between us, and Sintra said that if we weren't careful we'd be at the warehouse all night, packing. So we called a halt, promised to do another *tasjeel* the next day, and returned the table and chairs to the mini-supermarket.

By now the temperature on the forecourt was in the high twenties. The hotel verandah was crowded with people sheltering in the shade of the awning; others sat on the ground with their backs to the wall of the supermarket, fanning themselves with sheets of cardboard. As Sintra, Ian and I squeezed into Charly's car, wrapping ourselves around the usual chaos of blankets, tents and water bottles, a man asked us to buy a tarpaulin and string to construct an awning over his group of tents.

Charly drove at her usual high speed and in less than ten minutes we were at the Czech store. It was on the main road on the outskirts of Polykastro, opposite the Park Hotel, where many of the volunteers who worked at the main Idomeni camp were staying. The store had previously been a nightclub, and the word 'Playboy' could still be made out in faded paint over the entrance. The Czechs ran the store according to some very simple rules. Incoming donations were sorted and stored in cardboard boxes in various categories: women's shoes, men's shoes, children's shoes; waterproofs; blankets; women's T-shirts; men's T-shirts, and so forth. If a European walked into the store it was assumed you were a volunteer, and nobody asked any questions. You could help yourself to any items you needed for the refugees in the camp where you were based, with absolutely no formalities. What was not allowed, on the other hand, was to give out items to refugees directly from the store. This could be tricky, as a slow stream of refugees passed by all day, on their way into Polykastro from a government-run camp at Karvalla, just a mile down the road.

Charly produced plastic bags and we got out our order books and set to work on the pavement in the hot sun. Some items were in plentiful supply, such as T-shirts and socks. Others were almost non-existent. We went through the order books list by list, making up the packages as best we could, leaving them open so that we could add the toiletries which we planned to buy later, in FYROM.

It would have been an easy task, but for the heat. When I started to feel dizzy, I took a handful of plastic bags and a bottle of water and retreated into the cool of the store. I set myself up by a tall stack of tea chests, from where I could observe the comings and goings of the other volunteers while I worked.

It was difficult to tell who was who. A slim, short-haired Czech woman seemed to be in charge, judging by the way she moved swiftly from box to box, clearly familiar with the contents, and by the way she greeted people when they walked in off the street. Her body language suggested a warm, practical woman who was determined to get things done. More than once I heard her telling a group of newly arrived volunteers that she needed help, and that if they were willing to give a hand for a few hours, it would make a big difference. She would laugh with an air of veiled frustration, exclaiming 'It's not the most exciting job in the world, I know that, but it has to be done!'

In one corner of the store a couple of men were rummaging through a box of sleeping bags, talking in Spanish. A large mural of a pole dancer, a relic of the night club, adorned the wall behind them. Through a doorway in another room, a woman was talking excitedly on the phone in Italian. I observed it all with quiet fascination. It astonished me that so many Europeans were streaming in to help the refugees, when, with the exception of Germany and Sweden, our governments were busy building fences and doing deals to keep them out.

I was pulling women's T-shirts out of a box, trying to find some that were long enough to cover the hips, when it struck me that I might do better by looking through the dresses. When I found the correct box, some were unsuitable, with skimpy shoulder straps and plunging necklines. But at the bottom of the box I found a couple of dark tunics with long sleeves and high necks. One was voluminous, in a dark green cotton – perfect for Fatima, or so I thought. I was just folding it up when a bulky British woman I hadn't seen before burst into the store, talking at the top of her voice.

'Things can hardly get much worse, can they?' she screeched. 'First I had my phone stolen, then I lost my wallet! Everything's gone, passport, the lot, I can't even get any money out of the bank. Now I know what it's like to be a refugee!'

Instinctively I put my head down and burrowed further into the box.

'No money, no home, nothing to even say who I am!' The woman, who was about forty, had narrow hips encased in tight red jeans and short, purple hair. She threw her arms around as she spoke and turned in a circle, as if trying to garner the attention of everyone in the store. 'No money, no home, and I'm supposed to be running this place!' I heard a loud, hyperbolic sigh. 'Oh well, what can I do? Guess I'm a refugee now, just like all these people.' She paused as if expecting a response, whereupon I turned my back. 'But I'm not going to let it stop me, I'll still run the place!'

I peeked sideways, wondering what had become of the Czech woman.

'Guess you have to be a refugee to understand what it's like to be one!'

To my relief the woman strode into the other room as she ranted, presumably wanting more of a reaction than she'd got from me and the Spaniards. It was inevitable that the volunteer effort would attract a few needy characters, I reflected; but I hoped this one didn't venture into the camps.

When we got back to Hara, an hour later, I bought a plate of food from the kitchen and headed towards the bar for a cup of tea. The heavily made-up woman was talking on her mobile. Seeing me coming, she flicked the switch on the kettle with her free hand, flashed me a little smile and reached for a polystyrene cup. A couple of minutes later, as I was removing the tea bag with a plastic spoon, I felt a presence at my shoulder. Turning, I saw Bassem, the son of the family from Homs, who had a way of moving about soundlessly. Beside him stood a slight young woman in a long cotton dress and headscarf.

Bassem's mouth was close to my ear. 'Please,' he began, 'I need to speak to you.' From the anxious look on his face, he wanted to consult me about something personal, so I suggested we go and find a place to sit. He led the way onto the verandah, to the only table which was free. 'This is my wife,' he said, gesturing at the slight young woman as we sat down. 'Her name's Basma.'

I was taken aback, for Bassem seemed too young to have a wife. The young woman smiled shyly and stretched out a small, clammy hand.

'Basma's pregnant,' Bassem went on, 'and she keeps being sick.'

'You're pregnant?' I looked at her in surprise. 'Congratulations!'

Basma looked pleased. 'Ten weeks,' she murmured.

'That's fantastic.' She was pale and thin, seventeen at most.

'But every time she eats,' Bassem went on, 'she throws up. Today she threw up three times.'

'Oh, that's not so good. Mainly first thing in the morning?'

Bassem sucked his teeth emphatically. 'This morning, this afternoon, and just now. I don't see how the baby can grow, if the mother can't keep food down.'

'Where do you two get your meals?'

He tossed his head in the direction of the road. 'From the food van.'

'What's it like?'

His brown eyes gazed at me steadily. '*Yani*, it's okay.' He rested a hand on his stomach. 'But it's not the food we're used to.' He was almost as thin as Basma.

I regarded the young mum-to-be, wondering why she and Bassem were seeking advice from me, rather than his mum, the older woman with the long plait; or from *her* mum, for that matter – but I wasn't sure where she was. 'Is there any type of food you think you could keep down?'

Basma stared at me with a look of veiled exasperation. 'I want Syrian food,' she said at last, in a tone which suggested she thought it obvious. 'The things my mother used to cook . . .' Her eyes filled with tears and I decided not to go there.

'Look.' I leaned across the table towards Bassem and lowered my voice. 'Maybe the Greek food would suit Basma better. Please don't tell anybody, but I'm going to give you some money to buy a meal in the restaurant.'

Bassem inclined his head very slightly. 'Thank you, sister,' he whispered as I reached in my money belt. 'Don't worry, we won't tell anyone.'

I folded up a ten-euro note into a small square and passed it to him across the table. 'Their food's good,' I remarked, jerking my head in the direction of the kitchen. 'I'd had a tasty vegetarian meal for just three euros.

By now I couldn't remember what I was supposed to be doing, so I retraced my steps and bought a bottle of water. It was still hot outside and I was worried about becoming dehydrated. As I leant against the bar, I noticed a tall, slim man in spectacles watching me from a couple of feet away. He was drinking from a can of Fanta.

'So you don't speak Greek?' he remarked in English, with a faint trace of a smile.

'I wish I did, it would make life easier!'

'Ah, that's what we all wish.' The man removed his spectacles, blew on the lenses, buffed them with a cloth and replaced them on his nose. 'In Syria we study English in school, but if we'd known this was going to happen, Greek would have been more help to us!'

'But your English will be useful in the rest of Europe.' I smiled and took a swig of water. The man's cheeks were smooth and unblemished, but his neatly cropped hair was greying at the temples.

'Ha, if I ever get there!' He shrugged his shoulders. 'I used English a lot in my work in Damascus. Every day, sending emails and dealing with international companies on the phone.'

'What's your job?' Without thinking, I used the present tense.

'I'm an engineer. *Was* an engineer, I should say! I don't feel as if I am one any more, I've become a professional refugee!' He pressed the frame of his spectacles against the bridge of his nose, with a grimace of resignation. Then he held out his hand. 'Nizar Ali, pleased to meet you.'

As we shook hands I found myself telling him that he *would* work again, one day, without a doubt. I don't know where my certainty came from; my words were a response to his despair. That must be one of the hardest things, I thought, to lose your sense of identity through not being able to practise your profession. I asked how long it was since he'd left Syria.

'I set off three months ago, in January.' This time he forced a smile. 'And I've been at Idomeni thirty-seven days, to be precise!' I saw a sweetness in his face, only partially masked by the look of frustration. I thought he might be in his late thirties.

'You're not staying at Hara?'

'My tent's at Idomeni. I come to Hara every few days and book a room to get a good night's sleep and take a shower . . .' He grimaced in embarrassment.

'Are you . . . here by yourself?' I was never sure if it was wise to ask this question; but a man of Nizar's age was highly likely to have a family.

'My wife and our two little boys are with my parents in Damascus. My plan was to send for them when I arrived in Germany . . . but now, I don't know if I'll ever get there.' He picked up the can of Fanta, lifted it to his lips and put it down again.

'Are they . . . safe?'

'Much safer in Damascus than where we used to live at the beginning of the revolution. Back in 2011, we were in a small town in the Ghouta, about ten kilometres outside the city. Damascus is so expensive that all young couples wanting to settle down used to move to the Ghouta. I drove into the city to work every day.'

'Why was the Ghouta unsafe?'

Nizar looked at me steadily. 'Don't you know about the Ghouta? Okay, let me explain. During the first few months of the revolution, every Friday there were demonstrations in our little town. The marches used to come right past our house. During those early demonstrations, there were cases where shots got fired through people's windows in the chaos of the moment. The security forces wouldn't have been aiming into the houses, but mistakes were made. At first, if we heard there was to be a demonstration, we used to close the windows; then as the violence increased, we had to take refuge in the bathroom, in the centre of the house. Imagine – me, my wife and our two little sons, who were two and four at the time, crouched on the bathroom floor. My wife and I would sing to drown out the noise of the shooting going on in the streets. Sometimes I put my hands over the children's ears to stop them hearing the people shouting slogans, followed by the sound of shooting and screaming.'

My eyes were fixed on Nizar.

'We tried to distract the kids from the real reason we were sitting in the bathroom; but it didn't work. At those moments my wife and I were in the grip of extreme fear and of course the kids picked it up. So the point came when we decided it was too dangerous to remain at home during demonstrations. We used to get up very early on Friday mornings and drive to my parents' place in Damascus. We'd stay there till it was all over, and then go home.

'We continued to live in the Ghouta for as long as we could, but there were times when I didn't go to work for two or three days because it was too dangerous to go out. There were demonstrations all over the Ghouta, peaceful at first but eventually some elements in the opposition resorted to violence. The Free Syrian Army became active in our town, attacking the regime with bombs and rockets.

'One day I was returning home from work by car around six p.m. My wife called me in tears, yelling "Don't come home, it's really bad, I've been in the bathroom with the kids for four hours without a phone signal, they're fighting in the street outside." Then the line went dead. The regime used to cut the mobile signal in areas where there was trouble, to punish the residents.

'I was beside myself with worry and didn't know what to do. I phoned a friend, who convinced me to stay put and not try to go home, although I felt terrible about my wife and kids being alone there. I waited in the car for two hours, trying to call her every few minutes, although mostly I couldn't get through. Eventually I reached her and she said things had calmed down and it might be ok to try to drive home. By now it was completely dark, as the regime had cut the electricity supply to the area and mine was the only car on the road. On the outskirts of our town I came to a road-block. Six armed men jumped out at the car and forced me to stop. I was terrified, but I managed to explain I was just going to collect my family. The men fired questions at me till an older man's voice from the darkness behind them shouted "Let him go to his house", and they let me go, telling me to take a back street.

'When I got home, my wife and the boys ran from the bathroom to the front door, sobbing. We hugged each other and then we ran out to the car. I drove like a maniac to my parents' place in Damascus.

'That was the last time my wife and kids saw our home in the Ghouta. I had to go back a couple of times to fetch our clothes and documents. Initially we imagined we'd be able to live there again after a few months; but things got worse and worse and eventually the regime sealed off the area. Anyone seen going in was assumed to be with the regime, and anyone seen coming out was assumed to be with the rebels. So it became a no-go area.'

By now my stomach was in a knot. I kept thinking how difficult it must have been for Nizar to leave his wife and kids behind in Damascus. I asked him what he'd felt about the revolution when it started.

Nizar took off his spectacles and polished them again. 'Look, when the children wrote on their school walls in Deraa, nobody thought it would become a big deal. The Assad regime had created stability over forty years and in general people were not thinking about change. The middle classes were quite well off and in the last ten years people had started to buy mobile phones and new cars, to eat out two or three times a week and shop in malls. New Arab banks were opening and people had deposits in them. Life was good in Syria before the revolution. Okay, we worked hard, most middle-class men had two jobs. I only had one, but I used to work ten hours a day, six days a week, with just Fridays off – that was the norm.'

'But what about the poor?'

He replaced the spectacles. 'Even the poor had enough food. They might earn as little as two to three dollars a day, but they could live on that, without saving anything. Nobody was below the bread line.'

'What about in the countryside?' Nizar's description was at odds with what I'd read. I'd understood there had been widespread rural poverty, especially with the impact of the drought.

Nizar pursed his lips. 'In the rural areas, people were not desperately poor, but there was a lack of services, sometimes no internet, inadequate schools.' He placed his Fanta on the bar and rubbed the back of his neck. 'Look, when it started in 2011, the country divided into two groups. The group I was in said: "We don't need a revolution, look what happened in Iraq and Libya; we don't like our government, but it won't be any better under anyone else – who would rule us, if not the Assads?" There was also concern about where a revolution might lead: it seemed so uncertain. The older people said it wasn't worth the risk, and so did many people my age.' He looked at me intently. 'Many of the poor also felt like this. They were preoccupied with meeting their basic needs and had no time to think about change.'

'And what did the other group say?'

'The other group said, "This is our moment, if we don't rise up now, we'll miss the chance. Our children's futures are not looking good; we should rise up."'

I asked Nizar if his group's view of the regime had changed over time.

'Yes of course, but let me explain how it happened. At the beginning in March 2011, the trouble started in Deraa. We got the details of what was happening from Facebook, because the regime censored the news. Then there was the first demonstration in Damascus, in which the demand was simply for a liberalization that would improve people's lives. People wanted freedom to think and to develop their country. *Nothing* was said at that point by the demonstrators about wanting regime change. Most of them had a lot of faith in Bashar – he was young, westernized, handsome, and he'd made many promises of reform, however vague.

'At the beginning, let's say 20 per cent of people were with the revolution and 70 to 80 per cent were neutral. Then the demonstrations started to get more frequent and much bigger in Damascus. The brutality of the regime response was extreme, with many demonstrators imprisoned and tortured. All this made the people who had opposed the idea of a revolution think again. When the government tried to say it was all down to foreign agitators, people became very angry. On one occasion, the regime said on national TV that the demonstrators were not demonstrators, rather that they had come out to thank God for rain, after years of drought! Another time they said the demonstrators were "viruses" and that they were "going to exterminate them". So, gradually, people lost faith with the regime and more and more people started to support the revolution. At the same time, the demonstrations spread to Homs, and Deraa was besieged by the government. As more and more people were killed, the demonstrations became much bigger and the regime used ever more savage violence, particularly in the countryside.

'But, you know, it needn't have been like this. If Bashar had come out in the early months and said to the people, "You're right, I will punish those who killed and tortured demonstrators, and then I'll liberalize and give you more freedom", it would all have ended, even after seven or eight months. If he'd done this, then there would be a statue to Bashar in every town in Syria.'

I asked Nizar when his view of the regime had started to change.

'I was like everybody else, my view changed because of the brutality. And eventually I became afraid for my life, and for my wife and children's lives.'

'What was it like when you moved to live with your parents in Damascus? Did you feel safe?'

'Thankfully there was nothing going on in the area where my parents lived. But we heard gunfire most nights coming from other areas of the city, and small or big explosions. By now the kids were showing signs of being affected. They had nightmares and difficulty sleeping. They would wake, crying, for no obvious reason. Even when they were awake they were jumpy, for instance, if a door banged.'

'That must have been so painful for you to see!'

'Of course. The worst thing for me was always the suffering of my children.'

We stood in silence for a moment and then Nizar tapped the screen of his mobile, which lay in front of him on the bar, and scrolled through some photographs. 'This is my oldest son,' he said, 'my wife sent me the photo the day before yesterday.' He slid the phone towards me and I gazed into the face of a boy who stared shyly at the camera from the seat of an expensive-looking Louis XIV upholstered chair, in a sun-filled drawing room. He had golden skin and his father's sensitive face.

'What a beautiful boy! How old is he now?'

Nizar raised his eyebrows and frowned. 'Let me see, he was nine, but he turned ten last week.' I glimpsed a trace of pride in his eyes.

'And the younger one?'

'My younger son is seven.' He scrolled through his pictures again and showed me a shot of a small boy dressed in football kit sitting cross-legged on a sofa.

By now Nizar's expression was one of distress, so I gave him back the phone and changed the subject. 'Are the schools operating in Damascus?'

'School, work, everything is normal. In certain areas, that is.' His tone was clipped.

'Do they teach English in primary school?'

'Sure, in both primary and secondary.'

'What about French?'

'French too; but it's not so popular these days.' His features relaxed as he studied my face, presumably wondering how much I knew about his country. Then his upper lip twitched slightly. 'We don't have happy memories of the French!'

5
A Young Helper

For the next couple of days, life followed something of a pattern. In the mornings we shopped in the supermarket in Gevgelija, the little town beside the Motel Vardar. Charly had a small fund from donations made to NLA by well-wishers, which we used to buy shampoo, soap, deodorant and hairbrushes; then we added these to the packages made up the night before and drove to Hara.

The distribution was easy. By the time we'd set up the white plastic table and placed our huge cardboard box of packages on the floor behind us, a crowd was forming. Women held their white order papers aloft, eager to get to the front. The only difficulty we had was that every day, a few of the people who'd made orders failed to reappear. When at the end of the distribution, an unclaimed package remained in the box, someone would always make out that it must have been intended for them. Sintra, who had a strong sense of order, would ask to see the person's paper, and frown when no paper was produced. 'I lost it' was a common excuse, followed by 'I tore it up by mistake.' Sintra and I would look at each other and weigh up whether we believed the person. We were meeting so many people every day that we couldn't always decide whom we recognized. If we were unsure, Sintra would say 'No, sorry, we can only give it to the person with the paper.' On the other hand, if the person looked familiar, she'd hand over the package.

The process could easily result in frayed tempers on both sides of the plastic table. By now I'd acquired a young helper, an eleven-year-old Kurdish boy called Dilshad. We'd got talking one day and since then he'd taken to appearing every time we pulled up in the car at the entrance to the camp, ready to help with whatever task I was about to undertake. If I had a pile of blankets or a box of packages to carry, he would insist on taking one end, while I took the other. He was short, sturdy and remarkably strong for his age, with a warm, open face, short, spiky brown hair and pale skin. He loved to play football, but would even abandon a game if he thought I needed help.

When we did the distribution, Dilshad was invariably at my side, helping to select the right package from the cardboard box and advising me on who I should serve next. To my amusement, whenever someone tried to persuade us to give them an unclaimed package, Dilshad would urge us to refuse, sucking his teeth with an air of contempt as they gave their reasons for having mislaid their order paper. Sometimes he would tug at my sleeve and mouth the word '*kaʒab*' (liar), raising his eyebrows in a gesture of disapproval. He was clearly enjoying his new-found power, and I felt sure his judgement of who was telling the truth was better than mine.

After we'd finished the distribution, I would retreat into

the hotel to pick up the mood of the day from the people seated at the restaurant tables. Word had got round by now that I spoke Arabic, and Syrians I'd not met would greet me warmly as I passed. I always smiled and asked how they were. I was basking in a sense of being noticed and appreciated, something I don't experience too often in the UK. Today, as I walked towards the hotel, I saw Juwan standing on the verandah. He smiled warmly as I stopped to greet him. He was wearing the same striped shirt and jeans as the previous time I'd seen him, yet something in his appearance was slightly different.

'I took a shower!' The smile developed into a big grin. 'I'm clean!'

His sense of triumph was so palpable that I laughed. 'Where did you manage that?'

He tossed his head in the direction of the road. 'Eko, the other petrol station on the big highway. The owner there's very nice, he lets us use the showers for free. Cold water, of course.' He pretended to shiver, clenching his teeth. 'But it's worth it!'

'I bet it is.' His hair had a fluffy, freshly washed look.

As I stood there smiling he added, 'Sintra was looking for you a moment ago, she's bought you a tea. Come, I'll show you where she's sitting.'

I followed Juwan into the bar, where Sintra was perched on her usual sofa. Three polystyrene cups steamed in front of her.

'Oh, there you are!' she called out, 'Come and drink your tea.'

I pulled up a chair and sat down. 'I think it's time for part two of Juwan's story, don't you?'

'Definitely!' Sintra pushed one of the cups towards him. 'We want to hear it all. Every detail!'

'Well, every detail you want to tell us,' I muttered, feeling a bit sorry for Juwan. But he seemed pleased by our interest.

'Okay,' he began, 'although it's a story of too many problems, I had unbelievable bad luck.' He sat down beside Sintra at an angle, so that he was facing both of us. 'So, I told you I packed my bag and set off for Turkey in December 2011. I crossed the border legally and made my way to my mother's relative in the coastal city where he lived. The relative was a wealthy man, but within a few days he started to act strangely, complaining about the fact that my mother had asked him to help me. I was very uncomfortable and didn't know what to do.'

Juwan's features drew tighter and I wondered if it was fair to ask him to relive a bad experience.

'I felt lost, because I didn't know Turkish and in that town nobody understood English. One day, the relative gave me a bit of money and asked me to buy him some beer in the local shop. When I got there, I overheard the shopkeeper speaking Kurdish. I was so happy to hear my own language!' He took a swig of tea. 'So I decided to ask him for help. I explained that I was newly arrived and needed a place to live. I had very little money, just enough to pay the rent of a room for about a month. The shopkeeper said he knew I was staying with his neighbour and that he could find me a job. I said that just a room would do, but shortly afterwards he offered me a job in his family's café-bar.

'As a teenager I'd always wanted to work, but my parents had refused to let me. They used to say, "We'll take care of money matters, we want you to concentrate on your school work and come top of the class!" Looking back, it would have been much easier for me in Turkey if I'd had some previous experience of working. Syrians can't work legally in Turkey, so the employer has the upper hand.[1] Suddenly I was plunged into working fourteen hours a day, seven days a week. I was a waiter and general dogsbody and because I didn't have anywhere to live, I slept in the bar at night. The only good thing about it was that I picked up Turkish very fast. Actually, it was okay at first, because it was winter and the hours weren't so long; but the following summer they expected me to work till the bar closed at two or three a.m. and then be up and working again at seven in the morning. All for twelve dollars a day!'

Sintra was frowning. 'It's a miracle you didn't get sick!'

Juwan nodded. 'I got more and more exhausted, and at times I felt really desperate. Eventually, I decided I just couldn't carry on any longer so I packed it in, said my farewells and took a bus to Istanbul, thinking I might find an easier job there. But in Istanbul it was the same: I could only work illegally and jobs were few and far between, especially for somebody like me without a specific skill. In desperation, I began to wonder about going to Europe via Greece. I made contact with one of my uncles who was also outside Syria and asked him to lend me 1,000 euros. He wanted to help but he, too, was trying to get to Europe. He'd just paid a lot of money to a smuggler for a trip which hadn't worked out, so he was short of cash. He sent me 300 euros, all he could manage.

'By now it was the summer of 2012 and my parents had left Syria and were in Iraqi Kurdistan. When I realized I wasn't going to find a job, I decided to try to join them. So I packed my bag again and took the overnight bus from Istanbul to Silopi in the far east of Turkey, a journey of twenty-five hours. I took a risk because I didn't have a visa for Iraq and wasn't sure they'd let me in.

'At the Turkish border post I showed my passport, which had a Turkish tourist residence permit in it. The official stamped my passport, but a few seconds later, without any explanation, he added a cancellation stamp, saying there was a warrant out for my arrest. Apparently this was because the police had been to the address I'd given when I got the residence permit a few months earlier, and been told I was no longer there. I said to the official, "Well, here I am, do you want to question me?" But he insisted I had to go to the Migration Office back in the coastal city where I'd worked in the bar. I couldn't believe my bad luck.

'By the time I came out of the border post I was beside myself with anger. I'd done that twenty-five-hour bus journey for nothing.

'That night I spent most of my remaining money on another bus ticket, and went back to the coastal city, a thirteen-hour ride. When I walked into the Migration Office the following day, I was too furious to feel worried. The person I saw there said I had to pay a fine, because I hadn't notified them I was no longer living at my original address. I was boiling inside and I lost my temper. "You people won't let me work," I said to the official, "and now you won't let me leave the country! Why don't you put me in prison?"

'The official said he couldn't send me to prison and that I *was* free to leave the country, but first I had to pay the fine. I demanded to see somebody more senior and was taken to the chief officer. We had a heated exchange, but then he told me to sit down. He looked at my passport and said I *was* free to go to Iraq, and both his junior official and the people at the border had got it wrong. I would only have to pay the fine, if and when I came back to Turkey. He sent for the junior official and gave him a dressing down, which I enjoyed watching. Then he told me to wait while he made a few phone calls. Finally he said the reason I'd had a problem was that all the staff at the border post near Silopi were new to the job and didn't know what they were doing. He gave me his telephone number and said to call him if I had any further problems when I got back there.

'I thanked him and left. But when I counted what remained of my money, I realized I didn't have enough to get back to Silopi. I racked my brains as to what to do. In the end I decided that the only option, if I didn't want another horrendous job in a bar, was to go and live in a refugee camp, while I tried to raise some money. So I made my way to a town in Hatay province where I believed there was a camp for Syrians. When I got there, to my horror, an official told me that the camp had been moved to a new location. Not only that, when I showed him my passport, he said that I wasn't eligible to enter a refugee camp, because I had a valid tourist residence permit for Turkey!

'While we were speaking, two Syrian families arrived on foot. As newly arrived refugees entering Turkey illegally, they *were* eligible to enter a camp and preparations were made to transport them to the new camp, which was ten or twelve hours' drive away. Meanwhile, the officials called the mayor, to ask what to do with me. He said I should travel in the truck with the two families and the governor of the new camp would decide whether to let me in. We arrived at night, exhausted, and were left to sleep in a hall. In the morning, I persuaded the captain who ran the camp to let me in. Now at least I didn't have to worry about shelter or food.

'It was a closed camp, so once I was registered there, I couldn't go out. As camps go, it was a good one. They gave me a decent tent, and the food was fine, although the other Syrians complained because they wanted Syrian food. The place was clean and the medical care was good. There was no electricity, it was summer and the weather was very hot. There were 18,000 refugees, divided into neighbourhoods of 2,500, each one with a Syrian *mukhtar* (community leader) who was responsible for liaising with the camp authorities.'

'Eighteen thousand people?' I butted in, thinking perhaps I'd misheard. 'That's the size of a small city!' Then I remembered that Turkey has two and three quarter million Syrian refugees.

'They're all huge, the camps in Turkey.'

I gazed at Juwan, thinking he must have felt incredibly alone, knowing nobody, broke and effectively a prisoner. 'Did you feel okay there?' I asked.

He hesitated before replying. 'It's not easy living in a refugee camp as a single man, cut off from your family and your community. There was nobody from my part of Syria; and in a situation like that, people are suspicious of each other. I had to be especially careful in relation to the girls and women. If anyone thought I was talking to their daughter, they might not like it and they could make problems for me.

'After I'd been in the camp a few weeks, because I spoke good Turkish, the Red Crescent clinic asked me to help out as an interpreter. One of my tasks was to interpret for

Kamiran, a young Kurd who needed regular medical treatment at the local hospital. We were allowed out of the camp together for the hospital visits and soon became friends. Kamiran became very attached to me and used to say that he loved me and would never forget me. As time went by, I grew to feel the same way. His father was a smuggler based in Syria and one day Kamiran suggested that, after his medical treatment was completed, his father could smuggle both of us to a safe country. I had no wish to remain in Turkey and I thought it was a great idea.

'He was due to have an operation in a Turkish hospital in a city close to the Syrian border. We knew that I would be allowed to stay in the hospital with him during the operation, so we made a plan. When he was discharged, instead of returning to the camp, we'd run away to a place where his dad would meet us and help us to go to Iraqi Kurdistan and maybe from there to Australia or Europe – or wherever, just somewhere safe. I trusted Kamiran and liked the plan. But it never came to fruition: ten days before Kamiran's final operation, I was deported.'

Sintra had been listening in silence. Now she frowned and shot Juwan a look of disbelief. 'You were *deported*? How come? And where to?'

Juwan frowned, clearly touched by her reaction. 'I know,' he said, 'it's unbelievable that I had so much bad luck.' He took the fingers of his left hand one by one between his right thumb and forefinger and tugged at the joints until they clicked. 'I was deported back to Syria.'

In the latter months of 2011, while Juwan was making plans to leave the country, Syria's non-violent uprising gradually metamorphosed into an armed struggle against the regime.

In order to understand what the Syrian revolutionaries of spring 2011 were up against, it's important to appreciate that the vast majority of them, whether old or young, had no experience of active involvement in politics. For nearly fifty years, since the Ba'athists had come to power, independent political expression had been either banned or co-opted. The strongest manifestations of opposition, namely the campaign by the Muslim Brotherhood in the late 1970s, the Damascus Spring in 2001 and the Damascus Declaration in 2005, had all been crushed, with surviving activists going into exile.

From the early 2000s, however, partly in an attempt to develop a progressive image, the regime had encouraged the growth of an apolitical *civil* society. Asma al-Assad, wife of Bashar, had helped to establish NGOs in the areas of education, culture, health and social work. The stated aim was to engage youth in the big cities and to supplement inadequate state services.

Alongside the NGOs, unofficial social welfare groups had been able to form at grass-roots level. Their activists worked to meet the needs of the poor, the unemployed and those who had recently migrated from the countryside to the cities. Although the uprising began in spring 2011 as a spontaneous expression of popular anger, activists from the social welfare groups swiftly played a role in helping to coordinate the protests. As early as April 2011, numerous *tansiqiyat* (local coordination committees or LCCs) had formed in city neighbourhoods, towns and villages. These were forced to operate in secrecy, using the internet to liaise with *tansiqiyat* in other areas.

A typical *tansiqiya* might consist of as few as five full-time activists, often young people who quit their jobs or studies in order to focus full-time on the revolution.

Gradually, a group of activists close to the female human rights lawyer Razan Zaitouneh set up LCCs throughout the country. They promoted dialogue among the opposition, documented human rights abuses by the regime and tried to communicate what was going on to the outside world. After decades in which the media had been rigidly controlled, there was now an eruption of citizen journalism. Members of the LCCs moved around the country providing technical training and equipment and lessons in internet security.

In the early months, the main focus of the LCCs' work was organizing protests and demonstrations. Passionate believers in non-violent civil disobedience,[2] LCC activists struggled for unity among the protesters, without regard to sect or social background.

Across the country, extensive use was made of social media, particularly Facebook, to debate and vote upon the title of each Friday demonstration. The titles chosen, such as 'The Friday of Anger', 'The Friday of Dignity' and 'Your silence is killing us' were often a message to the outside world. The protesters adopted the pre-Ba'ath Syrian flag as a symbol of the revolution.

Juwan and Nizar both recounted how the regime reacted to the popular demonstrations with extreme violence. The regime bussed gangs of mainly Alawite thugs known as *shabbiha* (ghosts) to sites where demonstrations were anticipated, with specific instructions to beat up and kill participants. Soldiers were instructed to shoot to kill, and those brave enough to refuse were shot dead themselves without more ado. This is the position Juwan would have found himself in, had he not fled to Turkey. Mourners at the funeral processions for martyred demonstrators were frequently attacked by the security forces, so that in the more rebellious towns and cities life became a long cycle of protests followed by funerals followed by more protests and more funerals. Meanwhile, thousands were taken to detention centres, where they were subjected to the most extreme methods of torture. Women prisoners were raped. Thousands of Syrians, young and old, perished at the hands of the regime: a report by Amnesty International in August 2016 claimed that over 17,000 Syrians had died in detention in the five and a half years since the uprising began.[3]

In rebellious areas, life was made very difficult for ordinary Syrians in every way possible. Whole communities were subjected to collective punishments such as the cutting of the electricity, water and food supplies; internet and phone lines went down and checkpoints were set up, at which the security services monitored who was entering and leaving the area.

But the leaderless character of the uprising meant that it could not be stopped by the imprisonment or execution of individuals, nor by the paralysing of a particular LCC: if activity in one town or city was temporarily suppressed, demonstrations and protests would quickly erupt in others.

In the early months of 2011, the regime cast around for means by which to shore up the loyalty of those citizens who had not yet sided with the revolutionaries. Public promises of reform were made repeatedly, although little was delivered. Assad met with figures from public life such as judges, religious leaders and members of the business community, regardless of sectarian identity, in order to demand their loyalty. Big pro-regime demonstrations were organized, drawing in part on the large workforce of government employees. The loyalists called themselves the *menhebaki-yyeh* (Arabic for 'those who love you', the 'you' being Assad). Assad told this group of people that only he stood between them and the total collapse of the state. If the rebels were allowed to succeed, he warned, Syria would descend into the chaos which had recently affected Afghanistan and Iraq. This message played into real fears felt by the middle and upper classes, for whom life in Assad's Syria had been relatively tolerable, as described by Nizar. The result was that, in the early days, many moderate Sunnis were willing to support the regime.

Assad also courted those minorities whom he perceived as reluctant to join in the unrest. An agreement was made with Druze leaders in the south to prevent their lands becoming a battleground; and 300,000 Kurds in the north-east were offered citizenship, which hitherto they had been denied.

At the same time, the regime sought to vilify the protesters in every way possible. Assad variously sought to characterize the uprising as a foreign conspiracy by the US and Israel, and as the work of gangs of criminals. But undoubtedly the most pernicious element of the regime's propaganda war was its attempt to characterize the uprising as sectarian in nature.

In the years preceding the revolution, the various sects which make up the Syrian people had managed to coexist with a reasonable level of harmony. Tensions existed beneath the surface, and there was resentment on the part of Sunni Muslims about the extent to which the regime had packed out the army and security forces with Alawites and, to a lesser degree, Christians. In their daily interactions with each other, however, most Syrians were not unduly preoccupied with sectarian identity.

When the uprising began, although most of the protesters were working-class Sunnis, their motivation was not sectarian. Mosques were used as rallying points, but in the main the young people on the streets were not supporters of radical Islamist ideology. The demands were for freedom, dignity and a process of liberalization. Activists coordinating the protests went out of their way to ensure that banners and slogans were as inclusive as possible, so that members of minority sects would feel able to participate.

The regime, however, sought to play on the underlying fears of the minorities, claiming that the rebels were Sunnis bent on jihad. Their aim, it claimed, was to turn Syria into a Salafist[4] state. This was a clever tactic. By 2012, in several cities, armed Christian groups took to patrolling their own neighbourhoods, while Alawite women joined a defence force in Homs. Fear was perhaps deepest among the Alawites, who were told by the regime that victory by the Sunnis would lead to their slaughter.

The regime's efforts to sectarianize the conflict went beyond mere propaganda. A strategy was adopted of deliberately pushing the protest movement into the arms of the small minority of Syrians with radical Sunni Islamist views.[5] To this end, the regime released a substantial number of Salafist prisoners in the early months of the uprising, in what it presented as a gesture of liberalization.[6] Some of these were foreign jihadis who had been permitted to cross Syria years earlier, en route to fight US troops in Iraq, and who had been imprisoned on their return. It has been claimed that the regime went so far as to assist the newly released jihadis in their creation of armed brigades.[7] A number of them went on to become the commanders of major radical Islamist militias.[8]

The attempt to strengthen the hand of radical Sunni Islamists was an astute strategy on the part of the regime, intended to dampen the enthusiasm of western states for supporting the rebels.

At the same time as releasing Salafists, with utter cynicism the regime was killing, torturing and imprisoning mainly secular LCC members. These people were arguably the most able and progressive of Syria's youth, the very people who could have helped to unify the country and bring about democratic change.[9]

Every time I walked past the mini-supermarket, I caught sight of Fatima sitting at one of the café tables at the front, often with a couple of her friends. Usually the baby was on her lap; sometimes the toddler was running around in the dirt nearby. She'd been pleased with the dark green tunic I'd brought her, but even in warm weather she wore the coat dress over it. As I passed by she would wave, and sometimes I stopped for a chat. I would ask how she was and she would smile bravely, shrug her shoulders and utter the fatalistic '*Alhamdulillah*', followed by a question about how I was doing. Sometimes she asked about the buggy situation. By now I had a list on my phone of women who badly needed buggies, with Fatima's name at the top. Every time I went to the store I enquired, but invariably the answer was, 'We don't have buggies at the moment.'

Tonight as I sat down beside her, I could tell Fatima was in pain. She had her bad leg stretched out under the table and was sitting awkwardly on the plastic chair. The baby was asleep in her arms.

'Your leg's bothering you, isn't it?' I asked bluntly.

She looked at me through her thick-rimmed glasses, winced and raised her eyebrows very slightly. 'Always. I never have a day without pain.'

I shook my head, wondering how her leg had been injured. 'Have you seen the doctor?' I asked, nodding towards the place where MSF parked during the day.

'They gave me painkillers, that's all they can do.' She shrugged her shoulders. 'It's okay, I'm accustomed to it. But if you can bring me a buggy, that will be very good.'

When I stood up to go, she pulled me towards her with a smile which was at once warm and brave and kissed me on both cheeks. 'Thank you, sister,' she murmured.

6
Children's Corner and a Smuggler

Every day, after registration was completed, we would get into Charly's car and head a couple of kilometres up the road to the village of Efzoni, for lunch in a cheap restaurant. Over Greek salad and chips we'd discuss how the morning had gone and try to make plans for the rest of the day. So much needed doing, and there were only four of us. After lunch, those of us on packing duty went to Polykastro, while the others returned to Hara for a new project of Charly's called 'children's corner'.

The idea was to engage the younger children in calm, creative activities for an hour or so, both to amuse them and to give their exhausted parents a break. For equipment we relied on a set of interlocking rubber mats which we laid on the ground, some giant lego and a box of drawing materials. The first time we did children's corner, around seven children took part. Some played with the lego, others drew and a couple spent their time climbing on Ian's slender back. Ian's manner with both children and adults was good-humoured and utterly unassuming and everybody liked him.

On the evening of the fourth children's corner, it was almost dusk when Ian and I set up. No sooner had we taken the rubber mats out of the car than a trail of twenty children followed us across the tarmac, skipping, seizing our free hands and clamouring for pencils and lego. We chose a spot between the hotel and the dustbins and assembled the mats. Two or three parents arrived with very small children. I was giving out sheets of copy paper and trying to explain that, because our supplies were very limited, each child could have only one pencil. They had to choose a colour and if, later, they wanted another, they had to give back the first one. Some of the kids took a colour from the packet of pencils in my hand, looked wistfully at the other colours, then threw themselves down on the mat and started to draw. But others stood and argued, saying they had to have red as well as green and look that child over there has a purple and a blue. I did my best to be even-handed, but occasionally I turned a blind eye to injustice.

One little girl caught my eye that evening. She was probably five, well built, with astonishingly thick black hair neatly plaited in two fat ropes and tied at the ends with blue elastic bands. At first she hovered on the edge of the mat, watching and not speaking. Eventually I persuaded her to sit down and draw. She seemed to enjoy herself, drawing a love heart and a flower with vigour. By the end of the session, I discovered that she'd got round my system and made herself a hoard of eight coloured pencils.

The two long-haired boys from the Homsi family were with us that evening. Iyad, the youngest, forced his way into the middle of the mats and sat on his haunches, bare arms and legs very brown against his turquoise singlet and red shorts. He loved to draw and worked with great enthusiasm, but his concentration span was less than a minute. I'd seen enough of his behaviour on previous occasions to know he needed watching closely. I was sitting on the edge of the circle with one of my hands resting on the box where we kept the pencils and paper, when a new child tapped me on the shoulder to ask for a pencil. I then made the fatal mistake of turning away. Within seconds there was a howl of pain from a little boy of three a couple of feet in front of me. Iyad had sunk his teeth into the boy's arm, leaving a visible indentation.

The three-year-old's dad was not far away. He picked up his son, calmed him down and didn't seem bothered about meting out punishment to Iyad. After that I decided to conduct an experiment. I took Iyad by the hand and led him over to the far side of the mat where I sat him down, facing me, and asked if he'd like me to do a drawing for him. He nodded. So I drew an English picture book cottage, with four windows, a door, a chimney and a little path winding across a front garden. I talked as I drew, thinking that for a child from a Syrian city, an English cottage might seem rather alien. I told Iyad this was a picture of the house where I live in my country, and he watched with close attention.

When I'd finished, I gave him a clean sheet of paper and asked him to draw something for me. I sat close enough to grab his arm if he lashed out at another child, and close enough for him to feel contained. He seized the sheet of paper and set to work with passionate enthusiasm. When he'd finished, he proudly showed me his work, in response to which I lavished him with praise. We carried on like this for twenty minutes, each taking it in turns to draw for the other. There was no more aggression, and Iyad's face took on a look of absorbed contentment.

By the time we'd packed up it was dark, although the forecourt was still thronging with people. The wind was getting up and I wondered if it was going to rain. As Ian and I climbed the steps to the restaurant, Hasan appeared through the crowd on the verandah. He grinned at us warmly and clapped hands first with Ian, then with me. 'Salam,' he cried. 'Where've you been, I was looking for you?'

'With the kids,' Ian replied. 'We had twenty-two this evening! We're going to the bar. Coming?'

It took us a couple of minutes to fight our way through the crowded restaurant to where the Greek woman sat on her stool, drawing on one of her extra long cigarettes. She nodded when she saw us, got to her feet and started to line up polystyrene cups.

While Ian ordered the teas, Hasan told me there'd been a fight on the verandah half an hour earlier. It had started with an argument between two men about whose turn it was to use the restaurant's socket to charge their mobile phone. One of the men had come close to hitting the other in the face with a plastic chair and for a few moments punches were thrown, until Stassos lost his temper and threatened to call the police.

I translated the story for Ian as I took my tea. 'I guess everybody's stressed out,' I said to Hasan.

'Stressed out, tired, worried about their situation. Still, people shouldn't be hitting each other, should they?'

'No, of course not . . .'

Ian passed Hasan his tea, fanning away the smoke from the barwoman's cigarette. 'I don't know how I'd cope if I had to live like this.'

A stockily built man who'd been standing with his back to us turned and looked at Ian. 'You'd cope!' He spoke in English with a Syrian accent. 'If someone had asked me a few months ago if I could live in a tent on a petrol station forecourt, I'd have said "no way!"' The man caught Hasan's eye and repeated himself in Arabic. 'By the way, how's your head?'

Hasan ran a hand through his hair. He sucked his teeth, indicating that the bruise no longer bothered him. I hadn't noticed the man at the demonstration and asked if he'd witnessed the incident with the car.

'Sure, I was sitting beside Hasan in the road. I saw you guys, too.' He smiled broadly and held out his hand. 'My name's Burhan. Pleased to meet you.'

I shook Burhan's hand and watched him as he turned to Ian. He was pale-skinned and solidly built with shoulder-length hair and a beard, aged about twenty-one.

'Your English's very good!' I said in Arabic. I wasn't sure which language to use. If we spoke English, Hasan might feel left out. He'd learned English at school, but his understanding was limited.

'I was studying for a degree in English,' Burhan replied. 'Planning to become a teacher.'

'In Damascus?'

'Aleppo. I enjoyed it so much.' He took a swig from a plastic water bottle. 'But then this war happened and I had to stop. I'm struggling now to remember my English.'

Ian grinned. 'It sounds pretty good to me. You know, Hasan here has promised to teach me Arabic. Perhaps we should start some kind of a school . . .'

'A school? In this shithole?' Burhan chuckled. 'Are you serious?'

'Why not? There are maybe 200 kids of school age at Hara. They're missing out on their education.' Ian was semiserious. 'I could teach history; you could teach English . . .'

Burhan stared at him with a mixture of amusement and disbelief. 'No, man,' he said slowly, 'I don't think so.' He cleared his throat. 'People are in too much of a mess.' He swept one arm in the direction of the crowded restaurant tables behind us. 'Everybody's trying to figure out what to do, shall I go with a smuggler, shall I wait for the border to open, how long's my money going to last . . .'

Ian nodded. 'Okay, I was half joking.' He put down his tea and rested his back against the bar. 'But, seriously, we keep trying to figure out what we should be focusing on as a group of foreign volunteers. What d'you think is the thing that's most needed at Hara? Right now?'

Burhan gazed at Ian for a moment, then placed a large hand over his stomach. 'Food. Everybody's hungry. Every single person. All we get to eat is the shit from that food van.' He glanced at me as if concerned I might be offended by his language. 'Sorry, but *you* don't have to eat it!'

'Is it that bad?'

Burhan wrinkled his broad nose. 'I have stomach ache *all* the time.'

Ian and I looked at each other.

'If you can do something to get us more food, and *better* food, that will be a great service.'

I glanced at Hasan. 'What d'you think of the food?'

Hasan hesitated. 'It tastes okay, but there's not enough of it.'

'Are you hungry?' As I put the question I felt a pang of discomfort. What was I going to do if he said 'yes'? Buy him a meal? I didn't want it to get round that I was prepared to feed people – I would run out of money in a day.

'*Yani*, I could eat a lot more.' He grinned. It was obvious, I reflected, from the hollows in his cheeks that he wasn't getting enough food, or enough sleep. He was the same age as my son and I felt bad for him. 'But I like the school idea,' Hasan went on. 'I want to learn English.' His expression brightened. 'Ian said he'd teach me.'

I put this to Ian. For me, the fact that the refugee children were missing out on education was a major issue. It wasn't just a problem here in Greece: many of the Syrian children in Turkey, Lebanon and Jordan were also losing out.[1] What hope would there be for a stable post-war Syria if a whole generation missed out on education?

'Sure thing,' Ian replied, 'I'll teach him English. And I want to learn Arabic. Tell him I'd like to do a swap.' He reached in his back pocket for the notebook and pencil he carried everywhere.

Burhan brightened. 'Here, Hasan, Ian wants to learn Arabic. Show him how to write his name.'

Hasan put his tea down on the counter and picked up the pencil. Soon he and Ian were hunched over the tiny pages of the notebook, while Hasan demonstrated how to form the letters of Ian's name.

'That's cool!' Burhan grinned at me. 'But Arabic's hard, I hope Ian's good at languages.'

'He speaks Turkish,' I said, 'I think he's pretty clever.'

'He looks clever.' Burhan grinned. 'And you? What other languages do you speak?'

'French and Spanish.' I stirred my tea, struggling to formulate a question. 'Tell me,' I began. 'You were hoping to become a teacher – and hopefully you will, one day. Doesn't it worry you that all these youngsters are out of school?'

Burhan's face fell. 'Of course. It's a disaster.'

'This is the generation who will have to rebuild Syria after the war.'

'Ha, when it ends! I don't think that's gonna be any time soon.'

I would go on thinking about the issue of education long after I left Hara. It seemed to me that if western governments genuinely wanted to help Syrians, then helping refugees in camps to provide education for their children ought to be a top priority. Hara, like other camps, was brimming with bright and able youngsters who were crying out to be engaged and occupied. An education programme needn't be massively expensive: there were plenty of experienced teachers among the refugee adults. Initially, the issue would be to create a level of order and provide safe, calm spaces where children could be engaged in constructive activities for a few hours a day.

Burhan was signalling to me with his eyebrows to look behind me. I swivelled round. At a table a few feet away, a man in jeans and a leather jacket was deep in conversation with a couple of Syrians. 'Smuggler,' Burhan murmured.

'Oh.' I looked again, keen to observe more closely a member of this curious profession. The man was black, short and stocky.

'Where d'you think he's from?'

'Sudan. Most of them are.'

I was surprised. If he was Sudanese, didn't that mean he was a refugee, too? And how would someone who was not from the Balkans know the mountains well enough to guide people across them at night? 'I guess they use local guides?' 'Of course.' I glanced back at the smuggler. I would have liked to listen in on his conversation with his clients, but the bar was crowded and I could barely hear the people close to me. Beside me, Ian had mastered his name in Arabic script and was writing a simple sentence in English for Hasan. And now I saw Charly beckoning me from the double doors to the verandah. She was going back to FYROM early this evening and had promised to give me a lift.

7

A Burning Summer

In addition to providing refuge for an ever-increasing number of refugees, from mid-2011 Turkey became host to both the political and the military wings of the official Syrian opposition.

By the late spring of 2011, there were many divisions within the broad movement opposing Assad. Chief among them were those between Islamists and secularists; and between insiders and exiles. Some of the latter had been living outside Syria for decades, and had little or no relationship with the activists on the ground inside the country.

A series of conferences were held in Turkey in the summer of 2011 in an attempt to unify the opposition, and resulted in the birth of the Syrian National Council (SNC). It was largely made up of exiles from the long-exiled and well-financed Muslim Brotherhood (MB), secular activists from the Damascus Declaration and representatives of the LCCs. It is noteworthy that the MB appeared to have been taken unawares by the beginning of the uprising and had played no role during the first six weeks. Nevertheless, it now sought to dominate the movement against Assad.

The stated aim of the SNC was the 'overthrow of the regime, its symbols and its head', but from the start it was hampered by two difficulties. The first was its domination by exiles and the second was its failure to attract the participation of Kurdish groups.[1] The latter difficulty was hardly surprising, given that the SNC was led by Arabs who refused to give any guarantee that Kurdish cultural and political rights would be respected in a post-Assad Syria. They insisted that Syria should retain its previous denomination as the 'Syrian Arab Republic'.

Another criticism of the SNC voiced by some Syrians was that the MB was allowed to play too big a role, with the result that minority groups such as Christians, Alawis and secular Sunnis felt reluctant to participate.

During this period, certain Middle Eastern states adopted pro- and anti-Assad stances which they would maintain throughout the war. Iran stood firmly beside Assad, while Turkey, Qatar and Saudi Arabia all turned against him by the end of the summer. For reasons which will become clear later, these three states shared two convictions which turned out to be erroneous: firstly, that the Syrian regime would crumble quickly; and, secondly, that military intervention by the west was highly likely.

Returning to the Syrian rebels, there was much debate both within the opposition generally and within the SNC as to whether violent means should be adopted by the revolution. In the eerily prophetic words of the writer Emile Hokayem:

Many activists who spearheaded the popular mobilization . . . feared that resorting to arms would cost the revolution the moral high ground; play to the advantage of a militarily stronger regime; radicalize the movement; shift power from civilian activists and politicians to armed commanders; put at risk and antagonize the population; cause immense material destruction and the collapse of state institutions; and create an opening for foreign involvement, including for jihadi fighters looking for a cause in the Arab world.[2]

At a conference in June 2011, the SNC made a commitment to 'peaceful revolution' and rejected the idea of western military intervention. As the months went on, however, and the violence developed, senior figures in the SNC came to the view that western military intervention, if it could be achieved, was their best hope of success.

Meanwhile, in the late spring and summer of 2011, appalled by orders to shoot their fellow citizens, soldiers had begun to defect from the Syrian army. In the late summer, the Free Syrian Army (FSA), was formed in Istanbul by some of these defectors, the vast majority of whom were Sunni and from the lower ranks of the army. By mid-2012, it was estimated that between 30,000–60,000 had defected. I was later to meet the wife of a defecting officer on my second visit to Greece, in January 2017.

The defectors were soon joined by civilian combatants, most of whom would have done two years' military service but who nonetheless had only basic fighting skills.

Early in 2012, elements in the SNC, mainly from the MB, advocated the endorsement of a military strategy. They pointed to the growing regime violence and the need for self-defence, as well as the fact that the anticipated western intervention had not materialized. By now, Saudi Arabia and Qatar were both calling for the rebel groups to be supplied with weapons. Some activists and representatives of LCCs strongly resisted this, but their pleas were not heeded[3] and by March 2012 the SNC had abandoned its opposition to the use of violence.

On the ground inside Syria, peaceful demonstrations continued in early 2012, alongside the armed struggle.

In August 2011, the US called for Assad to stand down. This was echoed in a similar joint statement by Britain, France, Germany and Canada and was wrongly interpreted by many countries as an indication that the west was indeed planning a military intervention. It appears to have influenced the decisions made by Turkey, Qatar and Saudi Arabia to break ties with Assad and support the rebels.

Turkey played a crucial role in the militarization of the opposition. Having hosted the FSA at its inception, it then allowed opposition militias to transport weapons and personnel into Syria across the 910-kilometre border between the two countries, and to use Turkey as a base to which they could retreat. It offered sanctuary to deserters, and its military intelligence agencies turned a blind eye to rebel activities in Turkish refugee camps.

Despite Turkish support, the FSA had huge problems from its inception. There were serious difficulties in reconciling the different approaches taken to fighting the regime by, on the one hand, relatively disciplined former members of the military and, on the other, civilian combatants who were more inclined to risky behaviour. The FSA's leadership was inexperienced and it was unable to exert more than nominal control over the armed groups which loosely operated under its banner. The proliferation of these groups was so fast that by the end of 2012 they are thought to have numbered around five hundred. By then there were also another five hundred armed opposition groups which were *not* affiliated to the FSA. The groups varied greatly in size, geographical location and ideology. While many had a Sunni Muslim identity, not all were motivated by radical Islam. Some groups were disciplined in their behaviour; others chaotic. Concerned about atrocities committed by some of its member groups, the FSA announced that it would respect international law as it governs armed combat, but it had no way to enforce this.

I assumed that some of the men I met at Hara had spent time fighting with rebel militias. Given that they'd now decided to seek asylum in Europe, I didn't think they'd want me asking them about it.

Initially, the rebel militias obtained their light weapons from regime arsenals or bought them on the black market. Workshops were set up to produce bombs and ammunition. Heavier weapons came from abroad, but initially the supply of these was modest. In order to obtain funding, whether from the west or Arab countries, each rebel group had to promote itself through social media, and some groups deliberately adopted Islamist-sounding names in order to appeal to potential funders.

Many Syrian individuals living in western countries and the Gulf sent funds to the rebels. In the US, a NGO known as the Syrian Support Group sent funds via Military Councils created in 2012, because these were seen by the US government as 'moderate'.[4]

Despite the SNC's endorsement of armed struggle, attempts to create links between the SNC and the fighting groups which were now emerging were unsuccessful. As it became clear that Assad's regime was not going to crumble quickly, the weakness of the SNC became more and more apparent and some members resigned. It also became evident that the activities of the anti-Assad states – Turkey, Qatar and Saudi Arabia – were dividing the Syrian opposition.

Two whole days went by before I managed to sit down again with Juwan. Late one afternoon I found him at a table on the verandah with a couple of friends. He held out his hand. 'How are you?'

'Good,' I replied, 'and you?' As he replied I glanced at the other young men. 'Are you free now?'

Juwan looked amused. 'Why, d'you want to hear Part Three?'

I smiled. 'I'm dying to know why Turkey deported you. Are you in the mood for talking?'

'Sure, I'd like to tell you the rest of the story. But where's Sintra?'

'Packing clothes in Polykastro.'

'Ah, okay, I'll talk to her another time.' He pulled out a chair for me, explaining to his friends that we had something to talk about. As they got up he rubbed his chin. 'We got to the point where I was living in the camp, didn't we?'

I nodded.

'I spent a burning summer there.'

'The heat?'

'The heat, living in a tent . . . And things went so badly for me!' As he puckered his forehead, the scar above his left eyebrow disappeared. 'To begin with, I was on friendly terms with everyone, including the captain who ran the place. Not many of the refugees spoke Turkish, so I helped out by interpreting, mainly at the Red Crescent clinic—'

'Tell me,' I butted in. 'Was there a Free Syrian Army presence in the camp?'

'Yes.'

'What did you think of them?'

'In general, I had a very high opinion of the rebels at that time. My idea was that they were extraordinary people, very good. I thought the FSA were the true men, who had ideal ethics and morals. They were sacrificing their lives for the sake of the Syrian people and I was in awe of them.'

'Did you meet some of them?'

'Not really, I felt I couldn't approach them, because I was impure and not a real man! They were fighters and I was not.'

'So you spent your time interpreting?'

Juwan shifted in his seat. 'Yes. And it was all fine for a long time, until two things happened that caused me a lot of problems.' He grimaced. 'The first involved a young Syrian girl who came to the clinic every day to help fold the gauzes used by the nurses when they made dressings. I didn't know her well, but I always said hello to her. She was beautiful. One day a Turkish security guard asked me to get the girl's phone number for him. When I asked him what he wanted with her, he said 'marriage', but I was convinced his real intention was simply to have sex with her.

'I didn't like the guard and I was worried for the girl. So, in order to put him on the spot, I offered to go to the girl's father and try to convince him to let the guard marry her. As I suspected, the guard was horrified, saying, "No, no, don't do that." Afterwards he stopped asking me to get her phone number, but he started to make problems for me. I was alone in the camp, without relatives to stick up for me, which made me an easy target. For example, one day there was a fight in the camp and when the police were called, the same guard said *I* was one of the trouble-makers. Luckily they didn't believe him; but then something else happened, which put me in a very vulnerable position.

'One of the nurses who worked in the Red Crescent clinic was a Kurdish woman called Aya, in her mid to late thirties. She was from the city of Diyarbakir, in south-eastern Turkey. Aya liked me and one day she invited me to visit her family. I would need a special permission to travel outside the camp, and she said she'd try to get it for me. At the time I didn't think too much about it, although with hindsight I wish I had.

'Like I said, I was on friendly terms with the captain who ran the camp. After Aya applied for the permission, I bumped into him and he asked how I was. Then he added "I think we have to move you to another camp." I protested, saying I'd got to know people here and wanted to stay. He said "Yes, yes, but there are people in the camp who're making problems for you."

'A little later that morning, Aya came and found me. She said that her request for me to visit her family in Diyarbakir[5] had raised some eyebrows among camp officials. She'd had a visit from intelligence men, who'd wanted to know why she was interested in me. They'd subjected her to an interrogation, in the course of which they'd accused her of having slept with me, which was totally untrue. Their line was that she was trying to seduce me, with the intention of later getting me to join the PKK. The whole thing was a complete fabrication, but very unpleasant for her. I told her I was so sorry she'd gone through that on my account.

'Early the next morning, the security guard who'd asked me to get the girl's telephone number came to my tent with four or five other guards. He woke me up, saying I had visitors. I thought that was very odd – who would come to visit me? The guard said I should get up and they'd drive me to the visitor tent. Once I was in the truck, I started to have doubts. There was another refugee with us, who was accused of burning down somebody's tent; and instead of taking us to the visitor tent, they drove us both to the gendarmerie. I went inside and was immediately told to kneel, facing the wall. I had no idea what it was all about, but of course I felt very worried. Then a group of soldiers started to beat me from behind. The beating went on until a voice called "Enough!" I was shaking, terrified and in pain, when suddenly a soldier accused me of fighting for the PKK.

' "You came here as a refugee", he yelled, "and then you went to the mountains to fight for the PKK! You came from your country to fight our country!" They started to hit me round the back of the head, on the ear, which was very painful. Then just as suddenly they stopped and the corporal called me over. He said he would deport me to Syria. "We'll send you to the Free Syrian Army," he sneered, "and they'll kill you, we don't need to kill you ourselves." He gestured at another guy who was the Syrian *mukhtar* of my neighbourhood. I didn't know if this guy genuinely had FSA connections or not, but the prospect that he might tell the FSA to hurt me was terrifying. Then the corporal asked how come I spoke fluent Turkish. I told him I'd been in Turkey for nine months, but he replied it wasn't possible to learn to speak a language so well in such a short time.

'I vigorously denied having anything to do with the PKK. I said, "If you can prove I fought with the PKK, then feel free to cut my throat." After I said that he calmed down a bit but said he didn't want me in the camp. I replied, "Well, I can't go to Syria, death awaits me in Syria!" After a few moments he said he would send me to another camp. I still didn't want to go, but anything was better than being deported to Syria, so I said, "Ok, send me to another camp."

'The corporal handed me to a guard who took me to the office responsible for transferring people to different camps. But he was told I couldn't be transferred, because the other camp was full. I was in a lot of pain from the beating and the guard was about to take me back to the gendarmerie, where I thought I'd be beaten again, so I said, "Ok, I'll go back to Syria. Take me to Reyhanli (in Turkey) and send me over the border towards Bab al-Hawa (in Syria)." I knew this area was in a liberated zone, so I would be safe there from the regime, if not the FSA.

'The office made me sign a paper saying I agreed to be deported the following day, and let me go.

'I staggered about in a state of disorientation. I'd been beaten, I was terrified and suddenly I was running a fever. I lay down in the shade in my tent and thought what the hell is going on, why am I so unlucky, and *what am I going to do now?* I wanted to cry, but my throat was tight and I couldn't.

'Later that day, I saw Kamiran. I told him about the deportation and asked for his father's phone number. He said, "Call him when you get to Syria, he'll pick you up near the border and take you to our house. After my operation I'll do my best to join you there." Then I went to the clinic to get an injection for the fever – I didn't mention the beating – and while I was waiting to be seen I met the captain. He asked how I was and I started to tell him about the beating, but his phone rang. While he took the call, I had the injection, thinking I could continue speaking with him afterwards. But when I came out, I couldn't find him. Somebody said to try the restaurant, but he wasn't there, nor was he at the Red Crescent tent. I tried the technicians' tent, as I knew some of the plumbers. But when I opened their door, the corporal who had questioned me barked at me to go out and the guy who was with him started to laugh. I fled. The only place I didn't check was the military tent, and I didn't dare go there. I felt terrible.

'Each time I saw Kamiran that afternoon, he kept saying that he and his family would help me. Osman, who lived in the tent next to mine, also said he would try to help, by getting the deportation revoked. I wasn't sure they could do anything and I went to bed that night expecting to be deported the next day. Early in the morning, the same security guards of the morning before came to my tent and told me to take all my stuff and go with them. I shoved a few things into a plastic bag – two T-shirts, a pair of flip flops, trainers, a towel and my phone. I was in the habit of leaving my cash with a friend, rather than in the tent, for fear of being robbed, so all I had on me was a handful of coins. My passport was with the camp administration.

'The guards took me to the gendarmerie and told the officer in charge I'd informed the captain about them beating me. I denied it, but the captain's interpreter was present and he confirmed that I'd spoken to the captain. At least they didn't hit me this time. They told me to wait outside the tent till the deportation bus came.

'While I was waiting, Osman came along and asked what was going on. I told him I was waiting to be deported and asked if he'd been able to do anything to help me. He said he was trying to get the deportation revoked, but he needed to phone someone. So I gave him my phone to make the call. To my horror, as he started to talk on the phone, he walked away. I was shocked, but I daren't follow him or I'd have the guards after me. Osman wasn't that good a guy, but I never thought he'd steal my phone. I felt sick as I waited and waited and he didn't return. Later in the morning, I was moved to a cabin close to the exit, ready for the deportation.

'Three other men were with me. They fully deserved deportation: they'd tried to rape a disabled child. I was wondering if there was any way I could get permission to go to my tent to get my phone back off Osman and get my cash from my friend; but the guards would only let me go if I agreed to be handcuffed, and I couldn't bear the humiliation.

'A security guard passed by and mentioned to an army officer that I was in the same cabin as the other three deportees just for convenience. He said, "Sorry you're being deported with these three assholes, I know you're a decent human being."

'At midday, they put the four of us in a van with some refugees who were returning voluntarily to Syria. The rapists were Sunnis from Latakia and the returning refugees were from Latakia, too. Latakia has a population of both Sunnis and Alawites, but it was under the control of the regime and there was no way I wanted to be taken anywhere near it. I thought it was agreed that I would be dropped off in Bab al-Hawa, just over the border from Turkey, but the van kept going and going and the sun went down and it got dark. I didn't try to speak to the driver because I was in such a state of disorientation, feeling completely lost. Eventually, several hours after dark, the van stopped and we were told to get out. When I realized we weren't at Bab al-Hawa, I asked the driver why he hadn't let me out earlier. He shrugged his shoulders, saying he was told to take everyone to the same place.

'We were on a mountain top which, as the crow flies, was one kilometre from an area under regime control. The other deportees had no problem with the regime, so it was okay for them to be dropped here; for me it was extremely danger-ous. As I stood on the side of the road in the cold night air, all I had with me was the plastic bag with my few clothes; no jacket, no boots, no phone and no documents except my Syrian ID card and military book. And I hadn't eaten for a day and a half.'

8

Turkey, Saudi Arabia, Qatar and Iran

In order to understand how and why the internal Syrian conflict became an international war it is necessary to look at how the regional balance of power stood in 2011. That, in turn, is best understood by tracing how things had changed during the previous decade.

After the collapse of the USSR in 1991, the US had become the dominant power in the Middle East. This had enabled George W. Bush to launch his war against Saddam Hussein in Iraq in 2003. By 2011, however, Barack Obama's administration had brought home all US troops from Iraq. Obama was deeply reluctant to engage in any further Middle Eastern adventures. This left a power vacuum in the region which several regional states sought to fill, under the watchful eye of Russia.

After toppling Saddam Hussein, in 2006 the US had installed a Shi'a-dominated regime in Baghdad under the premiership of Nouri al-Maliki. He pursued an aggressively sectarian policy which angered the Sunni minority who had dominated the country under Saddam.[1] Civil war erupted, in the course of which hundreds of foreign jihadis entered the country – many via Syria – to fight on the side of the Sunnis; but ultimately the Shi'a remained in control of the country.

Historically, Sunni-dominated Iraq and Shi'a-dominated Iran had been bitter enemies; and as such they'd contained each other's ambitions. With the installation of Nouri al-Maliki, the enmity came to an end and Iran became Iraq's close and influential ally. Ironic though it is, Iran was the main beneficiary of the ill-planned US intervention. Iranian influence in the Middle East now increased substantially and, from 2005, Iran's new hardline president Ahmadinejad felt freer to pursue his ambitions than his predecessors had done.

One of the results was that the long-standing rivalry between Iran and Saudi Arabia intensified. Saudi is mainly Sunni and closely allied to the west. The ruling Saudi monarchy had long been suspicious of Iran as a Shi'a power and afraid of its potential influence on Saudi's own repressed Shi'a minority, who make up 15 per cent of the population. A further Saudi concern was about the vulnerability of its lucrative oilfields in the Persian Gulf, which are relatively close to Iran and located in a Shi'a-majority area.

Iran has had a long-standing alliance with the Assad regime in Syria, based largely on both countries having traditions of opposition to Israel and the west. Another of Iran's key allies is Hezbullah (the Party of God), the Lebanese Shi'a party-cum-militia. Hezbullah was established in the early 1980s by Lebanese Shi'a seeking to expel the invading Israelis from south Lebanon, and has always depended on Iranian support. It is the only political party which was allowed to retain its militia after the ending of the Lebanese civil war in 1990. Although Hezbullah plays a major role in Lebanese parliamentary politics, Lebanese governments tend to have strong alliances with Saudi Arabia and the west. The result is that Iranian supplies of weaponry to Hezbullah cannot be flown into Beirut, but rather are flown into Syria and transported from there to eastern Lebanon by road. Thus, for Iran, maintaining good relations with Syria is vital to enable it to continue to support Hezbullah.

Iran's support for Hezbullah and for the Palestinian groups Hamas and Islamic Jihad (both of which had head-quarters in Damascus at the beginning of the revolution) reflects its desire to maintain a high level of pressure on Israel and, indirectly, the US. As Iranian influence in the region rose following the toppling of Saddam Hussein, Iran acquired popularity on the Arab street by berating Arab regimes such as Saudi Arabia with strong links to the west. But the new popularity was dented when Iran put down its own unarmed protesters during their 'Green Revolution' in 2009.[2]

Around this time, Israel's premier Netanyahu began campaigning for Iran to be made the subject of UN sanctions due to its nuclear enrichment programme. He succeeded in 2010. By early 2011, partly due to the sanctions, Iran's leadership was feeling less confident about its country's future as a rising regional power. Given that insecurity, and given the long history of close relations between Iran and Syria, after some internal debate, Iran decided to support Bashar al-Assad in preference to the Syrian rebels. This was not an easy decision to make, because supporting Assad would destroy any remaining popularity Iran enjoyed on the Arab street.

After 2003, Saudi Arabia had become deeply troubled by the prospect of Iran acquiring a nuclear capability. In response, the Saudi monarchy invested heavily in the military, increasing its arms imports from the US ninefold in the period from 2008 to 2011.

Relations between Saudi Arabia and Syria had historically not been easy, due to their opposing alliances during the Cold War and Syria's close links with Iran. But both sides were capable of opportunism, and, in 2009–10, visits were exchanged between Bashar al-Assad and the Saudi King Abdullah.

In the vacuum created by the decline of American power after 2003, and under cover of the increased rivalry between Iran and Saudi Arabia, a tiny Sunni Muslim emirate, the peninsular state of Qatar, had begun to expand its political role in the region. Qatar, which hosts a US air force base, has only 300,000 citizens (plus over a million migrant workers), and such immense wealth from natural gas that its people enjoy the highest per capita income in the world. Qatar's then leader, Emir Hamad, had for some time wanted to distance Qatar from Saudi Arabia and had hosted the outspokenly anti-Saudi media outfit *al Jazeera* from 1996. In 2010–11, the highly ambitious Hamad was hoping to take over the role previously played by Saudi Arabia as regional mediator. To this end, he participated enthusiastically in pushing for the NATO intervention in Libya in 2011.

Sunni Muslim Turkey, like Iran, saw the fall of Saddam as an opportunity to expand its political role in the Middle East. After decades of secularism under the influence of Kemal Attaturk, Turkey had now been governed by the AKP, a moderate Islamic party, since 2002 under the premiership of Recep Tayyip Erdogan. Despite Turkey's westward-looking orientation, its membership of NATO and its close alliance with the US, by 2011 Erdogan was interested in developing closer links with his Middle Eastern neighbours, apparently hoping to renew some of the regional influence his country had enjoyed in Ottoman times.

Historically, relations between Turkey and Syria had been strained for a number of reasons. The two countries were on opposite sides during the Cold War; the issue of the formerly Syrian province of Hatay which the French had ceded to Turkey in 1939 remained unresolved; there was competition for water resources and, most problematic of all, Hafez al-Assad had allowed the PKK to operate from bases in Syria and Lebanon, until Turkey threatened an invasion in 1998. With the advent of Bashar to the Syrian presidency, however, both countries had pursued rapprochement. By 2011 Turkey enjoyed a thriving trade with Syria and the two leaders were on friendly terms, even holidaying together.

In the early months of 2011, Saudi Arabia, Qatar and Turkey all publicly maintained their support for Assad, while privately urging him to halt the violence which his security forces were meting out to the demonstrators. But by the late summer, all three countries had turned on the Syrian president and were calling for his departure.

Initially, Abdullah had been concerned about the potential threat to all Arab regimes, including his own, posed by the

Arab Spring, and he had been minded to support Bashar. With this in mind, he had sent one of his sons to Syria three times, hoping to convince Bashar to end the repression. The prince got nowhere with Bashar, however, and Abdullah took offence. By now he felt the threat to his own monarchy from the Arab Spring had passed and his chief concern was the thwarting of Iran. He decided the best way to achieve this was to support the Syrian opposition.

In Qatar, Emir Hamad believed he had grown in international stature as a result of his role in the Libya crisis and was keen to play a role in Syria, too. This was despite his recent close relationship with Assad, whom he had cultivated for the previous few years. By the late summer of 2011, Hamad decided to support the rebels, and in particular, those rebels who were affiliated with the MB.

When Turkey cut ties with Syria, one of the reasons was frustration at Assad's repeated refusal to take notice of Erdogan's pleas to reduce the violence and another was the latter's belief that the regime would soon fall. Erdogan believed that the winds of change represented by the Arab Spring would inevitably result in the sweeping away of autocratic Arab regimes, and he did not want to risk compromising his own considerable popularity in the Arab world by being seen to support a violent dictator. Erdogan hoped that, when Assad fell, he would be able to play a role in ensuring that the regime was replaced by a moderate Islamist democracy – preferably one dominated by the Muslim Brotherhood, with which he had good relations.

On 18 August, a call was made by Obama for Assad to step aside. At the same time, a similar call was made by

Britain, France and Germany. These two calls were interpreted by a number of Arab countries as indicating that the west was planning a military intervention in Syria. Although there was no such plan, Turkey, Qatar and Saudi Arabia felt confirmed in their inclinations to abandon Assad. On the ground in Syria, the rebels' hopes were falsely raised.

By early 2012, long before various sanctions against Syria put in place the previous autumn had had time to take effect, Saudi Arabia and Turkey were playing active parts in supporting armed Syrian groups. Given that neither state, nor Qatar, had in-depth knowledge of Syria nor any substantial experience of proxy warfare, the wisdom of their actions was questionable, to say the least. Their policy seems to have been based on a belief that the Syrian regime was about to crumble and an assumption that the US would be more likely to intervene if there were already an armed insurgency underway. Neither notion proved accurate.

It is difficult to establish when weapons were first sent to the rebels by external powers. By mid-2012, the opposition was reporting that only 15 per cent of their arms were supplied in this way. Large sums of money were donated to the rebels, some by individuals in friendly countries, others by governments. This enabled rebel groups to purchase weapons on the black market and to pay their fighters, who had families to support. As time went on, Qatar and Saudi Arabia both announced numerous schemes to fund the FSA. A Turkish NGO also donated money.

Of the weapons that were supplied by foreign states, some came from Libya, transported via Qatar into Turkey.

The Turkish government denied any involvement in making arrangements for the weapons that were flown or trucked into their country, but members of the Syrian opposition disputed this, claiming that by the summer of 2012, Turkish intelligence was organizing the distribution of weapons supplied by Qatar and Saudi Arabia to particular groups.[3] Less substantial deliveries of weapons reached the rebels through Jordan, northern Lebanon and Iraq, some sent by Saudi Arabia, via its tribal connections. Military command rooms were set up in Ankara, Istanbul and Amman.

Inevitably, the choices made by Qatar, Turkey and Saudi Arabia as to which groups to arm or finance were determined by their own agendas, with little regard to the impact on the course of the conflict nor to the suffering of the Syrian people. Qatar, for example, would gradually support the more radical of the Islamist militias, even those linked to al-Qaeda, many of which operated outside the FSA. Saudi Arabia was alarmed by this, predicting accurately that jihadis would become involved in the conflict.

Although Saudi Arabia had sent jihadis to fight the Russians in Afghanistan in the 1980s, by 2011, the monarchy was deeply concerned about the potential political impact on its own repressed population of jihadis who returned to the Kingdom preaching jihad against it. They did not want to see jihad in neighbouring Syria, and developed an intense dislike of the Muslim Brotherhood.

There was little or no coordination between the states which armed the rebels, and in some cases their activities served to fuel rivalry between opposition groups, rather than assist in the overthrow of Assad. The same applies to these states' activities in the political sphere. Of the three, Qatar and Turkey had the strongest links with the Muslim Brotherhood. In addition to providing military supplies, each state used their links, and, in Qatar's case, generous funding, to steer the politics of the SNC in directions that accorded with their goals.

Meanwhile, Iran had sent military advisers to assist the regime very early on in the crisis, and by 2012, western officials claimed that it was supplying Assad with rockets, rocket-propelled grenades, anti-tank missiles and mortars, even though this would have been in breach of UN sanctions. In May 2013, Hezbullah admitted that its militiamen were fighting in Syria on the side of the regime.

Iran also sent foreign Shi'a – from places such as Pakistan and Afghanistan – to fight for Assad. After numerous defections and desertions from the Syrian army, there was a serious shortage of manpower, with troop numbers reduced by almost 50 per cent by 2013. Iran and Hezbullah strengthened what remained of the Syrian army by providing training and equipment and advising on military strategy. Iran also provided assistance with the monitoring of internet and other communications, intelligence sharing and counter-insurgency advice.[4] It is not clear how many Iranian personnel were sent to fight in Syria, but rebels have reported encounters with soldiers in Syrian army uniforms who only spoke Farsi. One Iranian commander, Qassem Suleimani of the Quds force, played a major role in reorganizing the Syrian army. He has been described as having become more powerful in Syria than Bashar al-Assad himself.

It was on the advice of the Iranians that Assad accepted that he should no longer try to defend against rebel attacks on army bases in remote rural areas, particularly in the north and east of the country. Having already abandoned some of the north-east to the Kurds, he now allowed the rebels to establish 'liberated' areas, while he focused on maintaining control over Syria's fourteen provincial capitals, most of which are in the centre and west of the country. This area has become known as 'rump Syria'.

Western countries also provided support to the armed rebels. In March 2012, Hillary Clinton claimed that the US would focus on humanitarian needs; but it appears likely that the CIA and other western intelligence agencies assisted with the distribution of weapons in Turkey. In July 2012, Clinton came up with a plan for the CIA to vet, train and equip a group of 'moderate' Syrians, but Obama rejected this, fearing that the weapons would get into the wrong hands.[5]

Britain and France provided non-lethal aid to the rebels and in 2013 persuaded the EU to lift its embargo on sending weapons to Syria.

As the rebellion expanded and fragmented from the spring of 2012, the Syrian opposition attempted to establish a Military Council (MC) in each province. These were run jointly by high-ranking defectors from the military and civilian commanders. The aim was to bypass the FSA command and to improve organization and communication. Many of the opposition's secular and nationalist militias joined the Military Councils, whereas some Islamist groups refused to do so. In December 2012, a Supreme Military Council (SMC) was formed, when several hundred rebel commanders met in Turkey in the presence of Western and Arab officials.

In November 2012, a meeting was held in Qatar, hosted by Hillary Clinton and Emir Hamad, to which the Syrian opposition and the SNC were invited. The result was a new organization to replace the SNC, known as the National Coalition for Syrian Revolutionary and Opposition Forces (NC). It was headed by Ahmed Moaz al-Khatib, an independent-minded imam who was well respected by both Islamists and secularists. Efforts were made to prevent the Muslim Brotherhood holding too much sway within the new body; the intention was that the NC would work closely with oppositionists active *inside* Syria. At a 'Friends of Syria' meeting in Marrakesh in late 2012, the NC was granted recognition as the 'sole representative of the Syrian people' by 140 countries.

Sadly, despite promising intentions, the NC was soon controlled by the anti-Assad regional states in the same way that the SNC had been, and Khatib was pushed aside. All his successors were protégés either of Saudi Arabia or Qatar as the two states became increasingly rivalrous for control of the Syrian opposition.

Both the US and the Saudis felt frustrated with the NC's domination by the MB and by its failure to form links with activists and fighters on the ground in Syria. In May 2013, a NC delegation was invited to Riyadh, where it was persuaded to reduce the strength of the MB within the NC and to try to include more minority representation. This was achieved, and in the new NC the FSA got fifteen seats, while one seat went to each of Syria's fourteen governorates, and a Christian opposition organization was given thirteen seats. In July 2013 a new, pro-Saudi president of the NC was elected.

While the influence of the MB was now reduced and that of Saudi Arabia increased, the NC still had little credibility as the legitimate representative of the Syrian people.

9

'Here, have my boots!'

I stood in the dirt in front of the Czech store, waiting for a lorry to pass. The traffic was sparse this morning, but the lorry was approaching at a frightening pace, raising a cloud of dust. The road ran in a plumb straight line from the bridge over the international highway to the first shops in Polykastro. On the far side, a couple of groups of refugees walked along the verge in the hot sun towards the town, trailing small children, identifiable by the women's head-scarves and the slow, weary pace at which they moved.

I was about to step out into the road when a young woman addressed me in Arabic. She was dressed in jeans and a loose blouse which merged with the folds of a fabric sling, through which I could make out the shape of a baby's head. The woman's arms were outstretched, holding the hands of two small children.

'Please,' she smiled, 'I need boots.' She stretched out one leg and flexed her foot to show me that the sole of her trainer was detached from the upper. 'Are there any in the store?'

She jerked her head at the building behind me. 'I'm a size thirty-nine.'

I wasn't sure what to do, given the rule about not giving out items directly from the store. I glanced down at the old pair of running shoes I was wearing. They were thirty-nines. I could give them to her, but then I would be shoe-less, as I'd already given my walking boots to someone in the camp.

'I'm really sorry,' I said. 'There *are* boots in the store, but we're not allowed to give them out.' As I spoke, one of the children wrapped herself around her mother's shin and the other tugged at her outstretched hand. I felt like a cowardly jobsworth. I understood the reasoning behind the rule, but the woman's need was urgent. 'Which camp are you in?'

'Karvalla.' The woman tossed her head in the direction of the bridge.

'I'm really sorry I can't help you,' I said again. 'Perhaps it's worth going into the store and asking someone who works there.' I jerked my thumb at the building behind me. 'Show them your broken shoe, say you're desperate.'

The woman thanked me and set off towards the store. As I crossed the road a moment later, it occurred to me that I could have gone into the store myself with my half-empty shoulder bag and pretended I was taking a pair of shoes for a refugee at Hara. I wished I had.

On the far side of the road I headed across a gravel car park and onto the verandah of the Park Hotel, temporary billet for scores of volunteers. Young people in T-shirts and shorts sat at tables drinking coffee in conspiratorial groups, tapping out WhatsApp messages with their thumbs and talking in hushed voices in English and German. Tobacco smoke swirled in a fetid cloud over the tables. One or two gangling young men sat alone, hunched over iPads. As I walked by, nobody so much as looked up, let alone glanced in my direction. Habituated now to the warm greetings I received all day long at Hara, I took this badly. Self-obsessed youth, I thought to myself grumpily. *So busy saving the world* . . . I opened the French doors and glanced briefly at the barrage of volunteer notices pasted on the walls of the reception area ('Lift wanted to Thessaloníki Thursday morning'; 'Volunteer meeting daily 8 p.m., in bar'; 'Legal briefing on asylum applications at Idomeni camp Friday 10 a.m.'). This last one looked interesting, so I stopped to make a note of the details. Then I made for the office.

My reason for visiting the Park was to rent a car. Charly had left this morning for a week in Oslo and Sintra was on her way home to the UK, leaving Ian and me without transport. A couple of experienced Northern Lights volunteers who'd been away on holiday were coming to join us, but their car was tiny so we needed one of our own. When the paperwork was done and the car keys safely in my pocket, I filled my bottle with cold water in the bar and retraced my steps across the road. I'd just reached the safety of the yard in front of the Czech store when I saw the woman with the broken boots again. She was standing face to face with a woman from the store, who was speaking excitedly in Spanish. One of the little girls was seated on the ground, sucking her thumb, watching with huge bewildered eyes. The other hid behind her mother's leg.

My Spanish is good so I went up to see if I could help. The Spanish volunteer turned to me with a look of exasperation. 'This lady needs something urgently,' she began, 'but I don't understand what it is she's after!'

'She needs footwear,' I replied. 'Look, the sole's coming away from the toe of her boot.'

A look of relief spread across the volunteer's face. 'Phew, if that's all it is, perhaps I can help.' She was petite and sporty-looking with thick curly hair, dressed in cut-off trousers and a T-shirt. 'Although, we're not supposed to give stuff out directly.' She turned round and glanced in the direction of the store, then looked at me. 'Can you ask her what size she takes?'

'Thirty-nine. I spoke to her earlier.'

'Thirty-nine?' The Spanish volunteer stooped down and began to unlace her own boots, a pair of blue lightweight ones which looked brand new. 'She can have these!' she cried, 'I've a spare pair in the van.'

Meanwhile, the young mother had grasped what was going on. 'No, no,' she exclaimed, shooting me a look of dismay. 'I can't take the boots off her feet!'

'She's embarrassed,' I explained to the Spaniard. 'She says she can't take them.'

The unlacing continued. 'She should try them, at least!' The Spanish volunteer removed the first boot, pushed open the tongue and held it out to the mother with a warm smile. 'Tell her I have another pair!'

It was impossible not to be caught up in the woman's enthusiasm. 'Just try it,' I said to the mother, 'you need the boots more than she does.' I held out my hand. 'Here, lean on me while you take off your old shoe.'

Still a little uncertain, the mother rested her hand on my arm and bent down to remove her trainer. The volunteer squatted down with the new boot and in no time at all had it laced up around the mother's ankle. Then she sat back on her haunches, beaming through her mass of curls. 'Well? It's a lovely fit, isn't it? Try the other one!'

The second boot fitted as beautifully as the first. As the mother straightened up, a smile spread across her face, mixed with a look of uncertainty. 'But I can't . . .' she stammered. 'Yes you can!' We both chorused, one in Spanish, one in Arabic. I then translated the long stream of thank yous which the mother addressed to her benefactor. In response the Spanish woman flung open her arms, embraced the mother and gave her a kiss on each cheek. I did the same and then the mother took the children by the hand and walked away. As I watched I saw a new spring in her step.

The hire car was tiny, a tin box on wheels, just big enough to carry a couple of boxes of clothing on the back seat, the mats for children's corner in the boot and me and Ian in the front. It was years since I'd driven on the right and I went gingerly at first. I knew by now that the volunteers *en masse* had a reputation for driving too fast and making U-turns when it suited them. This was no different from the driving style of many Greeks, but it was out of order. If I still had any latent anarchist tendencies from my distant student days, they didn't apply to the rules of the road. So I tootled at forty kilometres per hour down to the bridge and onto the international highway. Ian was meeting me at Hara, and while I familiarized myself with the gearstick and the indicators, I was glad to be alone.

Twenty minutes later I pulled up at the camp, taking Charly's parking place beside the field. The Kurdish women were sitting on the ground in the sunshine, eating something wrapped in paper, while the old man stood as usual by his smouldering fire. I waved as I got out. Early that morning I'd bought a football for Dilshad, and I was hoping to give it to him before getting embroiled in *tasjeel*. The football was a present for all the help he'd given me, but there'd be trouble if I was seen handing it over.

I locked the car and took a few steps into the camp. On the far side of the forecourt, a long, double queue of refugees snaked towards the ADM van, the back doors of which stood wide open. I held my hand to screen my eyes from the glare and was scanning the various groups of tents when I felt a finger prodding my sleeve.

'*Marhaba*' (hello). Dilshad stood at my elbow in his navy blue shorts and sweatshirt, face upturned, cheeks pink, spiky hair standing on end.

'*Marhabteen!*' (two hellos) I replied. 'I was looking for you.'

'Did you bring the football?' Dilshad's voice was husky today, like a middle-aged chain smoker.

'I did!' I raised my eyebrows and smiled, enjoying the look of delight which spread across his face. 'Meet me at the car in one minute.'

It was a multicoloured football, which I'd found in a shop in Gevgelija. I gave Dilshad a biro to write his name on the plastic, in case anyone tried to claim it wasn't his. Then he wrapped his arms around the ball as if it were a new baby, thanked me and asked how soon we were doing *tasjeel*.

'Soonish,' I replied. 'But first I've got to find Ian.' Finding other volunteers could be remarkably difficult in the chaos of the forecourt.

'I-i-an? He's over there by the food van. Come, I'll show you.'

As I followed Dilshad towards the van, I saw Ian in the distance in his purple Northern Lights waistcoat. He had one of the Homsi boys on his shoulders and another holding his hand and he was talking with a group of men beside the Afghan tents. But before we reached him, a small European woman approached me from behind the food van. She was dressed in jeans and wore her auburn hair coiled in a thick rope around her head.

'You're with Northern Lights, aren't you?' The accent was British. 'Can I have a word?'

The woman's name was Cjara and she was with ADM. She told me that an official from Save the Children had approached her, saying they could supply milky rice puddings for the children of Hara, as a nutritional supplement.

'That would be great,' I said at once. 'People are hungry.' I hesitated, not wanting to appear critical of ADM, who were doing a great job with very limited resources. 'It's brilliant that you lot bring food twice a day,' I added, 'but everyone could do with more.' The previous day I'd had a chat with a French volunteer in Polykastro about the food situation. When she'd first arrived she couldn't understand why the World Food Programme weren't feeding the refugees.[1] She'd contacted them, only to be told that feeding refugees in Europe was outside their remit.

Cjara's smile was sparkling. 'Of course. The problem is' – and here she raised her eyebrows very high, as if to prepare me for a big ask – 'we can deliver the puddings to Hara in our van, but we don't have the capacity to give them out. We were hoping Northern Lights could do the distribution?'

I hesitated for a couple of seconds before replying. With so many children in the camp, distribution would be time-consuming, and even when the two volunteers returned from holiday we would only be four. But the thought of people's hunger outweighed any sense of caution I might otherwise have had. And I felt sure Charly would want me to accept: we'd agreed at lunch the previous day that food should be our top priority.

'I'm sure we can do the distribution,' I told Cjara. 'Who classes as a child?'

'That's up to you.'

I was taken aback. I'd never in my life been asked to decide who should eat and who must go without; but again my hesitation was brief. 'How about we say ten and under?' I would live to regret this arbitrary cut-off point. How I managed to forget, even under pressure, the legendary need for food of growing adolescents, I cannot explain.

'That sounds fine,' Cjara replied. 'You'll need to do a head count, so that you know how many puddings to give to each family. If it's hot, like today, I'd give them out as quickly as possible after we bring them.' She wrinkled her nose. 'Anything made with milk will go off quickly in this heat . . .'

'Can you bring them towards the end of the day? We don't have any storage, so we'll have to put them in our cars.'

'Hopefully, yes. We'll try to bring them with the evening soup run.' She smiled, but then a worried look passed across her features. 'You know, you'll need a well thought-out system for the distribution.' She gazed at me steadily, no doubt wondering if I had any experience in giving out food to the hungry. 'Be careful, you don't want to start a riot!'

Half an hour later, as Ian and I were setting up for *tasjeel*, the slight figure of Bassem pushed his way towards me through the crowd expectantly pressing against the plastic table. 'Sister,' he said when he got within earshot, 'I need to speak to you.' He shot me one of his piercing looks and inclined his head in the direction of the tent he shared with Basma.

'I can't come right now, Bassem, we're just starting *tasjeel*.'

'When can you come?'

'Later, when we finish.'

It was gone four when I climbed down the steps at the back of the hotel and crossed a pool of foul-smelling water to reach Bassem's tent. I was wondering why he didn't move it to somewhere cleaner, when I noticed that his family's group of three tents had gone, leaving a dry, empty space beside the boundary fence.

When I called Bassem's name, he unzipped the door and made a space for me on the threshold. Basma was lying on a blanket at the back.

'Your parents have moved,' I said to Bassem.

'Because mum had two snakes inside her tent. They're over there.' He jerked his head towards the Kurdish field.

'Why didn't you go with them?'

Bassem looked uncomfortable. He inclined his head very slightly towards Basma. 'They're not happy with us,' he murmured. 'The marriage.'

Oh dear, I thought. Perhaps this had been a love match, and Bassem's parents didn't approve. I smiled at Basma and asked her how she was. She sat up slowly, reached out her arms and kissed me on both cheeks.

'Thank you for coming to see us,' she said softly. 'I'm okay, but I'm so worried.'

'About the baby?'

'No, no, about my mum.'

Bassem explained that Basma's mum was still in Homs. She'd had a couple of strokes, and wasn't strong enough to travel.

Basma started to cry. 'I think about her all the time. I miss her so much.'

I asked if she ever spoke with her mum on the phone.

'I can't,' she replied, 'we don't have a phone. We lost it on the sea crossing.'

I unzipped the pocket of my bumbag and pulled out my phone. 'Use mine.'

But Basma shook her head. 'Thank you so much, but I can't do that.' She didn't give a reason and I looked at Bassem. He gazed at me steadily, giving nothing away.

'I think you should,' I repeated. 'It's hard to be pregnant with your first child and not have your mum around. She'll be so happy to hear your voice!'

But Basma was adamant. 'No, no, it's not that simple. I do want to speak to her, desperately, but when she hears my voice she'll be angry. So angry.'

I was wondering whether to ask what the mother would be angry about, when Bassem spoke.

'Sister, we need a telephone of our own. Please. You're the only person who can help us. Please can you buy us a phone?'

I was a bit taken aback. I had no idea where the nearest phone shop was, and I didn't want to set a precedent by buying items for individuals. I tried to explain this to Bassem and Basma, while thinking guiltily about the three-euro football I'd bought for Dilshad. They waited politely till I'd finished speaking and then Basma seized my hand and kissed it.

'Please, please,' she said. 'You're like my mother now, I don't have anyone else to turn to. Please help me. A cheap phone, something basic, that's all I need.'

As I walked away I racked my brains as to what this was all about. It wasn't great that Bassem's parents didn't approve of his marriage; but now I wondered whether both families had been against it. I did the maths. If Basma was only seventeen, and Bassem's family had been in the camp on the Turkish border for four years, had the pair married in the camp? Basma's mother had been too ill to travel, so perhaps Basma had fled Homs with other relatives. I'd heard of Syrian girls being married as young as fifteen. Perhaps the marriage had been arranged without the agreement of Basma's parents, or, worse still, without their knowledge. That would explain why she feared her mother's anger.

But it wouldn't explain why the pair refused my invitation to use my phone. I found that quite annoying.

Evening was a sociable time at Hara and the forecourt was crowded. I was on my way to visit an Afghan family I'd met during the *tasjeel*. The twelve-year-old daughter had interpreted for her mother and little brother, and the mother, who was a pharmacist, had invited me for tea. The whole family were at Hara, having fled Afghanistan after the father, a lawyer, received death threats from the Taliban.

With every few paces I took towards the Afghan tents, somebody stopped me to say hello. A little girl of three or four, whom I often saw wandering about the camp by herself, came up and took my hand. I couldn't understand her speech, but I got it that in the chaos of the forecourt she felt the need to cling to somebody. Her little hand was warm in mine. Ten feet away, the tall man in the baseball hat who had led the chanting at the demonstration caught my eye and waved. And now Hasan was at my side, with a smiling woman who held a toddler on her hip and in her hands the two halves of a pair of wire-rimmed spectacles, broken at the bridge of the nose. Hasan gave me a high five.

'T'reza,' he began, 'Om Shvan wants to speak to you. She's the mother of the boy I told you about, remember?'

I glanced at the woman and clapped my free hand over my mouth. 'I'm so sorry, I completely forgot!' Two days earlier Hasan had mentioned a teenage boy with broken glasses.

'I'm sorry to bother you,' the woman said, 'but my son can't see a thing.' She smiled, pushing a wisp of hair under her headscarf. 'I've tried to mend them,' she added. 'I taped them together with Elastoplast, but they broke again. He needs new ones.'

I thought for a moment. There had to be an optician in Polykastro, but how was she going to get there? 'I'm going into Polykastro tomorrow morning,' I told her. 'Give me the frames and I'll see if I can find an optician. If they can't fix them I'll ask if they can make your son a new pair.' I paused. 'What's your name?'

The woman smiled again. 'Yasmin, but people call me Om Shvan (mother of Shvan). Thank you so much, thank you, thank you!' She explained that Shvan was fifteen and she depended on him to help her with her younger kids.

'How many do you have?'

'Three boys, three girls,' she replied, still smiling. 'Their father's in Germany.'

'And you're all in the one tent?'

Om Shvan nodded. 'Over there, by the entrance.' She pointed at the cluster of Kurdish tents behind the one occupied by the very old woman and her family. 'Come and see us! Ask for Yasmin.'

10
Rice Pudding

In Polykastro the next morning, finding an optician proved difficult. After a number of false starts I was helped by a kind Greek woman I met in a shop, who drove me to the place she used. The optician declared the broken frames beyond repair, but when I explained they belonged to a refugee child, she told me to bring him for an eye test, promising to make him a new pair of spectacles as cheaply as possible.

When I got back to Hara I found Yasmin sitting in the doorway of her tent near the road, with a toddler asleep on her lap. Shvan, the teenager, sat cross-legged at the back. I greeted them, crouched down and explained about the eye test, promising that Northern Lights would cover the cost. Yasmin was very appreciative, and insisted I stay for a cup of tea, brewed by her neighbour on an open fire.

I sat down on the ground and smiled at her. 'Where in Syria are you from?'

'Qamishli, in the far north east. We're Kurds. But before we fled we were living in Damascus.'

'In the city itself?'

'In a neighbourhood close to Yarmouk.'

Yarmouk was a large Palestinian refugee camp established in 1948, in the south of Damascus. In the early months of the revolution, its people had endeavoured to maintain neutrality. But gradually it had become a place of refuge for displaced Syrians, with the result that its population swelled from 200,000 to 900,000. Suburbs neighbouring Yarmouk were repeatedly targeted by the regime until, in December 2012, a mosque, a school and a hospital inside the camp were hit. From that point on, the camp became rebel territory and the regime imposed a siege, preventing the entry of food and medical supplies. Hundreds of thousands of inhabitants fled, but many remained to face a slow death by starvation.

I looked at Yasmin with renewed interest. 'Were you caught up in the siege?' Behind her I saw a young girl winding her way towards us with two steaming plastic cups.

'Not the siege, but our neighbourhood was bombed by the regime, dozens of times.' She took the cups of tea from the girl and handed me one.

'Is that why you left?'

Yasmin nodded. 'It was the most horrific thing. Every time we heard the planes coming over I would gather all the kids around me and try to shelter them with my body, but it was impossible. One day our building was hit, and we were very lucky to get out alive.' She glanced down at the sleeping child. 'Even now, if we hear the sound of a plane, we all go into panic. A few weeks ago there was an earthquake here in Greece, a very small one, and we were terrified.'

After losing their home, the family had travelled to Yasmin's father-in-law in Qamishli. Yasmin's in-laws and their wives and children had made the same journey, and soon they were more than thirty in the grandfather's small house.

Yasmin wrinkled up her nose. 'It was very difficult, because we were so overcrowded; and money was tight, none of the men were working. After two years living like that, we decided that my husband would try to get to Europe, and I would take the children to Iraqi Kurdistan. We hoped things might be better there.'

'And were they?'

'No. We were welcomed in Iraqi Kurdistan, in a tent camp, but the situation was terrible. There was no work, no source of income and no chance of proper accommodation. As soon as I realized how bad it was, I decided we couldn't stay. That was tough, because by then I was on my own with the six kids, and Shiro was a small baby.' She took a swig of tea.

'How did you manage?'

'For quite a few weeks I didn't hear anything from my husband. That made me really anxious and I decided to go to Turkey. We couldn't cross the border legally, so I had to pay a smuggler.' She took a deep breath and glanced at me intently, as if wondering whether I was ready to hear a disturbing story. 'It was February 2015. In order to get to Turkey, we had to cross the river which forms the border with northern Iraq. If you enter legally you cross it on a bridge, but we were illegal.'

As she spoke I recalled the rickety metal bridge above a gorge which I'd walked over a number of times on my way in and out of Iraqi Kurdistan in the 1990s.

'The smuggler made us set off just before dawn, about

four in the morning. It was perishing cold and we had to
walk for two hours to the river and climb down the bank.
Then we had to wade across, with the water up to the children's chins. I was carrying a backpack containing half our
possessions, and the rest in two carrier bags, slung from my
elbows. 'When I stepped into the water and felt how cold it
was, I was so terrified that I couldn't move. My two little
girls were roped to me, and I had the baby like this' – she
crossed her hands and held them out – 'cradled in my arms,
to keep him out of the water.'

'The smuggler was beside me and when he saw how afraid
I was, he told me to shut my eyes and walk forward. It was
pitch black so we couldn't see much anyway; but the sound
of the water was deafening.'

'Where were Shvan and the other two?'

'They were just behind me. They are bigger, they were
roped together and they held each other's hands and kept up
as best they could.' She gazed at me steadily. 'It was the most
difficult five minutes of my entire life.'

As I pictured Yasmin and the children stepping into the
icy water, my eyes filled with tears.

'Somehow we made it to the far bank, where the smuggler's mate had lit a big fire. We stayed there for an hour,
waiting for our clothes to dry.' Then we had to walk a long
way until a truck came to meet us.'

'How long?'

'Maybe three hours.'

'And then did you travel straight to western Turkey?'

'Yes. We were in a camp there for a year, before we came
to Greece.'

*   *   *

Later, when I walked up the steps to the hotel, I noticed a new tent pitched to the right of the verandah. A woman of about sixty sat beside it, in a wheelchair. She was dressed in black with a white handkerchief knotted over her long, dark hair and she was watching the comings and goings on the steps with intense interest. She fastened on me the moment she saw me, summoning me over with a firm gesture of her hand. I tried addressing her in Arabic but she wagged her finger and said very firmly, in English, 'Arabic, no, *Farsi*!' My Farsi is non-existent and her English was very limited, yet she managed to make it plain that she both needed, and expected, a lot of help. Her name was Javaneh and she had a bad leg, hence the wheelchair. She was from Iran and her daughter and granddaughter were asleep in the tent. She needed a change of clothes and new underwear. I tried to explain that I could make a list and see if we had what she needed at the warehouse; it didn't seem fair to ask her to attend *tasjeel*, because she might find it difficult to queue.

After a few minutes the daughter emerged from the tent, wiping her face with a cloth. She looked about twenty-five and was one of very few women in the camp who didn't wear a headscarf. She spoke reasonable English and seemed a little uncomfortable in the presence of her mother. The small granddaughter lay asleep on a blanket.

'Please,' I said to the daughter, 'tell your mum that I've got things to do right now but I'll come and see her this afternoon and we'll make a list of the items she needs.' The daughter nodded. 'No problem,' she agreed, 'mum can wait, take your time!' She raised her eyebrows almost imperceptibly, with an expression which suggested she was weary of trying to humour her mother's demands. I smiled and walked away.

For the next couple of hours Javaneh kept appearing wherever I was, sitting bolt upright in the wheelchair, which was propelled by an assortment of obliging children – and not, I noticed, by the daughter. I was trying to do the head count of children of ten and under, with the assistance of an eighteen-year-old Syrian girl called Salma, who had noticed what I was doing and offered to help. We were going from tent to tent with a sheet of paper and a pencil, asking people how many children they had. The task should have been easy enough, but by now it was early afternoon and many tents appeared deserted. We started in the Syrian and Iraqi areas, close to the line of Portaloos. I was never sure what to do when faced with a zipped-up tent whose occupants were either out or asleep, but Salma was quite comfortable taking hold of a tent pole and giving the tent a gentle shake, while politely urging the occupants to open the door.

Each time someone responded, she would point at me in my purple Northern Lights vest and explain that I needed to know if they had any children under eleven. At this point I would usually butt in and explain that we would soon be supplying *helouwiyaat*, or milk puddings, because we knew the children were hungry.

Salma thought we ought to insist on seeing the children before we included them in our tally. If we just took each adult's word at face value, people might lie. I could see her point; but most of the children were out playing, either in the road or on the forecourt.

Several times, we turned away from a tent to find Javaneh blocking our path. Pied piper-like with her crowd of children looking on, she would hold her head on one side and fix her eyes on me with a look which was both whee- dling and insistent. Although I couldn't understand the Farsi, she seemed to be trying to convey something along the lines of 'Look, poor me, I'm in a terrible situation, surely you should see to my needs before you do anything else?' She would point to her long black tunic and frown, appar- ently meaning that it was dirty and she needed a new one. Then she would pick up the fabric of her trouser leg between thumb and forefinger, pull it away from her leg and point to some mud near the hem with an expression of distaste. 'Yes,' I would say, 'I'll come to you later on, I haven't forgotten.' Out of the corner of my eyes I saw Salma raising her eyes to heaven.

The head count took a long time. After we'd covered the Arab areas, we trawled through the Afghan and Iranian areas and then separated to trudge from tent to tent in the two fields. I went to the far one, which was partly Afghan, partly Kurdish. When we met on the hotel steps half an hour later, Salma said we should cover the back of the hotel, just to be sure. As we'd both suspected, here there were no chil- dren at all but plenty of Pakistani men who claimed to be under eleven, giggling and clutching their stomachs to let us know they were rumbling – which I didn't doubt. At last we were finished. Salma totted up the tallies, producing a grand total of 195 children under eleven.

At last I was free to go to Javaneh's tent. She greeted me with a look of scepticism, but warmed up as we made the list. As we did so I discovered that she knew more English than I'd thought. In addition to various items of clothing, she demanded a new tent, claiming the one she had was too small for her little family of three. I knew we couldn't help with that, so I tried to explain that there were many families of five or six sleeping in tents of the same size. Javaneh was unimpressed by this argument, and pleaded with me to make an exception. 'I must have tent!' she kept saying, her upper lip contracting with annoyance. 'Bring tent, please!' Seeing that I was getting nowhere, I stood up and told her I hoped to bring the clothing she had asked for the following day, after a trip to the warehouse.

'And tent, tent!' she called as I walked away.

As I read more about the crisis, one of the things which I found appalling was the extent to which the decision-making of the anti-Assad states, including the western ones, was based on inadequate information and miscalculation. Russian decision-making, by contrast, appeared to have been based on sound knowledge and clear analysis – whether or not one agreed with Putin's conclusions. It was no surprise that, by early 2017, Russia held the key to Syria's future.

Obama had come to power in 2009 with very little experience in foreign policy. Having opposed Bush's Iraq war of 2003, he now hoped to rebuild the reputation of his country in the Middle East and Islamic world. He had no intention of embarking on further military adventures in the region, and Middle Eastern oil was now of less importance to the US economy than previously, following the discovery of shale.

The series of uprisings that shook the Middle East from December 2010 posed dilemmas for Obama that presumably he would have preferred not to face. Some of Obama's advisers urged him to wade in with calls for the departure of autocratic leaders, while others urged caution.

Tunisia's President Ben Ali was the first to fall, on 14 January 2011, ousted by his people without foreign assistance. Egypt was next, the key Arab ally of the US, and recipient of a massive annual military subsidy from them. When Mubarak failed to resign as anticipated, Obama bowed to pressure from his more idealistic advisers, and had a call made to a senior Egyptian general demanding the president's departure. Mubarak quit the following day.

Three days later, protests by Shi'a in Bahrain alarmed the Saudis, who sent in troops. One day after that, on 15 February, the first protest occurred in Libya. Before the end of the month, France was calling for Gaddafi to go and Britain proposed a no-fly zone over the region. Meanwhile, inside Libya, which unlike Syria has a fairly homogeneous population, the opposition was coalescing into a unified grouping known as the National Transition Council (NTC).

It was with reluctance that Obama consented to the UN resolution now proposed by Britain, France and the Arab League, which would enable the NATO bombing campaign against Gaddafi.[1] On President Medvedev's instructions, Russia abstained from the vote, enraging Putin, who was prime minister at the time. Later, Russia would argue that the resolution provided for humanitarian intervention only, not regime change; but western states disagreed.

The ensuing NATO campaign culminated in October 2011 in the death of Gaddafi. It was misinterpreted by the Syrian opposition and the anti-Assad regional states as evidence that, even under Obama, the days of US intervention in the region were not at an end. This became the basis of a widespread conviction that Obama would ultimately intervene to oust Assad.

It is easy to comprehend that, by the time of the first major demonstrations in Syria, in the middle of March 2011, foreign ministers and foreign policy experts in western countries were struggling to keep abreast of developments in the Arab Spring. It is also understandable, given the NATO campaign, that Libya occupied much of their attention for the next six months. What is less easy to accept, however, is the level of ignorance about Syria by states such as the US, which should have made it their business to be well informed. In 2009, the US had just one person staffing its Syria desk,[2] despite the fact that, for the previous fifty years, Syria had deliberately maintained a veil of secrecy over its internal affairs.

The most disastrous consequence of ignorance about the regime was the widespread but erroneous assumption that it would crumble quickly in response to the protests. There seems to have been little grasp of the clever strategies which had been employed over decades by both Hafez and Bashar to protect the regime from an internal coup; nor of the loyalty to it felt by many of the Syrian minorities, and even by middle-class Sunnis. Obama and his advisers appear to have calculated that since the Egyptian regime had fallen quickly, so too would Syria's – despite the many fundamental differences between the two states, and, crucially, the fact that Syria had Iran and Russia for allies.

It seems that the best information available to the US in the spring and summer of 2011 was that provided by Robert Ford, the new US ambassador to Syria. Sympathetic to the protesters, he repeatedly advised that the regime was *not* about to fall; but, like his French and British counterparts, he was ignored.[3]

Interestingly, it appears that Turkey, Qatar and Saudi Arabia were almost as ignorant about Syria as the US, also believing that the regime would fall quickly.

Medvedev was pushed aside by Putin in the wake of the latter's fury about the NATO air campaign in Libya. As Putin saw it, the west was once again using its military might to bring about regime change in an independent country. In 2012, Putin stood and was elected for a third term as president.

From 2000 on, the Russian economy had grown considerably, thanks to increases in the market price of oil and gas. As a result, Putin had been able to modernize and re-equip his armed forces. During the same period he'd worked to reassert Russian influence in the Middle East. By the time of the Arab Spring, Russia had strong trading relationships with various Middle Eastern states, to which it sold both energy and weapons. Alongside this, efforts were made to improve Russia's image in the eyes of the Arabs, capitalizing on the deep unpopularity of the US following the debacle in Iraq. There was anxiety, however, in Moscow, about the links between Muslims in the North Caucasus and Middle Eastern Islamic radicals. A number of domestic attacks by Islamists on Russian soil had raised concern.

As to relations with Syria, Russia had sold weapons to Syria in the noughties, but greater quantities were sold to other Arab states. The Russian naval base at Tartous on the coast of northern Syria had been allowed to fall into disrepair in the 1990s. It was dredged in 2007, but then left in the care of a minimal Russian staff. Syria was no longer of special importance to Russia, and Putin made plain his dislike of Bashar.

Putin's view of the Arab Spring was very different from the western one. He saw it as primarily an Islamist uprising, rather than a movement for freedom and democracy. His view of the Arabs was that they were not ready for democratic government, which he considered would be at odds with their history and their attachment to Islam. Not only that: Putin believed that multi-ethnic societies such as Syria's were inherently weak and required a strong regime to hold them together.[4]

From a western perspective, and indeed from a democratic Syrian perspective, Putin's view of Arab culture was neither inspiring nor optimistic; but at least he had a clear assessment of what he was dealing with in Syria. Having said that, the key issue for Putin was his determination, in the wake of the Libya crisis and the Iraq war eight years earlier, to prevent another US-led campaign for regime change – recent Russian adventures in Georgia and Ukraine notwithstanding. He was fearful that if intervention in sovereign states for the sake of regime change became legitimized, then, one day, the guns might point at Moscow. It was for this principal reason that he decided to support the Syrian regime.[5]

It was to take some months before the west fully grasped Russia's position on Syria. This was partly due to clever diplomacy by Moscow, in which it frequently presented itself as willing to consider western proposals, despite having no intention to agree to them.

The US and EU began to impose sanctions against individuals within the Syrian regime as early as April and May 2011. In May and June, Britain and France put draft resolutions before the UN Security Council (UNSC) condemning Assad's human rights violations, but these were blocked by Russia and China. At this stage, US pronouncements were limited to calls for the violence to stop, and for Assad to engage in reform. As the violence continued unabated, and after an attack on the US embassy in Damascus in July, the wording of the US statements became stronger. But it wasn't until the administration was criticized in the US media for failing to condemn Assad more roundly that Obama made the 18 August statement mentioned earlier, which ended with the words 'the time has come for President Assad to step aside'. The statement was issued just hours before Obama went on holiday; and without the making of contingency plans, in case Assad should fail to pay heed.[6]

The unintended and unhelpful result of these statements was a hardening of positions by both Assad's supporters and his detractors. Russia and Iran became more determined to stand firm beside Assad, while the rebels and the anti-Assad regional states felt vindicated in their belief that the US intended to intervene. When, on 22 August, the UN Human Rights Council voted to launch an investigation into allegations that the regime had committed crimes against humanity, both Russia and China objected vigorously, issuing a joint statement demanding that the international community stay out of Syria's 'internal affairs'.

By now, it seems, the die was cast for a long and hugely destructive war in which the US and its Middle Eastern allies would confront Iran and Russia. Both 'sides' were labouring under the illusion that Obama intended a military strike for which in reality he had neither appetite nor plans. As a result, the somewhat tokenistic steps taken by the west and the anti-Assad states over the following months would not lead to Assad's resignation.

A ban on the US import of Syrian oil imposed in August 2011 was swiftly followed by a similar ban by the EU. In the autumn, Turkey imposed an arms embargo on Syria and froze all its government assets. At the same time, the Arab League imposed economic sanctions and shortly afterwards suspended Syria from membership. An Arab League Peace Plan was attempted in December with the reluctant consent of Assad, but it was so ill-conceived and under-resourced that it failed early in 2012. It is possible that Qatar, which held the presidency of the League at the time, and the other Gulf states only proposed the mission because they felt such a step would have to be taken before the west could be persuaded to intervene militarily. By now Qatar was already secretly sending some arms to the rebels.[7]

After the failure of the Arab League Peace Plan, former UN Secretary-General Kofi Annan was appointed as a joint Arab League/UN envoy to Syria in late February 2012. He saw that the war could not be brought to an end unless consensus was reached between the various foreign states now involved. The six-point plan which he devised was backed by Russia and China at the UNSC on 21 March; but in order to get their endorsement, Annan had avoided any reference to Assad's departure – thereby incurring the wrath of the opposition – or to military intervention. The six points were: a ceasefire under UN supervision; humanitarian assistance to the Syrian people; freedom of movement for journalists; respect for the right to demonstrate peacefully; the release of prisoners; and a commitment to an inclusive Syrian-led political process to address the legitimate aspirations of the Syrian people.

An attempt was made to put Annan's plan into effect from late April 2012, under the supervision of a force of just 300 unarmed UN monitors. The initial ceasefire lasted only two weeks, and was followed in late May by regime massacres near Homs. After this, the FSA resumed its defence of civilians, and the plan was aborted in August.

Annan received little support for his attempts to rescue the mission. His second initiative, the Geneva Communique, involved the creation of a contact group which included Russia, China, UN, Arab League, US and EU participants but excluded Iran, Saudi Arabia and all Syrians. Annan succeeded in getting the participants to sign up to the same six-point plan, but there were crucial differences of interpretation. US Secretary of State Hillary Clinton regarded the plan as requiring Assad's departure, whereas the Russians did not. When western diplomats sought a UN resolution to enforce sanctions against Syria if it failed fully to implement the plan, Russia and China exercised their rights of veto. Annan resigned in August 2012.

My days at Hara were numbered. The next time I bumped into Juwan, anxious to hear the rest of his story, I invited him to eat with me that evening in the restaurant in Efzoni. We slipped away from Hara in the early evening and walked the kilometre to the village. The spacious restaurant was almost deserted, the perfect place for a tête-à-tête. We ordered food and sat down at the back.

'You'd just been dumped by the Turkish driver close to the front line with the regime,' I reminded Juwan as he took out his phone charger and plugged it into a socket.

'Okay.' He frowned and cleared his throat. He looked tired today, and the scar above his left eyebrow was more pronounced than usual.

'It was totally dark around me, but in the distance I could see the lights of a village. I had no idea where I was, so I followed the other deportees along the road, without speaking. One man got out a cigarette lighter with a torch on its end, but the light was too weak to see by. Another snapped, "Put that out, or some sniper will hit us."

'I was stunned to learn I might already be in the line of sight of a sniper – this was the last thing I was imagining when I accepted to be deported to Bab al-Hawa, I really never thought the Turks would put me in the face of the Syrian army. We kept on walking till we came to a place where the road split into two. A group of men were standing about, speaking Turkish in low voices near a broken-down car. I assumed they were Syrian Turkomen and asked them how far it was to Afrin, a liberated town close to the Turkish border.'

'Why Afrin?' I butted in.

'Because Kamiran's family lived near there. They said, "About four hours." At first I thought they meant four hours on foot, but they said no, by *road* it was four hours. That's when it dawned on me just how far I was from where I'd intended to be. One of the men was perched on a rock at the roadside. "Go with the other deportees to the next village," he said, "from there you can take a service taxi to Latakia and a coach to Afrin."

'My jaw dropped open. "But I can't go to Latakia!"

'The guy slid off the rock and leant towards me. "Don't tell me you're wanted by the regime?"

'"But of course I'm wanted, why else would I be here? I failed to show up for military service."

'"Ri-ght", the guy said slowly, "then you definitely can't go to Latakia." He and his friends all began to talk at once, trying to figure out what I should do. I was listening attentively, hoping they would come up with a solution. One suggested I get a smuggler he knew to take me back to Turkey, and then cross again into Syria at a border post close to Afrin. He said I should stop there with him at the roadside, as the smuggler would probably show up in a few minutes.

'So I waited there with him. Ideas and thoughts were fighting each other in my head as I questioned how I'd got into such a dangerous, miserable situation.

'The smuggler arrived. He said he could get me back across the border, but that I'd have to make my way through Turkey to the crossing near Afrin by myself. Then he asked me how much money I had.

'I smiled ironically. "How much do you want?"

'"No, how much do you have?"

'"Seriously?"

'"Yes!"

'I took the handful of coins out of my pocket and showed him. He was shocked: "You only have this?"

'"You can check, if you like."

'"This will not even be enough for the trip inside Turkey."

'I shrugged my shoulders. "I'll sort that out when I get there." I was in a state of shock and not thinking wisely. Then the smuggler said he'd take me to Turkey for free.

'"Are you sure?"

'"Yes," he replied, "I'll do it for God," meaning it would be an act of charity.

'I felt a mixture of feelings, partly broken pride at being dependent on the kindness of a stranger, but also happiness that my problem was going to be solved. The smuggler asked me to walk along the road in the dark with him towards some huts made of branches, which I thought must belong to FSA fighters. Women and children milled around near them. I didn't feel at all comfortable because I didn't know who anybody was. It was the first time in my life I'd been in a war zone and I was worried about the FSA, especially after the threat made by the Turkish corporal. The smuggler left me with some Arab men who were sitting on the ground around a fire in the middle of the road, saying he'd be back in half an hour.

'At first I didn't look at their faces or try to talk, in fact I shrank inside myself. It was very cold and I was only wearing a T-shirt, light trousers and flip flops. I took out my towel to cover my bare arms, but I still felt cold, and very hungry and tired. After a few minutes, one of the men spoke to me. "Come closer to the fire." At that point I stopped thinking about my pride because I was so much in need of help. Another man was making tea on the fire. I heard him say "Aren't you thirsty?" pointing to the kettle. The idea of a glass of hot, sweet tea seemed like a big luxury and I accepted. A moment later, the same man asked if I was hungry.

'In Syrian culture, it's not polite to accept something you're offered the first time round. You should refuse; if you're offered it again you may then say yes; but if you're feeling very proud you may refuse twice and only accept the third time. I was so desperate that I accepted the tea and the bread and jam immediately they were offered! While I was eating, the other men round the fire tried to warn me that the smuggler was not going to come back. I was shocked and asked why, to which they simply said, "He's gone."

'Before they told me this I'd felt I had a plan; now, I was completely lost. I panicked, thinking, it's night, I'm in the middle of nowhere and I have no idea who these people are. Then the man who'd given me the tea and bread said, "Would you like to sleep?" I was exhausted from the long journey in the van and I still had a sharp pain in my right ear. So I said, "Yes, please." The man showed me to a hut right beside the fire. I couldn't see how big it was, but I could hear kids talking next door, through a wall of branches. I was so disorientated that I didn't realize the people helping me were refugees. Someone gave me a blanket and I wrapped myself in it, lay down and slept.

'Early the following morning, when I stepped outside, some of the men I'd met the night before were still there, so I gave them back their blanket and asked where I could find water. They gave me a bottle to fill and sent me down the hill on a narrow dirt track. The sun was just coming up and through the trees I could see houses and a mosque. It was the first mountain village I'd ever seen. At the bottom of the track I found a building housing a large water tank with civilians and a bunch of fierce-looking FSA men, dressed in camouflage, standing about. Two of the FSA men stripped off, jumped in and swam across the tank. Another was using soap in the water.

'I was astonished to see the fighters swimming. How could they be so irresponsible, I wondered – even a child wouldn't swim in drinking water. I filled the bottle and splashed water on my face. Seconds later I heard shooting, coming from the hill where I'd slept. I thought the FSA guys on my hill were shooting at the regime in the village.

'Then I heard a strange sound – *fzzzwooosh* – as a shell landed. Next a regime helicopter filled the sky above our heads. It was terrifying. I ran from the tank and crouched down by a small rock: there were no trees to hide behind. I heard someone say that a militia leader had attacked a regime van nearby and the FSA were firing at the regime to distract them.

'After the helicopter had gone, someone told me that the path I'd taken from the huts to the water tank was very dangerous, because the sniper in the village could see it. People were running up the hill on a different path which was covered by trees, so I followed them. When I got back to the huts, out of breath and frightened, I recognized the voice of the man who'd fed me. He was about forty-five, with a long blond beard and a bald patch, very likeable. He said the militia who'd started the shooting were mostly from one family. "The sons of this family", he complained, "started to shoot from our hilltop without considering that they're putting all these women and children at risk. If they want to shoot at the regime, they should do it from another hill, not from the one where all these families are hiding!"

'His words began to shake my view of the FSA. A few minutes later the shooting started again, and then mortars exploded and the helicopter came back. The bearded man told me to hide in the hut. It was just behind the hill, and the mortars were likely to fly over the top of it. Nothing exploded near me, but I kept hearing *fzzzwooosh* again and again. A young FSA man was running around screaming, spreading panic among the women. He was shouting, "Run to the Turkish border!" That would have meant one kilometre in the open, in full sight of the regime helicopter in the skies above. Luckily nobody took any notice. I was lying in the hut thinking how stupid, and the bearded guy was shouting "No, no, don't do that!"'

When the waiter arrived with our plates of lamb cutlet and Greek salad, Juwan stopped talking. We ate in silence, each busy with our own thoughts. When he'd cleared his plate, Juwan pulled his phone charger out of the socket and looked at me.

'After the helicopter had gone, I met the two guys whose hut I'd slept in. Both had fled Lattakia to avoid military service, one leaving a wife and daughter behind, the other one unmarried. We had breakfast with the people who'd befriended me the night before and I was introduced to everyone. The bearded guy, Abu Hadi, had five kids with him, some of whom were teenagers; another guy had three. They were so kind that I found myself telling my real story. They listened and became very angry on my behalf. Abu Hadi said he'd treat me like one of his sons. I was dealing with them as Arabs, but it turned out that Abu Hadi's ancestors were Kurds, who'd been Arabized.[8]

'They explained that they were part of a group of about 850 displaced civilians, men, women and children, who were waiting to cross into Turkey. The border post was only half a kilometre from where we were, but it was closed at the moment, because the refugee camps on the Turkish side weren't ready to receive people. Can you imagine – Turkey kept the border closed despite the fact that the civilians on the Syrian side were being shelled!

'Abu Hadi said the group had fled their villages a few weeks ago, after a battle in which the FSA had liberated a nearby mountain top. He criticized the FSA militia near us, saying they were a bunch of thieves, and that the serious FSA fighters were further inside Syria. The ones on the border, Abu Hadi said, were waiting to get their share of any aid that arrived and have their photos taken to send to funders abroad. My notion of the FSA changed a bit from hearing this. I decided there were probably some good FSA fighters, but others who were abusing their power.

'My new friends were very sympathetic. They even suggested I should change my name and go with them when the border opened. Their kindness really touched me, but I didn't dare risk going back to Turkey now that my name had been linked with the PKK. It was just too dangerous.

'I stayed with this group of people about a week, sharing the hut with the two men. Our situation was very vulnerable, as we were on the top of a hill, surrounded by rock, grass and bushes. The nearest trees were below us in the valley and the only thing hiding us from the regime troops was the hill itself.'

I swallowed my last mouthful and pushed aside my plate. 'It sounds terrible. Was it still summer, or autumn?'

'Early autumn. It was hot in the day time and very cold at night. Once a day the Red Crescent brought us bread and jam and water. The two families shared their food with us, sometimes potatoes or rice bought in a liberated village half an hour's walk away. We never got enough to eat, but we managed. I spent all day wracking my brains about what to do. I considered the option of joining the FSA, but I didn't think I could live with their attitude. Also, I knew nothing about being with a militant group. If I joined I would have to be the person who did the dishes or washed the clothes.

'One afternoon I was sitting in the hut, sheltering from the hot sun, when somebody said that the woman doctor had arrived. It turned out that she was really a Palestinian nurse and her job was to provide medical care to the displaced women and children. I didn't think anything more about her.

'The next afternoon I was sitting with Abu Hadi in his hut. We could see through gaps in the branches and caught a nice breeze. Abu Hadi looked out and said, "The Libyan doctors are here," explaining that the doctors were supported by some Libyan sheikhs – religious scholars who wanted to support their fellow Muslims. His wife wanted the doctors to see their children, who had diarrhoea and coughs. I was listening with one ear, but at the same time my mind was swimming somewhere else, thinking how to solve my problem. I knew that Abu Hadi and all my new friends were praying that the border would open as soon as possible. Privately, I was praying that the border *wouldn't* open. When it did, they would leave, and I'd be alone.

'Time went by, the sun set and we went out to collect firewood to start a fire. Some of the guys made tea. It got really dark and people settled round the fire. Somebody sat down on my right and Abu Hadi was on my left. I was staring at the fire, thinking about my situation, when Abu Hadi told me that the man on my right worked with the Libyan doctors. I glanced at the man, who was blond with blue eyes. Initially I thought he was Syrian – we have people with blue and even green eyes. I gave a cool "hello", in Arabic, and he nodded. Then I dived back into my thoughts.

'Abu Hadi spoke to the guy across me and this time he replied, in very bad Arabic, that he didn't understand. So without thinking I translated Abu Hadi's question into English; and the man's answer into Arabic. After a while Abu Hadi asked the man another question and again I translated it. Then somebody called the foreign guy and he left to see what they wanted. I went back to my thinking and Abu Ahmed started a conversation with somebody else.

'But a little later the foreign guy came back and tapped me on the shoulder. I got up and we stepped away from the fire. He said, "I noticed you have a good English."

' "Thank you."

' "Would you like to work with us?"

'As he spoke I felt as if somebody had hit me to wake me up. "*What?*" I exclaimed in disbelief.

' "Would you like to work with us?" he repeated.

' "But who are you?"

' "MSF. Doctors without Borders."

' "Yes, yes, I've seen you on TV, I've heard what you've done in many countries!"

' "So would you work with us? We're starting a new project in this area and we need a translator."

' "Of course, I'd be happy to help my country and my people, I'd be honoured to work with you!"

' "We'll pay you."

' "There's no need to pay me, just give me food and somewhere to sleep. How can I take money when you're helping my people?"

'But the blue-eyed man was insistent about paying, so in the end I said "Okay." He said he'd pick me up in two days' time.

'I was in shock as I watched him disappear into the night. It was like heaven had helped me, I was so relieved. Now I was finding myself with good people, I could live with them, I would have a life which I felt motivated to live. It was a miracle!

'When I went back to the fire my friends had guessed I was being offered a job, and they were extremely happy for me. They said I mustn't forget them. One guy asked if I would give him my flip flops and a T-shirt, which I did, there and then. I thanked them for being so kind to me and promised I would always remember them. It was very nice to have this warm reaction from people I'd only known for ten days; although in Syria people are like this.'

'How incredible!' I exclaimed. 'Your luck completely turned! What happened next?'

'Two days later, Paul, the blue-eyed man, came back to distribute some medical supplies with the Palestinian nurse. It was night and he asked me if I was ready. I grabbed my plastic carrier bag, put on my trainers and walked with them down to the water tank, where their truck was waiting. An old couple asked for a lift and got in the cab. The blue-eyed man and I climbed into the back and we set off on a road full of potholes. The driver couldn't put the lights on because we were so close to the regime-controlled area. Soon we came to a place where the trees on both sides of the road were on fire, with flames meeting in the middle above our heads. The heat was intense on my face and arms and the engine groaned, making me afraid we might break down. But then we were through the fire and a few minutes later we turned onto a better road, where it was safe to have the lights on.

'Paul pointed out to me the mountain which had been liberated from regime control two weeks earlier. We dropped off the old couple at a little house beside the road and gave a lift to two FSA guys who wanted to go to the next village. We were to spend the night in the MSF house there. When we arrived, I took my first shower in over a week. There was no electricity and anyway we couldn't use lights in case we were seen by regime troops. I was introduced to my new colleagues and we sat outside drinking tea.'

11

'Why won't the UK let us in?'

When I reached the store the following morning, I made a point of packing Javaneh's order first. I found everything she wanted, apart from the underwear. Back at Hara I tried to locate the daughter, hoping she could help me explain this to Javaneh, but she was nowhere to be seen. Eventually, a neighbour told me there'd been a massive row, culminating in the daughter snatching up her child and leaving the camp. I found Javaneh sitting on the floor just inside the tent, plaiting her long black hair with an air of weary resignation. She brightened when I gave her the clothes, shrugged at the lack of knickers and asked if I could bring her some pyjamas.

After that, she became even more demanding. Most days she turned up at the *tasjeel*, even if Sintra or I had already been to visit her. She would get her little band of children to push her wheelchair through the crowd assembled in front of the table. As soon as she was within shouting distance of me – or Sintra – she would sit up very straight, lean forward and call, in English in a sharp, insistent voice, 'Please, please!' We both tried to make her wait her turn, but it wasn't easy.

Privately I rather admired Javaneh's chutzpah, and to begin with I made a special effort to find her clothes which I thought she'd like. One day I brought her a long black crepe dress and a new pair of trousers. She seemed very pleased with the dress; but a second later it was *'shoes, bring shoes!'* She had a damaged toenail and wanted a well-fitting pair of lace-ups that wouldn't press on it. I wrote down her size and said I'd look on my next visit to the warehouse.

That evening I saw her out of the wheelchair, slowly parading up and down on the verandah in the new dress, smiling to herself. I was pleased she liked the dress, but a little surprised she wasn't even limping.

The following day I found her what I thought was a fabulous pair of almost new, black leather lace-ups. They were the right size and the toes were so stiff that protection for the toe nail was guaranteed. But when I gave them to her, Javaneh regarded them with a look of disdain, as if they weren't quite what she'd had in mind. Slightly indignant, I tried to explain that I thought they were just the job. She looked at me, sniffed, then forced herself to smile and blow me a kiss. A day or two later I saw her skimming her way round the camp in the wheelchair with her retinue of children, her feet in the new shoes resting daintily on the foot plate.

One of the most interesting aspects of the Syria conflict, and arguably the one most commonly misunderstood by westerners, is the question of why the Syrian fighting formations came to be dominated by groups which espouse radical Islam.

Until the mid-1960s, the Arab world was becoming increasingly secular. Arab nationalism was the dominant political ideology, and Ba'athism took hold in Iraq and Syria. This began to change in response to the humiliation felt by Arabs following their defeat in the 1967 war with Israel. Disillusionment with the politics of Arab nationalism and socialism became commonplace, while the poor felt increasingly angry about the failure of their governments to provide for their needs. Over the next decades, many turned towards Islam and, by the 1980s, an Islamic revival had taken hold in most corners of the Arab world. In police states such as Iraq and Syria, where freedom of expression was banned, religion acquired a new importance and radical Islam offered a vocabulary of resistance. Thus, in Syria in the late seventies and early eighties, as noted earlier, opposition to the regime centred on the Muslim Brotherhood.

Mindful of the potential threat of radical Islam, both Hafez and Bashar had been careful to nurture the loyalty of the Sunni *'ulema* (clergy), and Bashar continued this policy after the revolution began. Many urban Sunni clerics backed the regime out of fear: those who spoke out were soon dead or in exile. In the cities, the perception that some Sunni clerics had failed to speak out against the regime's devastating violence pushed protesters towards support for radical Islamist leaders who had not been co-opted by the state. It was different in rural areas, where the *'ulema* strongly supported the revolution.

The western media tends to dismiss radical Islam as an incomprehensible ideology which espouses mindless violence, the commission of atrocities and the oppression of women. While much violence is undoubtedly committed in the name of radical Islam, if we want to understand what has happened in Syria, we need to look more closely at what it means to its adherents there and why it attracts them. Many different types of Islamism were present in revolutionary Syria, but the one which came, over time, to dominate the armed struggle was Salafism. Salafism is a form of Sunni Islam which aspires to recreate life as it was lived (or is thought to have been lived) in the days of the Prophet, using force if necessary. In the early 2000s, as explained, the regime had allowed Salafists to operate inside Syria because it wanted to encourage their presence as a destabilizing force in US-occupied Iraq. Salafist fighters returning from Iraq to Syria were imprisoned; but a substantial number of them were deliberately released by the regime in 2011, apparently in an effort to 'radicalize' the opposition and thereby discredit it in the eyes of the west. A couple of years later, a number of these men were leading the most powerful Islamist militias, many of which explicitly sought to establish a religious state in Syria. Prominent among these were Jaysh al-Islam, Ahrar al-Sham, Suqour al-Sham and Jabhat al-Nusra.[1]

A moving account of why some of the Syrian protesters of 2011–12 turned to radical Islam is given by Robin Yassin-Kassab and Leila al-Shami in *Burning Country*:

Tormented, bereaved and dispossessed, the Syrian people turned more intensely to religion. This doesn't mean they became advocates of public beheadings and compulsory veiling; almost all were horrified by the appearance of these phenomena and most still expressed the desire for a civil rather than an Islamic state . . .

The first cause was the same one which powered militarization – the brute fact of extreme violence. In most cultures the proximity of death will focus minds on the transcendent . . . and more so in an already religious society like Syria's. Faith is intensified by death and the threat of death, and by the pain and humiliation of torture . . .

The sung slogan 'Ya Allah Malna Ghairak Ya Allah' (O God We Have Nothing But You) became ubiquitous among protesters facing bullets. An intense relationship with God became a survival framework for the detained. Religious slogans became cosmic rallying calls for the fighters. In the Syrian context, radicalization is better named traumatization.[2]

The leaders of the radical Islamist militias were committed to different variants of Salafism. It is impossible to know to what extent the individual fighters, lower down the ranks, actively supported their ideologies. Money and survival were undoubtedly big factors in the decision to join up: as the Syrian economy collapsed, young men who did not flee the country had few choices of employment in the 'liberated' areas, other than taking up arms. Some of the numerous militias paid only minimal salaries; in general, the larger and the more radical ones paid better, with ISIS paying the most. Having strong sources of external funding, often from Qatar, the radical militias were also better armed and equipped, meaning that their fighters had better chances of survival; by comparison, the FSA had been unable to establish a regular and reliable supply of weapons for militias affiliated to it. (The supply of weapons by the US to FSA-affiliated 'moderate' militias was intermittent and has been likened to a tap that was turned on and off, frequently leaving the fighters vulnerable and making it impossible for them to make sustained progress.[3])

Another factor in the choices made by young men as to which militia to fight for was the greater discipline and order which existed in the radical Islamist militias, compared to the looting, corruption and disorganization that characterized some of the secular and FSA-affiliated ones. Islamist militias generally did better in battle than their secular counterparts; some were also good at providing services to civilians and at creating security in the 'liberated' areas they controlled. The price was the imposition of strict Islamist values on the civilian populations; but in the chaos of war, where kidnapping, rape and looting were commonplace, this was not always, initially, unwelcome.

Of the militias which did not espouse radical Islamist ideology, many nevertheless used Islamic names, in some cases as a ploy to attract better funding from foreign states, and in others simply because Sunni Islam was embedded in the culture.

At Hara, I often found myself musing about the politics of the young Syrian men I met, some of whom had presumably been fighters. Which militias had they fought for, and did they subscribe to radical forms of Islam? I wondered about the women, too. Almost all wore headscarves, even the Kurds, but I was pretty sure this was due to the very public existence they endured in the camp, rather than an indication of hard-line religious views. (Most Kurds are Sunni Muslims. Kurds tend to take a relaxed approach to their religion and, in the west, few Kurdish women wear headscarves.) Much as I would have liked to, I didn't feel it was my place to ask questions of the women I was meeting. And what sensible refugee would talk openly about radical affiliations, while seeking asylum in a European country?

The sense of betrayal and abandonment which Syrians felt when the west failed to support them in the face of extreme regime violence contributed to the radicalization of the armed opposition. These feelings of betrayal were accentuated in September 2013, when Obama's threatened missile strike in response to the regime's use of chemical weapons was called off. This compounded anger felt six weeks earlier, when the west had failed to condemn with any real conviction the Egyptian military's forcible overthrow of the elected Muslim Brotherhood government of President Morsi. It is hardly surprising that many Syrians concluded that the west was utterly hypocritical, and that intensified armed struggle in the name of Islam was the best way forward.

Another consequence of the coup in Egypt was that relations between the anti-Assad states plummeted. As a keen supporter of the MB, Qatar had sponsored the Morsi regime. Both Qatar and Turkey's leaders were furious when it came to light that Saudi Arabia had sponsored the regime's ouster. The rift had repercussions in Syria, where, for the next months, militias funded by Saudi Arabia refused to cooperate with militias funded by Qatar.

Most 'extreme' among the radical Islamist groups fighting in Syria are Jabhat al-Nusra, which is linked to al-Qaeda and ISIS. Both of these are *jihadi* organizations, which means that they subscribe to an ideology of warfare across existing state boundaries with the aim of creating a single Islamic state. That is not generally the case with other radical Islamist groups active in Syria, whose stated primary goal is to bring down the regime.[4] The Islamic Front, for example, initially gave mixed messages as to its political position on a number of issues, and notably on democracy. In May 2014, however, seeking to distinguish itself from ISIS and Jabhat al-Nusra, it signed up to a 'Code of Honour' in which it rejected 'extremism', said it aimed to achieve 'freedom, justice and security for Syrian society' and did not call for the creation of an Islamic state.

The origins of both Jabhat al-Nusra and ISIS are tied up with events in Iraq in the years preceding 2011. During the civil war in Iraq from 2006, the al-Qaeda-affiliated organization Islamic State in Iraq (ISI) fought alongside the Iraqi Sunnis against Shi'a militias and the US-installed, Shi'a-dominated government, until in 2007 ISI was defeated by tribal militias backed by the US. Some of ISI's fighters were Syrians. When the uprising began in Syria, Abu Bakr al-Baghdadi, the Iraqi leader of ISI, sent a Syrian member to Syria with generous funding and a brief to set up an al-Qaeda–style operation there. This was the beginning of Jabhat al-Nusra,[5] which was listed as a terrorist group by the US in 2012.

Nusra had access to a large arsenal acquired both from Iraq and from private donors in the Gulf. Its fighters were highly experienced, having fought in Afghanistan and Iraq; soon they seized military installations in eastern Syria and became active in Aleppo, acquiring more recruits through their successes. Although Nusra's Salafist ideology was unappealing to many Syrians, they were seen as a powerful force to help defeat the regime. Cleverly, they provided services to the desperate Syrian population, in stark contrast to the FSA.

Large numbers of foreign jihadis were now rushing to Syria to fight. They included veterans from Chechnya, Afghanistan and Iraq, together with would-be jihadis from Arab states,

Europe, the UK, Australia and the US. Most of them joined Nusra; some formed smaller jihadi groups. These fighters had not been invited by Syrian activists or rebels, and they became an additional source of torment for the population.

In April 2013, al-Baghdadi publicly announced that ISI was the parent organization to Nusra and that the two would now merge, with him as leader, to form Islamic State in Iraq and al-Sham (ISIS). But Nusra's leader refused to have his new militia absorbed into ISIS and he was backed up in this by the original al-Qaeda. At this point, most of Nusra's foreign fighters left to join ISIS.

One late morning, as I was fighting my way through the crowd on the verandah with a hot cup of tea in my hand, the tall man in the baseball hat who'd led the chanting at the sit-in caught my eye. I knew by now that his name was Abu Anas. Our paths had crossed at some point every day, and we always exchanged greetings and smiles, but we'd still not had a proper conversation. He was often on the forecourt, chatting with the other Syrian men, drawing on a cigarette and watching the scene with a taut, restless energy.

'T'reza!' he called out now, from the table where he sat with a crowd of younger men. 'Come and sit down! Let's have a chat.'

Abu Anas intrigued me, so I accepted. Privately, I'd nick-named him 'Abu Taweel' (Father Tall) as he was noticeably taller than most of the other men in the camp. His physique and body language reminded me to a quite uncanny degree of an old friend of mine who lived in France.

'How's it going?' His brown eyes were full of warmth under the brim of his baseball hat. There were deep crow's feet at his temples and his neat beard and moustache were flecked with white. He must have been very handsome, once upon a time.

'*Yani*,' I smiled, 'I'm tired, but it's going fine today. And you?'

'*Alhamdulillah*, I'm still alive!' He picked up an open pack of cigarettes, pulled one out with his long, bony fingers and lit it, gazing at me steadily all the while. 'We've been trying to figure out what to do.' He inclined his head to indicate that 'we' included the other men seated at the table, most of whom I knew by sight. 'But everything depends on whether they open the border.' He sighed and blew a raft of blue smoke in my direction, which I promptly waved back. 'Sorry, sorry, you don't smoke, do you?'

'No, I don't.' I loathe the smell of cigarette smoke, but I felt more fascinated than annoyed. The last person who'd blown it in my face so casually was my friend in France, at a café table in Paris: he, too, was an incorrigible chain smoker. And if you simply changed the colour of the eyes, the person opposite me could be the same man, a few years on. Everything about him, from his denim shirt and jeans, to the way he lounged against the back of his chair, to the lines on his gaunt, darkly tanned face, were virtually identical. I smiled again and took a swig of tea, vaguely wondering if Abu Anas would turn out to have the same ferocious temper as my friend.

'What's your view, T'reza? What d'you think the Macedonians are up to?' He rested the smouldering cigarette in an ashtray and pushed it towards his friends. 'When d'you think they'll open the border?'

'I really don't know.' I shook my head. 'It's probably a question of *whether* they'll open the border, not when.' As each day passed it struck me as less and less likely that FYROM would reopen its border to refugees.

'You're from Britain, aren't you?' Abu Anas was studying my face again. 'Where did you learn Arabic?'

He listened politely as I gave my usual explanation. 'Don't apologize, you speak very well! Arabic's not an easy language. And look at us, we don't speak English, we don't speak German . . . Okay, Mahmoud here speaks a bit of German' – he nodded at a bearded man sitting at the end of the table, who was listening with an air of amusement – 'but the rest of us don't.' He leant towards me across the table. 'We're delighted to have you here helping us, T'reza. It's a treat to meet a western woman who speaks our language. Everyone comments on it – everyone!'

This was not the first bit of appreciation I'd received, but it was the bluntest, and it touched me. 'I'm so sorry you can't all come to the UK,' I said by way of response. 'You know, lots of ordinary people in Britain want to take in Syrian refugees. It's our government that's the problem.' I hesitated. 'Okay, there are some people who don't want refugees, but many of us would like you to come.'

A square-jawed man to Abu Anas's left interrupted. 'Really? They want us?'

'Everyone has seen the pictures on TV. They understand how desperate things are for you. So it's not really the people that you're up against, it's the British government.' As I spoke, I hoped I wasn't gilding the lily. The desire to take in more refugees was certainly common in the circles I moved in. I should stress that this conversation took place before the shock of the Brexit referendum.

Abu Anas picked up his cigarette. 'So what is it with the British government, why won't they let us in?'

'*Yani*, lots of reasons, but a big one is fear. Especially after the attacks in Paris and Brussels.'[6] All the men around the table nodded. 'They think that if they let you in, there'll be more attacks.' As I spoke I thought how illogical this was; the majority of the perpetrators in both incidents had been French- and Belgian-born European Muslims of North African descent. Just two of the men involved in the Paris attacks had registered as Syrian refugees in the Greek island of Leros a few weeks earlier. If they'd been barred from entering Schengen, would the attacks have been aborted? I doubted it.

Abu Anas sucked his teeth and shook his head. 'But members of Daesh (ISIS) don't travel like this, trudging across Europe on buses and sitting in refugee camps.'

I was intrigued. 'How do they travel, then?'

Several of the men spoke at once, but Abu Anas' voice was the loudest. 'In luxury, by aeroplane! They have lots of money, they can buy decent forged documents.'

I took a swig of tea, picturing a bunch of men dressed in Daesh's signature black, beards newly shaved off, sitting with legs outstretched in the first-class section of an aeroplane, dozing or playing on their mobile phones.

Abu Taweel seemed to read my thoughts. 'I take it you know there's an agreement between Bashar and Daesh? They don't attack each other's forces, do they? Have you noticed that?'

Now all the men around the table joined in. 'It's well known,' Mahmoud announced, leaning forward in his chair. 'Bashar never touches Daesh. Look, if you think about it,

Bashar's very happy to let them sit there in the north-east. Why? Number one, because he gave up on that region long ago. Number two, because, as long as they're there, with their so-called Caliphate, the west will let him control the rest of the country.'

Another man chimed in. 'It's like an insurance policy. Daesh is insurance for Bashar. So long as Daesh is there, Bashar can stay too. Mutual protection, you could say.'

I'd not heard this theory before and my heart sank as I listened.

ISIS arrived in Syria in spring 2013 with large quantities of food, medicine and cash with which to buy the support of the population. Soon to be joined by more foreign fighters from all over the Islamic world and a few converted westerners, by May 2013, ISIS was the dominant force in 'liberated' Raqqa. The city's large Christian population fled. Strict Sharia law was imposed, with smoking and alcohol banned, and women forbidden from appearing in public with anything more than their eyes visible.[7] A reign of terror ensued, in which ISIS attacked Nusra, the FSA and the Islamic Front, not to mention civilian activists, journalists, humanitarians and westerners. ISIS was now a major third force in the war.

Although it went largely unreported in the western press, during the winter of 2013–14, Syrian forces in the 'liberated' areas invaded by ISIS mounted a remarkable challenge to its domination, driving it out of Idlib and Aleppo and achieving some success against it in Raqqa and Deir Ezzor.[8] But subsequent events in Iraq turned the tide in favour of ISIS.

It is interesting to note that some of the leading military

strategists of ISIS are Sunni Iraqis who formerly, under Saddam Hussein, held positions in the Iraqi army and intelligence services.[9] The de-Ba'athification of the army carried out at the insistence of the Americans had left these men angry and humiliated, divested of their former positions of authority. Their rage was compounded by the installation of the Shi'a regime of Nouri al-Maliki and the downgrading of the status of Sunnis in Iraq as a whole. Thus, although ISIS officially espouses Salafist ideology, its military expertise derives partly from the skills of a group of men who previously thrived in Saddam's secular state and whose motivation is presumably political, more than religious.

It is also noteworthy that, according to former Guantanamo detainee Moazzam Begg, no less than seventeen of ISIS's top leaders are survivors of torture endured in US-run prisons in Iraq.[10] Many of these men first met while in those prisons.

Sunni Iraqis rose up against their government in 2010, and by 2013 their intifada was growing stronger. In 2014, ISIS lead a coalition which drove the Iraqi army out of sizeable areas of the north and west of the country. The city of Mosul was occupied by ISIS in just four days in June, by a force of 1,300 men fighting against a nominal 60,000 Iraqi army and police, many of whom simply fled for their lives.[11]

This campaign gave ISIS control of the Iraqi–Syrian border. After seizing the weapons left behind by the Iraqi forces and the money in Mosul's banks, ISIS stormed back into Syria, where it declared its 'Caliphate' at the end of June. Despite vigorous resistance by the FSA and Islamic Front (whose requests for weapons from the US were refused), by July 2014, ISIS had control of one-third of Syria and one-third of Iraq.

The horrific atrocities perpetrated by ISIS in Syria are well known in the west and I don't propose to describe them here. What is less well known is the point made by Abu Anas and his friends, namely, that an agreement of mutual tolerance was indeed reached between ISIS and the regime, and held for many months.[12] Evidence of this is the fact that while the regime regularly bombed schools and hospitals in Raqqa, they avoided the large and ill-concealed ISIS headquarters.[13]

After ISIS took control of the majority of Syria's oil wells, in July 2014, the regime purchased oil from them. Shortly thereafter, following a massacre by ISIS of 220 regime conscripts, the mutual tolerance came to an end. From now on, the regime fought ISIS in areas of Syria that it wished to hold; in other areas, however, it allowed ISIS to attack the FSA, sometimes joining in by bombing the latter.[14]

It is not difficult to see just how useful the arrival of ISIS in Syria was to the regime. It served as the fulfillment of their prophesy that the revolution would facilitate the rise of Salafis bent on establishing an Islamic state; and it helped to terrify members of Syria's minorities, secularists and moderate Sunnis into loyalty, since all were potential targets of ISIS.

12

Skype Calls Go Unanswered

As I climbed the steps of Motel Vardar with Ian, a small party of Macedonians burst through the double doors and lurched, giggling, onto the terrace, clearly the worse for wear. We passed five or six smartly dressed couples, swathed in a cloud of brandy-infused cigarette smoke, the men in formal suits, the women in knee-length skirts and high-necked blouses.

It was ten p.m. and Ian and I were exhausted and hungry. After dumping our Northern Lights vests in our rooms and collecting laptops, we met again in the empty dining room, choosing a table by a pillar at a safe distance from the screen.

The headwaiter hurried over to take our order, smiley as ever in his grey pinstripes. When he'd gone, Ian lifted the lid of his laptop and looked at me over the top of his beer glass. 'I should blog,' he said softly.

'So should I.' I pulled my little MacBook out of my shoulder bag, grateful to have a companion who felt as compelled to write as I did. For the next twenty minutes, we sat in silence, tapping away at our respective keyboards. We had known each other all of five days and a gulf of decades stretched between us, but a shared fascination with the Middle East seemed more important.

There was always far more to record than I had time for, and the words rushed through my fingertips onto the screen. When the food came, we pushed our laptops aside, tucked in and started talking: not unusually, there was a problem to be solved. The next morning we were planning to attend the 'legal briefing' at Idomeni, where UNHCR were going to explain the legal options for the refugees. From there we'd go to Hara, where we hoped to disseminate the information. The problem was, how? The information would be complex and we didn't have a common language with the speakers of Urdu, Farsi and Dari.

'Maybe UNHCR have something in writing we can give out,' Ian suggested. 'They must have translators.'

'If they haven't, we could get Juwan to translate stuff into Arabic,' I added. 'His English is amazing.' I'd persuaded Burhan and Juwan to come with us to the meeting, hoping they'd be able to repeat the information in Arabic to the Syrians and Iraqis. I'd also tried to invite a young Afghan woman and a Pakistani man, but wasn't sure if they'd understood the importance of the meeting.

Ian grinned. 'Juwan's a pretty remarkable guy. He's read more books in English than I have.'

Most of the refugees were still asleep when Ian and I reached Hara the following morning. The forecourt was oddly silent, with the majority of the zipped-up tents still in shadow. Behind the camp, by contrast, the fields were bathed in sunlight. We'd arranged to meet Hosni, Juwan, the Afghan woman and the Pakistani man at eight thirty, to allow us time to walk across the fields to Idomeni. Greece had passed a regulation making it illegal for volunteers to carry refugees in their cars, so this was the only way for us all to get there.

I found the young Afghan woman on the steps of the hotel, her chiffon headscarf draped loosely over her head and shoulders. She couldn't come with us, she said, because her mother needed her to take care of her little brother. I went looking for the Pakistani, without success.

It took Ian twenty minutes to rouse Burhan and Juwan, both of whom had overslept. The morning was fresh, but it would be hot when we walked back in the middle of the day. We set off through the Afghan/Kurdish field, passing a row of zipped-up, silent tents and taking a track of baked mud through a ditch. The land was flat, the soil red. In all the surrounding fields, bright green shoots of new wheat pushed up in neat straight rows. It was the first exercise I'd had in five days, and I was happy to be moving.

Burhan was in an upbeat mood. 'It's so great to be going somewhere!' he told Ian, resting a brotherly hand on his shoulder. 'This is the first time I've left Hara in three weeks!'

'I go to Idomeni every couple of days,' Juwan chipped in. He was bundled up in a bomber jacket, despite the sunshine which was now warming our cheeks, and looked half asleep.

'What d'you go for?' Ian asked.

'I have friends there, but also I go for the food!' Juwan grinned. 'Distribution is much better at Idomeni than at Hara. You can get all sorts of nice things to eat . . . and imagine, they have a stall giving out *free tea*!'

After half an hour in the fields we crossed a main road. Skirting more fields, we reached a line of bushes and trees that screened the railway line which had been the main feature of Idomeni village prior to the border closure. Here flies buzzed in our faces and a smell of excrement hung in the air. Every few yards, in among the undergrowth, lay piles of human shit.

At last Juwan led us up the bank through a gap in the bushes onto the shingle beside the tracks, a hundred metres from the low stone buildings of Idomeni station. In the distance, a vast tent encampment stretched for as far as the eye could see. In the foreground, small tents were scattered here and there, some beside the tracks, some even straddling the rails. The sun was high by now and people were waking up, unzipping their doors and looking out. A woman boiled water on an open fire. Children played across the rails.

It might have been a peaceful scene if it hadn't been so bizarre. I knew that the trains weren't currently running into Idomeni, but nevertheless I found the sight of tents pitched on railway tracks unsettling.

In a few minutes we were in the bustling centre of the camp. Juwan led us to the shipping containers which housed the UNHCR offices, and from there we followed a warren of little alleyways to a white marquee, where chairs were set out in preparation for the meeting. We took seats and waited as a dozen international volunteers drifted in.

The meeting was chaired by a young Greek lawyer, who looked as tired and drawn as the child protection lawyers I worked with at home. She was dressed in jeans and a T-shirt, her lovely face masked by horn-rimmed spectacles. She spoke with a strong accent, but her English was impeccable;

so good, in fact, that at times I got carried away following the structure of her perfect sentences, delighting in the way she got to the end of each one without making a single error. She had once worked for the Greek Asylum Service, she told us, but was now employed by UNHCR.

'Greek asylum law is *very complicated*,' she warned us in a sing-song tone, wagging a slender brown finger. 'And the EU–Turkey agreement has made it worse. But there are some basic principles you'll be able to understand.' She paused for breath. 'If you're working with Syrian or Iraqi refugees who arrived in Greece *before* the 20 March deadline, they're subject to special measures and there are just three legal routes through which they may be able to leave the country.'

On arrival, whether in the Greek islands or at the land border with Turkey, she explained, these Syrians and Iraqis had been given a paper called a *hatiyya* which allowed them to remain in Greece for six months. During that time, they must either apply for 'Family Reunification' or 'Relocation' or 'assisted repatriation' to their country of origin. (Some few individuals had already opted for this last choice.) Family Reunification was available to those who had a 'close family member' living legally in another European country, defined as a spouse or a child under eighteen. Relocation meant being placed in one of the European countries which had agreed to take a quota of refugees (something the UK had expressly refused to do). Those who elected Relocation would have no choice over which country they were sent to.

'In order to take up any of these options,' the lawyer added, 'there is one system, and one system only. You have to begin by making a Skype call to the Greek Asylum

Service.' She removed her glasses and gazed around the circle, making eye contact with each of us individually. '*Please tell people this.* If they don't have Skype on their phones, they need to download it. When they make the call, they will be asked to give their names and dates of birth, and their photograph will be taken.' She paused, replaced the glasses and looked down at her papers. 'And then they'll be given an appointment, to attend at the nearest office of the Greek Asylum Service for interview.'

A bearded man sitting on the far side of the circle cleared his throat. 'Where's that?'

'We don't yet know. There's one in Athens, and one in Thessaloniki, but I don't know which one they'll be told to go to. The appointment is at 7 a.m., for every single person. *All appointments are at 7 a.m.*'

A stir of disapproval went round the room and the bearded man spoke again. 'Is transport laid on?'

The lawyer raised her eyebrows and shrugged her shoulders, clearly embarrassed. 'This also, is not yet clear.'

I exchanged glances with Ian and shook my head. How were the lone mums of Hara, many of whom had completely run out of money, to get to Athens for a 7 a.m. appointment with their large broods of children? Even getting to Thessaloniki by that time of the morning would be a major headache.

'Okay' – the lawyer raised her hand with forefinger outstretched – 'clearly, transport is a huge problem; but there is another difficulty, of which you must be aware. If you look on the Greek Asylum Service website, you'll see that there is a time allotted for each different language group to make their Skype call – for example, Arabic speakers are to call between ten and twelve on Mondays, ten and eleven on Tuesdays or nine and ten on Thursdays.' She paused for breath. 'The difficulty is that, at present, the GAS does not have sufficient staff to answer the calls. Many refugees are trying to make the Skype call, but cannot get through.'

Several of us gasped. 'So what are they supposed to do?' I enquired.

The lawyer turned to me. 'You have to tell them to keep trying. *Every* day, when it's the right time for their language group, they must try to make the call.' She raised her eyebrows and her shoulders shot up. 'The Greek government is aware of this problem. They are trying to recruit more staff.' She lifted her hands from her lap, fingers outstretched in a gesture of despair, leaving me in no doubt as to her deep sympathy with the refugees. 'This is the way it is, in Greece.'

At the first appointment at the GAS offices, the lawyer added, refugees would be given a pink card. This entitled them to work and to send their children to Greek schools, but no financial support would be provided. They would be asked which of the three options they wished to pursue and, if it was Family Reunification or Relocation, to make out their case. A couple of months later they would be required to attend a second appointment, at which they would be asked more detailed questions. The whole procedure for those opting for Family Reunification might take up to eleven months, during which time the refugee would have to remain in Greece. Relocation might be quicker, but places on the scheme were only available when the receiving European countries indicated that they were ready to take their quota of refugees; and this was not happening at the speed anticipated.

Those who didn't qualify for Family Reunification or

Relocation could opt for asylum in Greece. This would give them the right to work and to free education, the lawyer said, but there was no financial support and no housing. It was pretty obvious, I thought, given the dire state of Greece's economy, that all but the most resourceful would be destitute, living on the streets as beggars.

I was making notes as the lawyer spoke. Given the length of time the whole procedure would take, she said, it was probably best for the Idomeni and Hara refugees to move to the various military camps being opened by the government. Nobody would be forced to move, but conditions in those camps would be better than here at Idomeni. Lastly, anyone who didn't make the Skype call before their *hatiyya* expired would be liable for deportation.

The position of the Afghans, Iranians and Pakistanis was much worse. Refugees from these countries had been given a *hatiyya* allowing them just one month to remain in Greece, after which they became liable to deportation. They weren't eligible for Relocation. A few might be eligible for Family Reunification; the rest had to choose between asylum in Greece or repatriation.

It was late morning when we staggered out of the marquee into the bright sunshine. Juwan led us to the stall which supplied 'free tea' and we sat on the ground, sipping the hot sweet liquid as we tried to take in the full enormity of the refugees' situation. I was already doubting the wisdom of our decision to prioritize food at Hara. People urgently needed information about their legal position and instruction in the use of Skype.

We set off back to Hara, ambling slowly along the dry mud tracks, swigging water and talking intermittently about how to disseminate the information. It was so hot that Burhan knotted his sweatshirt, *kefiyyah*-like, over his head. Shortly before we reached the road, a trio of men appeared in the distance, walking towards us. For a second I felt nervous, but for no good reason: the track was the shortest route between Hara and Idomeni. When the men reached us, I recognized two of them as Syrians from Hara. The third I didn't know, but he was the spitting image of an Iraqi I'd met years earlier during my days in Kurdistan. He had thick, jet black hair and fleshy cheeks. After he'd shaken everybody's hand, including mine, he announced he was a singer and hoped we'd like to hear a song.

It was hot and we were hungry, but we all said yes, do please sing for us. So the man put down the plastic bag he'd been carrying, straightened his shoulders and opened his mouth. The voice which issued forth was rich and beautiful. He sang with great feeling, one of those passionate Iraqi songs that speak of the desert and love, with the rhythm of a caravan of camels moving slowly through an endless, arid landscape. We listened intently, as the man's sonorous voice drifted on the hot, dusty air. It was like stopping in the middle of an arduous journey for a cool drink at an oasis. When the song ended there was a moment of silence and then we all clapped and thanked him. He bowed, picked up his plastic bag, smiled a lot and ushered his friends back onto the path, gesturing in the direction of Idomeni.

After lunch in the bar, I went to fetch my bag from the car. I'd parked it in shade beside the Kurdish field early in the morning, but by now the sun had moved. When I opened the door and slid into the driving seat, it was like entering an oven. I grabbed my bag from under the seat, got out and locked up. As I was walking back towards the camp, my eyes lighted on the very old woman with the orange headscarf whom I'd first seen queuing to see the doctor. She was sitting on the ground in the doorway of her tent, looking at nothing in particular with her pale, watery eyes. The younger woman sat a few feet away on her usual log with her back to me, stirring a blackened cooking pot.

The extreme age of the old woman fascinated me: I thought she might be ninety-five, the age my mum had been when she'd died the previous spring. I slowed my pace and walked towards her. We'd never spoken before, but it shouldn't be difficult to squat down in front of her and make conversation for a moment or two.

But when I came within a few feet of the old woman, and before she saw me, tears sprang to my eyes. The emotion was sudden and powerful and I couldn't control it. Just in time I turned sharply away, wiping my eyes with my fingers. I stumbled back towards the road, ignoring the shouts of children who demanded to know where I was going. I strolled towards Efzoni in the still, warm air, seeing my mum's lovely face in my mind's eye. I missed her so much.

I cast my gaze across the fields, hoping the sight of young green shoots pushing up through the soil would have its usual grounding effect on me. I would have liked to turn my back to the road and head towards the hazy blue line of the mountains, but I'd promised to organize the rice pudding distribution. After a few minutes I turned back towards the camp. The ADM van was due in half an hour.

*   *   *

When the van appeared around a bend in the road, I was standing in the shade at the back of the hire car. Dilshad was at my side, as were Hasan and a handful of his teenage friends. I'd put out the word that I needed help to distribute the puddings, and they'd shown up immediately, full of enthusiasm at the prospect of doing something constructive. I was relieved to have their help, but unsure whether my 'distribution plan' would prevent the riot Cjara had warned of. I'd divided the camp into sections, and now I explained to the boys that they should work in pairs, restricting the puddings to children of ten and under.

The van pulled up behind my car, facing the other way, and reversed towards us in a cloud of dust. Suddenly Cjara was at my side, neat and smiling, with a scarf wound round her hair. Two lads sprang out of the cab and opened the back doors of the van to reveal a stack of black plastic crates that reached to the roof.

'Save the Children have sent a lot of puddings,' Cjara explained as the men began stacking the crates on the ground, 'more than I thought. I don't know if they'll all fit in your car.'

A large cardboard box of unclaimed packages blocked my back seat, together with the items for children's corner. There was nothing for it but to take them out and stack them on the edge of the field, with Dilshad standing guard. Soon Hassan and his mates had formed a chain between the transit and the car, and one of the ADM lads was bent double, cramming the crates onto the seats. Each crate contained fifteen white plastic tubs. They were much larger than I'd imagined, each one enough to feed two small children. When the car was completely full, the ADM lads dumped the last two crates at my feet and thrust a couple of bags of plastic spoons into my hands. By now I was panicking at the enormity of the task ahead and wishing I'd roped in Ian to help me, or Eric and Kim, the two experienced volunteers who'd recently returned from holiday. I locked the car, thanked the lads and waved to Cjara, who was climbing back into the transit. 'Good luck!' she shouted through the window. 'I'll be in touch, we may come earlier tomorrow.'

A crowd was forming around the car, and I knew we had to get started. I gave the crates at my feet to two of Hasan's friends and asked them to do the round of the Kurdish field.

'What do we do if a kid says he's ten, but we know he's eleven?' one of them asked me.

I frowned. 'I guess you refuse to give him a pudding. You'll have to use your judgement. Be strict to begin with; if we find we've got puddings to spare, then we can always go round again and give them to the older kids. I've never done this kind of thing before!' I passed him a bunch of spoons. 'We'll learn as we go along.'

'Cool.' The boy grinned, picked up the crates and set off into the field.

Several more teenagers now offered to help, strong-looking lads in cut-off jeans and T-shirts. I chose two whom I knew by sight, unlocked the car and gave them the two crates from the driver's seat. 'You guys go to the Afghan field,' I said. 'Please be sure to go round every tent, Afghans, Kurds, anyone else who's camping there.' I didn't want the non-Syrians to get less than their share.

Dilshad was sitting with a glum expression on the box of unclaimed packages. I'd promised he could help with the distribution and he wasn't happy about being left with the much duller task of standing guard. So I got Hasan to move the box closer to the car, gave him the keys and said it was his job to receive the empty crates from the teams of helpers when they returned. Dilshad and another teenager, Samer, a tall, gangling boy in a stripy football shirt, would come with me to distribute puddings on the forecourt.

Our task went smoothly at first. Dilshad and I carried one crate between us, while Samer took a second. We picked our way between the tents under the canopy, giving a tub of pudding to every child who approached us. It was the time of day when people liked to sit in the open doorways of their tents, enjoying the late afternoon sun. Seeing us coming, parents called out, claiming they had two or three or even four children under eleven. At first I accepted these claims at face value. Our crates were soon empty and Samer ran back to the car to get new ones. While we were waiting, Dilshad tugged at my arm. 'T'reza,' he said, 'that man in the blue tent was lying to you. He's only got two children, not four. We should *see* the children before we give out the puddings.'

When the distribution was done I surreptitiously rewarded the helpers with a pudding apiece, told them to eat it out of sight of other teenagers and escaped to the restaurant for a cup of tea. I was pleased with how the distribution had gone, but worried about the legal information. How were we going to disseminate it? Our original idea had been to call a big meeting of all the Arabic speakers and get Juwan or Burhan to explain what we'd been told, but now, in the chaos of Hara, it seemed unrealistic. Where could we even hold such a meeting?

I was stirring my tea and staring into space when Muna, a young Syrian mum whom I'd met several times during the clothing distribution, pulled out a chair on the far side of the table. She wore a billowing blue *gelabba* and a white head-scarf knotted under her chin. We exchanged greetings and I asked how she was.

Muna shook her head. 'Not good. I don't sleep well at night and all day I'm dragging myself around feeling tired, so tired.'

'I guess you're very uncomfortable in the tent?'

'The ground is hard as rock, and we only have two blankets to cover the three of us.' Muna was alone at Hara with her boys aged eight and eleven.

'You're cold?'

'*Yani*, it's okay till the early hours, then the temperature drops and I feel so cold I can't relax.' She sniffed. 'And I'm worried sick. I keep asking myself how I'm going to get my boys to Germany. Their father's desperate to see them.'

'Are you in touch with him?'

'By Facebook.' She pulled out a smartphone with a cracked screen.

I took a deep breath. 'I went to a meeting today', I began, 'with the UNHCR at Idomeni.'

Muna looked at me sharply. 'What did they say?'

'They told us about your legal options.' I did my best to explain what the lawyer had said about Family Reunification. I started to explain the importance of the Skype call, but she frowned, so I told her that Skype was a system of making a call without paying, using the internet.

'But the internet signal's hopeless! Every time I try to connect, it cuts out.'

The hotel's wifi password was pasted up beside the double doors, but I too had never managed to connect. 'You may have to go somewhere else to get a proper connection,' I said. 'The first thing is to download Skype onto your phone.' I added that there were only certain times of day when the Greek Asylum Service had an Arabic-speaking interpreter available. The more I explained, the more furious I felt about the hopeless inadequacy of the system.

An expression of deep unease was spreading over Muna's features. 'So if I make this call, and they give me an interview,' she said slowly, 'how long before they send me to Germany?'

I hesitated before replying, sliding my tea cup around the table while I asked myself if I could fudge the issue. I decided I could not.

'Up to eleven months.'

Muna gasped, rested her elbows on the table and sank her face into her outstretched hands. Her shoulders shook as the tears dripped from her wrists onto the table. I watched, aghast, wishing I'd said I didn't know.

13

Rain and an Encounter with the Greek Secret Service

The western response to the chemical attack on civilians in the Ghouta in August 2013 created a major turning point in the war. Up to that moment, the threat of military intervention by the west had seemed to most parties to the conflict to remain a real possibility. Afterwards, it became abundantly clear that the threat was hollow, at least under the Obama administration. One of the results was a boost to the power of the radical militias among the Syrian fighting groups.

With the help of the USSR and Egypt, Syria had developed a substantial arsenal of chemical weapons under Hafez al-Assad, as a counterweight to Israel's nuclear arsenal. There was international concern about them getting into the hands of Islamic radicals, and from the middle of 2012, Obama had repeatedly warned Assad that the movement or use of chemicals would be seen by the US as the crossing of a 'red line', from which serious consequences would result.

In August 2013, following a number of reports that chemicals had been used by both Assad and rebels, a UN team entered Syria, at Assad's request, to investigate. Three days later, on 21 August, approximately 1,400 civilians choked to death on the nerve agent Sarin at three locations in the rebel-controlled Ghouta, provoking an international outcry. Suspicion fell on the regime, particularly because the equipment used in the attack was complex and unlikely to have been in rebel possession; but Russia blamed the rebels.

The UN team were now directed to focus primarily on this incident. Meanwhile, four US and two British warships were sent to the eastern Mediterranean and a plan was announced for a forty-eight-hour cruise missile attack on the regime to begin on 2 September. British prime minister David Cameron, who had long wanted Obama to take military action on Syria, sought endorsement from parliament for British participation in the attack, but he narrowly lost the vote and had to withdraw the British warships.

It appears that Obama's conviction was shaken by the British vote, as he then decided to put the matter before Congress, something he need not have done. During the ensuing week's delay, Obama met briefly with Putin at a G20 summit. Three days later, John Kerry, Obama's secretary of state, who had been pushing for closer cooperation on Syria with Moscow since May, made a pointed remark that Assad could prevent the bombing by handing over his chemicals to the international community. This was seized on by the Russian minister of foreign affairs Sergey Lavrov, who now called on Assad to comply. The Congress vote was put on hold, and within a couple of weeks the US and Russia announced a framework for the destruction of Syria's chemical weapons under international supervision. Syria was ordered to comply by a UN resolution passed unanimously on 27 September, and the destruction process began on 6 October.

The background to Obama's vacillation over the military strike is important. By early 2013, events on the ground had made the US administration even more reluctant to intervene in Syria than previously. Libya was now in difficulties, with Islamism on the rise, while in Syria jihadis were coming to dominate the rebels. The US feared that, if Assad went, Syria might descend into a chaos in which the jihadis would thrive.

The US' failure to strike in September 2013 came as a boon to Assad. One inevitable consequence was that he could now be confident that, for the next nine months, while the chemical destruction teams did their work, he would not face further threats from the west. By contrast, the failure to strike was a big blow to the rebels and their backers, who saw it as a major betrayal. Many Syrian rebels felt angry, abandoned and demoralized. The anti-Assad states, some of which had offered to reimburse the US for the cost of the military strike if it had gone ahead, were furious. Their response was to move away from their existing policy of supporting 'moderate' rebel militias, pursued hitherto in the hope of preventing jihadism, pleasing Washington and attracting a US military strike. Instead, and despite its general nervousness about Salafist fighters, Saudi Arabia now backed the merger of a number of radical Islamist militias to form a Salafist grouping, Jaysh al-Islam (Army of Islam).[1] This was intended to be an alternative to Nusra

– which was aligned with al-Qaeda – and to ISIS. Later in the year Saudi Arabia approved the formation of a new Islamic Front. These new organizations rejected affiliation to the FSA and the Supreme Military Council.[2] Turkey also felt deeply let down by the US. In November 2013, to the horror of the Turkish government, the PYD announced the creation of Rojava, an autonomous Kurdish region, in the liberated areas of northern Syria under its control. From this point on, Turkey had little hesitation in allowing ever more radical Islamist militias to move in and out of Syria across the mutual border. These militias were Arab, not Kurdish; and Turkey was not sorry when eventually it saw the biggest one, ISIS, clash with the YPG. As Christopher Phillips puts it:

> With the prospect of a PKK quasi-state on its southern border, Turkey turned an ever-blinder eye to the radical groups criss-crossing its border with Syria. Clashes between ISIS and the PYD from autumn 2013, for example, were not wholly counter to Turkish interests.[3]

In the wake of the chemical weapons deal, there was a brief moment of increased cooperation between the US and Russia. Kerry and Lavrov agreed to hold a peace conference, 'Geneva II', based on the six points in Annan's Geneva Communique. But the run-up to the conference was fraught. In September 2013, a number of Syria's radical Islamist militias had rejected the National Coalition (NC) and called for a new political opposition with Sharia law as its basis. At the same time, the FSA had come under attack from the Islamic Front. Now that the radical militias were in the ascendancy, it was politically difficult for the weakened NC to agree to attend talks with representatives of the regime. In the event, the NC did attend, but without the full backing of all its members.

Another problem was vigorous disagreement about whether Iran should be invited to attend the conference, particularly as its government refused to accept the idea of a transitional government for Syria (one of Annan's six points). Here, the NC stood its ground and Iran's invitation was revoked. This meant that when the talks finally began in late January 2014, one of the key parties to the war was absent.

Assad's representatives spent the conference insulting the opposition and its foreign backers, making plain that they had no concessions to offer. The talks collapsed in mid-February, with Lakhdar Brahimi (who had succeeded Kofi Annan as special envoy to Syria in 2012) publicly apologizing to the Syrian people for their failure. Russia went into the Crimea a few weeks later, Russian–US cooperation came to an abrupt end, Brahimi resigned and the war continued. For its part, the US had rewarded the NC for attending the talks by resuming the supply to the FSA of non-lethal assistance in January. A month later, the supply of lethal assistance was also renewed.

The west's attitude towards the Syrian regime altered in the summer of 2014, after ISIS returned to Syria in force. If this were the alternative to Assad, no western government would now seek his demise. The US began to bomb ISIS in Iraq in August 2014, with Obama arguing that US interests were at stake: ISIS was threatening the Kurdistan Regional Government in Iraqi Kurdistan and destabilizing the whole of Iraq, in which the US had invested so much since 2003. On 22 September, the US and some of its Arab allies overcame their previous reluctance to intervene in Syria and began bombing there, too, arguing that the jihadis' international reach threatened US citizens everywhere.[4] Officially, the raids were aimed at ISIS, but on the very first day, Nusra was hit and, later, Ahrar al-Sham, both of which were at war with ISIS. Oil facilities and grain silos were also hit. While these had been profitable for ISIS, they had nevertheless provided essential fuel and food for civilians.

Given that by now the regime had killed at least 200,000 Syrians without attracting intervention from the US, it was hard for Syrians to stomach Obama's decision to bomb their country for the sake of targeting ISIS. ISIS was hated by most Syrians, but it had done them a great deal less harm than had the regime.[5] In some quarters, the cynicism and fury felt by Syrians lead to an increase in support for radical Islamist groups. Some young Syrians joined ISIS.

Unwilling to send in ground forces, Obama now committed half a billion dollars to a programme to train and equip 'moderate' Syrian rebels to fight ISIS. This move was regarded with huge suspicion by existing Syrian militias and later had to be abandoned.[6] Meanwhile, the regional anti-Assad states continued to urge the US to destroy Assad, whom they saw as a greater threat than ISIS.

Turkey refused to allow the US to use its bases in the bombing campaign until one of their soldiers was killed by ISIS in July 2015. Many Kurds believe that Turkey was in league with ISIS, which it undoubtedly saw as its best defence against the growing military strength of the PYD/YPG.

The border between Turkey and northern Syria remained porous, so that it was easy for would-be foreign fighters to reach ISIS-held territory; and for wounded ISIS fighters to be evacuated to Turkish hospitals.

In September 2014, the Turkish army stood idly by while ISIS launched a vicious attack on the PYD's stronghold city of Kobane, sending 200,000 Syrian Kurdish refugees fleeing into Turkey. Ankara would neither allow Turkish-based PKK fighters to support the YPG forces, who were stretched to their limit, nor would it send its own troops to their assistance. This caused major damage to Erdogan's relationship with Turkish Kurds, who demonstrated in considerable numbers. By late October, he allowed some FSA and Iraqi peshmerga forces to enter Kobane, but by then the damage had been done. This brought an end to a PKK ceasefire which had endured since March 2013. There was now an upsurge in nationalism among Turkish Kurds.

American and allied air power proved useful in the battle to regain Kobane from ISIS. Bombing raids were coordinated with the YPG, Iraqi peshmerga and FSA, who fought alongside some international volunteers. This was the beginning of a positive relationship between the US air force and the YPG. The YPG has an all-women counterpart, the YPJ, which played a considerable role in the fight against ISIS in Kobane. Ironically, given that the PKK remained on the US list of designated terrorist organizations, the US now found in the YPG/J a well-organized, secular, local force with which it could operate effectively against ISIS. In January 2015, ISIS was driven out of Kobane; then out of Hasakah in April and in June out of Tell Abyad, a crossing point into Turkey. Needless to say, the positive relations between the

US and the YPG/J caused Turkish–US relations to came under strain.

Predictably, ISIS's slick propaganda machine milked the western bombing campaign for all it was worth, presenting it as yet another example of Crusader-imperialists attacking Muslims, and using it in their recruitment drives. It is estimated that by late 2015 up to 30,000 foreign Muslims from eighty-six different countries had voluntarily relocated to the 'Caliphate', including a number of young women from the UK and some who attempted to travel there with children. On 3 December 2015, following the attacks in Paris in which 130 were killed, the British parliament endorsed UK participation in the coalition air strikes.

The rain started in the early evening. Women retreated into their tents, while men gathered on the verandah and in the restaurant. As I walked about the forecourt, I felt the mood of the camp sinking. A few young boys still raced around, oblivious to the cold they would suffer when their only sets of clothing got wet through. Most of the tents were flimsy affairs, the sort you could buy in a supermarket for thirty euros, designed for the odd night of fair weather camping. Some had fly sheets; others didn't.

The bad weather was forecast to continue all night and into the following day. While the rain grew heavier, we volunteers gathered in the bar to make a plan of action. As we weren't doing late-night tent duty, Ian and I would go to Polykastro first thing to buy plastic sheeting, plastic ties and a cheap Stanley knife. The sheeting would be cut into squares and distributed to those with single skin tents in advance of a heavy storm which was forecast for the early afternoon. But even with the plan in place, it was impossible not to feel a sense of guilt when we left Hara at nine p.m. and made for the solid walls and roof of the Motel Vardar.

After the predicted night of rain, in the morning the sky grew lighter. In Polykastro, Ian and I struggled to explain to the owner of the hardware store exactly what we wanted, until a customer who knew some English helped us. We sped back to the camp with enough plastic sheeting to cover thirty tents and the knife stashed in the glove compartment. A small crowd formed as we parked the car, the adults grey-faced with exhaustion: they'd spent the night lying awake on sodden bedding, with water running down the sides of their bodies or dripping onto their faces.

I helped Ian distribute the sheeting until the other volunteers arrived, along with a couple of new ones. It was time for *tasjeel*, and Leanne, a Canadian, offered to help. We set up the table in the usual place by the dustbins and took a lot of orders for warm, waterproof jackets, while above our heads the sky turned grey. When the rain arrived, we fled to a roofed-over outdoor staircase and carried on taking orders.

By three p.m. I was hungry and tired. Leanne was meeting the others for lunch in Efzoni and suggested I join them. I said I'd follow her in ten minutes with Ian, who was leaving that night for London and was going round the camp saying goodbye to all the friends he'd made.

It was still drizzling and the forecourt was almost empty. As I searched for Ian, a slightly built young man from Aleppo came up. We'd spoken several times before.

'T'reza,' he said, 'have you heard the news?' His red T-shirt clung to his torso, wet through.

I shook my head.

'Tomorrow, a big group of us, not just from Hara but the whole of Idomeni – 6,000, we're hoping – are going to walk to the border.' He lifted his arms above his head with his palms facing forwards. 'We'll walk like this, so it'll be clear we're not threatening violence. We're going right up to the fence, to see if we can't get them to open it for us.'

My instant reaction was one of anxiety. 'Be careful!' I exclaimed. 'What if the border guards beat you?'

'If they beat us, they beat us,' the young man replied. 'We can't sit here forever.'

I looked at his slender frame, wincing inwardly. 'No, of course not.'

'We're only refugees,' he added, 'trying to get to Germany. We haven't done anything wrong!'

A moment later, Hasan appeared from nowhere. 'Have you heard about tomorrow?' he asked me in a tone of excitement. The man from Aleppo smiled and walked away.

'I've just heard,' I replied, taking in the raindrops beaded on his T-shirt. 'Are you going to go?'

'All of us,' Hasan made a gesture with both arms outstretched that took in the whole of Hara. 'It's the only way.'

At that moment Ian waved from the hotel steps, and Hasan and I walked towards him. The thought that Hasan might get hurt disturbed me. 'Please be careful,' I said. 'Those border guards can be violent. I don't want you to get hurt!'

Suddenly Hasan looked upset. 'I don't want to get hurt, either,' he replied. 'I will be careful, I promise.'

A minute later, Ian and I were in the car. As I pulled out onto the road, I told him the news and said I was worried. I was still feeling a bit shaken when Ian told me to look in the rear-view mirror. 'See that car behind us?' he said. 'They want you to pull over.'

A bolt of adrenalin shot through my system as I took in the headlights of the vehicle behind us and the vigorous, angry hand signals of the driver. Something unpleasant was about to happen. I pulled over to the side of the road and switched off the engine.

Within seconds, the other car stopped close behind us and four very large, unshaven, burly men in scruffy clothing swarmed around the car. We'd driven no more than 200 metres. I pulled the key out of the ignition, glanced at Ian and we both got out.

The car parked behind us was dark blue, dirty and unmarked. Two of the men approached me now, holding out small ID cards with Greek writing and, in the centre, written in English, the word 'POLICE'. '*Bolees, bolees,*' one of them shouted. I understood him perfectly well, but I didn't believe him. He was so large – about six foot four – and his manner so aggressive, that I assumed we were being kidnapped. Standing on the far side of our little car, Ian, as I found out later, was thinking exactly the same.

I felt terrified, but I knew I had to act as calmly as possible. 'What's the problem?' I asked. 'We're volunteers at Hara' – I indicated the camp behind us – 'and we're on our way to get some lunch.'

The men made out they spoke no English, yet somehow indicated that they wanted to see our documents. I handed over my passport and the green card for the car, wondering how on earth I was going to get them back. Ian spoke in his normal, quiet voice as he produced his passport. The calm of his manner astonished me: when I'm angry or frightened I tend to shout, so I determined to copy his example.

'I'm a lawyer, from Britain, and he's a student from the US,' I told the man who had my documents.

Then I heard Ian say, 'Would you let go of my arm please, you're hurting me?' The thug who had Ian's passport, who was perhaps only six foot two but bloated and grisly-looking, had clamped his fingers around Ian's forearm. It was obvious from his manner that he was spoiling for an excuse to punch him. My first instinct was to announce to the four of them that Ian was my son and that they must get their hands off him, right now; but our passports gave the lie to this. So instead I repeated that I was a lawyer and demanded to know what they wanted. Would they like to search the car? In which case, go ahead. Did they want to question us? We were ready.

The response was a flat refusal to search the car and an insistence that we had to go with them to 'the police station', in an undisclosed location. The thug still had Ian by the arm and the other guys were closing in on the car. I could just smell how belligerent they were, as if we'd personally done them some wrong.

There didn't seem any choice but to go with them. When we tried to get back into the car, they said no, one of them would travel with me in my car and Ian must go in their car. At this I lost my temper. 'No way!' I said. 'He's young and he's with me and he's coming in my car. You drive in front and we'll follow you.'

The men snarled, but in the end they allowed Ian to get into the back of my car, in the tiny space between the door and a box of second-hand clothes. One of the four, who was lean and well over six feet tall, with a venomous demeanour, got into the passenger seat. I started the engine and as I pulled away, Ian frantically tried to phone the other volunteers, to tell them what was happening. We still thought this was more likely a kidnap than a genuine arrest.

I followed the blue car a kilometre up the road until we reached the first of Efzoni's two restaurants. 'Hoot!' Ian told me. 'Pull up and hoot!' So I pulled in and leaned on the horn. This enraged the man in the passenger seat. He gave up his pretence of knowing no English and made it clear we'd now blown our chances of any leeway. From now on he was going to drive and Ian was to go in the car with the other three. Ian and I instinctively got out – it was less frightening than being trapped in the little car – but the other three, who had parked beside me, marched towards us and grabbed hold of Ian. There was some shouting, as we all collectively lost our tempers – apart from Ian, who kept up the appearance of extraordinary calm – and I was told to get into the other car. Now I put my moth-balled Greenham Common training into practice and flopped to the ground. One of the thugs swore at me in Greek, grabbed me by the armpits and dragged me into the back of his car.

The whole experience was so frightening that even a few hours afterwards I was unable to recall some of the details, but I know I sat beside him on the back seat of his car, my heart beating very fast, my arm gripped in his large hand, feeling sick about Ian. I don't know why, but I remained convinced throughout the incident that these men wouldn't seriously hurt a middle-aged woman, yet equally convinced that they were out to hurt my friend. Ian was young, foreign and physically smaller than them. The temptation to hurt him seemed to hold an irresistible appeal, as if they saw it as a measure of their manhood.

A few moments later, to my surprise, the car I was in was driven by one of our captors through the centre of Efzoni. After about a minute we pulled up outside a small, single-storey building with 'HELLENIC POLICE' written on the wall.

Relief flooded through me: so we hadn't been kidnapped. And now, as I got out of the car I caught the eye of a female, uniformed officer with garishly dyed red hair, smiling at me warmly from the outdoor patio where she stood beneath a fig tree. Her smile appeared sincere. Beside her was a young male officer, also in uniform.

My captor had let go of my arm, so I walked towards them. 'What's the problem?' I asked. 'These guys are so aggressive, and they won't tell us what they want.'

The male officer looked at me calmly and answered in English. 'No problem,' he said, 'no problem. See your bag.' He pointed at my bumbag.

'Fine,' I replied, taking it off and handing it to him. 'You're very welcome, and to search the car, I've already told them that. But why do they have to be so unpleasant?' I was still shaking, though slightly less than before. 'I'd like some water, please,' I added, looking around at the whitewashed houses of the village street, where a couple of the thugs were milling about in the road, conspicuously *not* bothering to search the car. Where the hell was Ian?

I shouted his name.

'I'm here,' he shouted back. 'I'm inside.'

I was relieved to hear his voice. With the benefit of hindsight, what I should have done was demand to see him.

Shortly after he shouted, as I found out later, Ian was subjected to a strip search, which he endured with the fist of one of the thugs rammed into his mouth. But in my shocked state I didn't ask to see him. Instead I began a conversation with the male uniformed officer.

'Why don't you ask us some questions?' I demanded, remembering my distant days as a criminal defence lawyer. 'What are we supposed to have done?' I took a step towards him, trying to make clear that I wanted an answer.

The officer stared at me blankly.

'Ask us what we've been doing at Hara,' I went on, feeling like I'd acquired a new job as a police trainer. Still no response. 'Okay, if you won't ask, then I'll tell you what we've been doing. This morning, everybody's tents were wet.' I pointed at the sky, wondering how much English the officer understood. The drizzle had stopped and patches of blue were beginning to appear. 'It rained all night, right?' I enunciated my words slowly and clearly. 'So we drove to Polykastro, we bought plastic sheeting, and we helped to cover people's tents.' I forced myself to smile at the officer and his female colleague. She was still regarding me with a kindly, reassuring air as she poured me a cup of water from a plastic bottle.

'Then I took orders for second-hand clothing.' I tugged at the sleeve of my blouse. 'The refugees need clothes, so we take orders and bring them from the store in Polykastro.' Through the branches of the fig tree I saw somebody open the boot of my car.

At last the officer shook his head. 'No problem,' he said. 'Just my boss want to check your car, then he let you go. Few more minutes.'

'But what *is* the problem?' I persisted. Then I had a flash of inspiration. 'Are you looking for activists?'

The officer's face lit up like a light bulb. '*Activists!*' he hissed, as if this were an English word for which he'd been searching. 'Yes, we looking for *activists!*'

I shook my head. 'Well, I'm sorry, but Ian and I are *not* activists. We're humanitarian volunteers. All we're trying to do is help the refugees survive.'

The officer looked at me. 'Ye-es,' he said slowly. 'But you know there lot of tension in this area. Tomorrow big action planned at Idomeni.'

I feigned surprise. 'Really? We don't work at Idomeni, we're at Hara.'

I drank the water and stood about with the officers. A few minutes later, my bumbag was returned to me, with all my documents in it, and I was told I could go. Now Ian came down the steps of the police station and I walked over to meet him. Outwardly, he still appeared very calm.

'Hi,' he said. 'We're free to go, but my iPhone's gone missing.' Courageous to the last, he turned to the thugs, who stood now in a group at the bottom of the steps, glowering at us. 'One of you has my iPhone. I'd like it back, please.'

For a few moments the men pretended not to have understood. I took out my iPhone and waved it in the air. 'This is what it looks like,' Ian said calmly. 'It was in my jacket pocket before you searched me, and it's not there now.'

There was a bit of growling and grunting. Eventually the largest of the four pulled an iPhone out of his pocket and handed it to Ian.

'Thank you,' Ian replied. 'And my worry beads, what have you done with my worry beads?'

This time the response was flat denial. Nobody had seen any worry beads. Ian kept repeating his request, until I said I thought we should cut our losses and leave. Reluctantly, he agreed, but not before going up to the men and attempting to shake hands with each of them. Three took his hand; the fourth, who had tried to steal his phone, refused.

When we opened the car we were surprised to find that the contents had barely been touched. Two items of clothing had been tossed onto the floor in the back. The Stanley knife lay in the glove compartment, exactly where we'd left it.

Five minutes later we discovered our fellow Hara volunteers in the other Efzoni restaurant, phones switched off, oblivious to what had happened. Ian was now running late to catch his plane, but over a quick plate of chips he told me that he'd noticed a couple of the men who'd arrested us at Hara, earlier in the day, chatting with the taxi drivers on the forecourt.

We both felt furious about the way we'd been treated. Later that evening, after Ian had left, I was summoned by the volunteer coordinator at the Park Hotel. She asked me what had happened and told me that around twenty other volunteers had been stopped by police today, mostly for alleged minor driving offences. Some were treated aggressively, others not. She thought it had something to do with the action planned for the following day.

Was I aware, she asked, that a few days prior to the river crossing in March, a group of 250 north European 'activists' had arrived at Idomeni? It was alleged that these people had distributed leaflets in several refugee languages, urging the refugees to cross the river. The Greek government had been outraged and, following the incident, had put a lot of pressure on the secret service to arrest the 'activists' involved. She thought perhaps Ian and I had been the victim of an attempt to pick up 'activists' in advance of any problems that might occur tomorrow at Idomeni.

Late that evening, after lengthy discussions about the best course of action, I went to the police station in Polykastro with a Greek volunteer. We decided to present ourselves as conciliatory, anxious to improve relations between the volunteers and the police.

In the reception area of the police station we found the man who'd driven my car, still in jeans, lounging in an armchair with a cigarette, surrounded by a group of uniformed officers. After ten minutes of animated conversation, the Greek volunteer told me that the man had asked her to tell me that 'nothing personal' had motivated my arrest, and that I shouldn't let it bother me. There was a lot of tension in the area, due to the planned action at Idomeni the following day.

As we left the station the volunteer turned to me. 'That guy is secret service,' she said. 'Here in Greece, they work very closely with the police.'

When I arrived at Hara late the following morning, a curious hush hung over the forecourt. I walked through the restaurant to the bar, wondering why it was so empty. Then it dawned on me that most of our refugees had gone to Idomeni for the action. I wasn't going, because I felt I'd be more useful at Hara.

In the middle of the afternoon, people started drifting back, weary, bruised and angry. Whole families had attended the action, with children of all ages. A large force of FYROM border guards had met them at the fence, using tear gas, rubber bullets and stun grenades to repel those refugees who'd lost their tempers and thrown stones. Getting through the fence had been out of the question. Now the refugees sat in the restaurant showing each other what they'd recorded of the event on their phones, and uploading images to Facebook.

A rumour was circulating that four refugees had died in the melee, but it turned out to be untrue. The incident was widely reported in the European media, which cited MSF as having had to treat 200 refugees, including women and children, for the effects of tear gas inhalation and over thirty for wounds caused by rubber bullets.[7] The Greek government was quoted as having described the Macedonian police's tactics as 'dangerous and deplorable'.[8] That evening, one of my teenage helpers showed me a bloody gash on his lower leg where a rubber bullet had hit him.

In the late afternoon I drove to Polykastro, on the trail of some second-hand buggies that I'd heard were being delivered to the Czech store. I felt drained from the events of the previous day and uneasy being alone in the car, but buggies were like gold dust and couldn't be missed. To my delight, the delivery had arrived and I crammed five of the precious articles onto the back seat.

By the time I got back to Hara, it was dark and drizzling and an atmosphere of chaos pervaded the forecourt. It was crowded, but I didn't recognize many of the faces I saw. In the wake of the action that morning, it seemed, a number of our refugees had left and new ones had arrived. I was on tent duty that night, which meant moving around the camp seeking out the newly arrived and checking if they needed tents. Eric would bring the tents between midnight and one a.m.

A little before midnight, someone introduced me to a petite woman in a long down coat and headscarf. She'd just arrived from Idomeni with her husband and two-year-old daughter. The child was asleep in a tent a couple of feet from where we stood, in the care of a kind Hara refugee who'd taken her in out of the rain. I promised the woman we'd give her a tent. 'Thank you,' she said, explaining she was an English teacher, from Mosul in Iraq, and four months pregnant. I suggested she go and sit in the restaurant till the tents arrived, but the woman didn't want to leave her daughter. So we stood and chatted. After a few minutes I asked her what life was like in Mosul under ISIS.

'The situation's terrible,' she replied. 'Nine months ago they stopped paying salaries to all the state employees. The only people receiving money are the pensioners.' The woman peered at me through the darkness. 'My husband studied engineering, but he couldn't get work: in the end he was forced to work as a baker. But people had no money to buy bread, so the bakery closed. We were obliged to go and live with my parents, along with my sister and her family. Imagine, the only income for all ten of us was my dad's pension. It was very, very hard.'

'And what about living under ISIS?'

'Very strict. If you do exactly as they want, they don't bother you. You have to follow their rules. Hijab for women, with only the eyes showing, and sometimes not even the eyes. And if you want to leave your home, a man must accompany you. But if you stick to their rules, they leave you alone.'

I glanced at the husband, who was standing quietly beside his wife, allowing her to talk. He had a kind face with a short, well-trimmed beard. 'Do they make the men fight?'

'No. The men only fight if they want to. My husband didn't want to, so he didn't fight.'

'How did you leave?'

'Leave?' The woman glanced at me as if astonished at my naivety. 'We didn't leave, we *escaped*! We arranged to go with a gas lorry. Twenty-three of us, all strangers, all trying to get out. The lorry had a little door from the cab into the cylinder. The children had to be given medicine to make them sleep, because we were in there for thirteen hours.'

'Thirteen hours?' I stared at the woman in disbelief.

'I had to sit like this' – she crouched down briefly on the wet tarmac, knees to chin – 'holding my daughter, and when they stopped us at an ISIS checkpoint as we left the city, we had to be absolutely silent. But my daughter started to wake up.' Even through the darkness I could see the woman's chin begin to tremble. 'She nearly died,' she whispered. 'The man sitting next to me put his hand over her mouth to keep her quiet and of course she couldn't breathe. I told him, "She will die if you do that," but he said, "Better for one to die than for all twenty-three of us to die."'

The woman began to weep and I put my arm around her shoulders to comfort her. 'But we got through!' she continued after a moment. 'They didn't hear us, and the lorry passed safely through the checkpoint.'

By now I had my free hand over my mouth, thinking of the little child who so nearly hadn't made it, asleep now in the tent of a kind-hearted stranger; and the new baby this brave woman was carrying. 'Thank God that you made it to Greece,' was all I could find to say.

'*Alhamdulillah*,' the woman replied.

14

Farewell to Hara

I was starting to feel very tired. There hadn't been much time to process the shock of being arrested and the fear that it had generated lurked in my system, making me uneasy, particularly when I had to drive alone. A general mood of disquiet didn't help: in the days following the 10 April action at Idomeni, tension pervaded the atmosphere in the area around the camps. Uniformed police stopped volunteers' cars on a daily basis, demanding to see papers. Crossing the border into FYROM and back attracted more questions than before. And at Hara, the community was in a state of flux, with people leaving and new ones arriving on a daily, sometimes hourly, basis.

My time was running out, but before I left, I was determined to distribute the information about the refugees' legal options. I'd found the material on the Greek Asylum Service website, including some in Arabic, Urdu, Farsi and Dari, but most Hara refugees had limited access to the internet.

One of the volunteers who'd been on holiday, a Dutch woman called Kim, suggested we print the guidance and make an information wall, taping it to the plastic sheeting that covered the verandah. I liked that idea, but thought we should also hand out as much information as possible. I spent a solitary evening in the restaurant at Vardar, where the internet signal was reliable, downloading documents from the website. The following morning, I drove to Polykastro. After stopping at the optician to collect the new glasses for Yasmin's son Shvan, I asked around for a print shop. I was sent to a toyshop where a plump young woman provided a printing service. We had the usual language difficulties, but we muddled through and she told me to email her the documents I wanted her to print and copy. I hadn't forgotten the story about the activists who'd allegedly distributed leaflets in refugee languages prior to the river crossing, so I decided to limit the numbers to ten copies of each document.

Even so, the work of printing and copying took over an hour, and the woman had to keep stopping to serve other people. *It's all from the Greek Asylum Service website!* I repeated to myself as my anxiety levels rose, imagining myself in a police cell, trying to persuade a Greek detective to let me show him where I'd found the information. The task was almost complete, the shop counter covered with piles of printed sheets, when the woman turned her back towards a couple of waiting customers, leaned towards me and whispered 'So sorry, police coming, two minutes. Want to see documents.' I forced myself to take a deep breath. The woman shot me a smile which was at once warm and apologetic. 'That's fine,' I nodded, 'I'm happy to show all this to the police.' I took out my phone and sent a text to a fellow volunteer saying I was probably about to be arrested again, while the woman went back to the till. But after fifteen anxious minutes no police had appeared and my documents were ready, all sorted in neat piles. I paid the woman at the rate we'd agreed, and asked whether she wanted me to wait. She beamed at me again. 'No, no, don't wait!' I offered her my phone number, thinking the police might search her computer and find my emails, but she waved me away.

The warm, sunny weather had returned and I drove slowly back to Hara on a quiet country road, holding my breath every time a car appeared in the rear-view mirror. But alongside anxiety, I felt a measure of fury. How was it possible that in a European country in 2016, people could fall under suspicion for attempting to give out public information from a government website to the very people that the information was directed at? And why did it fall to the likes of me and my fellow volunteers to give out such vital information? I was reluctant to blame the Greek government, given the massive economic problems they were facing, but where was the EU? UNHCR apart, why had they left the task of supporting and advising the refugees to unpaid volunteers?

Back at Hara, Kim and I asked Hercules if he'd agree to our taping the guidance to the plastic awning. The refugees were more likely to depart quickly, we told him, once they knew what their legal options were. He asked for a copy of each document and said he'd let us know the following day.

I was uncertain now about the wisdom of handing out the information I'd had copied. Late that afternoon I persuaded two or three volunteers that we needed to make a collective decision about what to do. I suggested we walk towards Efzoni and find a place to sit in the shade, away from the noise and interruptions on the forecourt.

We found a small shrine set back from the road and sat down under a tree. I was explaining what had happened in the toy shop, when Kim noticed a tall Greek standing beside the road, observing us through the lens of a mobile phone. She leapt to her feet and challenged the man, but he brushed her concerns aside. 'No, no,' he said in English, 'I'm not filming, I'm trying to get a signal. The heat is too much for me and I want to call a friend to come and pick me up.'

'Then please move further away!' Kim insisted. 'You're making us uncomfortable.' The man staggered, aping the symptoms of sunstroke. Ten minutes later he was still in the same spot, still filming us with his phone. We agreed to shelve distribution of the leaflets for the time being and walked back to the camp. The following morning I would see the same man at the border, filming cars waiting to cross into Greece from FYROM.

I felt sad and demoralized when we returned to the camp. But as we passed the Kurdish tents beside the entrance, I heard Yasmin calling my name. I remembered the new glasses for her son stowed in the glove compartment of the car and went to fetch them.

When I returned, Shvan was standing outside the tent beside his mother, blinking in the sunlight. He was a shy lad and had not had much to say when I drove him to the optician appointment four days earlier. Now he took the glasses and put them on with great care, as if afraid they might break.

'Well?' I asked. 'Can you see?'

A broad smile spread across his pale, sensitive face. 'Perfect!' he cried, turning to his mum, then back to me. 'I can see everything! Thank you so much!'

*   *   *

Shortly before the time I spent at Hara, in September 2015, Russia entered the war.

In the first half of 2015 the Syrian rebels had made significant advances both in the north and south of the country. In the north, in March, Idlib was the second provincial capital lost by the regime, falling to the newly formed coalition Jaysh al-Fateh (Army of Conquest), which included Ahrar al-Sham and Nusra as well as FSA militias. Jaysh al-Fateh succeeded in achieving high levels of cooperation between different factions and had a good supply of weapons. Its work was assisted by an easing of tension between Turkey, Saudi and Qatar and it went on to capture Jisr al-Shugour in April. Meanwhile ISIS swept into and vandalised the ancient city of Palmyra, while in the south the rebels were also making gains. Here a more moderate grouping called the 'Southern Front' had formed in 2014 and was committed to a pluralist post-Assad Syria. Many of its fifty-four factions were affiliated to the FSA. The Front was supported by the US, Saudi Arabia and Jordan. In March, the Southern Front captured a southern city, Bosra al-Sham, and the last regime-controlled border post with Jordan.

The regime, for its part, was now struggling with a severe shortage of manpower, which had worsened after Iraqi Shi'a militiamen had returned to Iraq to combat the Sunni uprising there in 2014. When a senior regime figure was arrested and then died in unexplained circumstances, there was speculation that the regime might at last be crumbling.

In the summer of 2015, agreement was reached between Russia and the regime for the Russian air force to enter the war. Russia was granted the use of Khmeimim air base near Latakia, which it took over and rebuilt in August and

September. The project was presented by Putin as a legitimate campaign against ISIS, on behalf of the Syrian government, which had formally requested his assistance.[1] He even went so far as to address the UN General Assembly in September, calling for the formation of an international coalition against ISIS.

Once the Russian air campaign began on 30 September, it soon became clear that the majority of the Russian bombs were aimed at anti-Assad rebels, not at ISIS. In mid-October, a joint ground offensive was launched by Iranian forces, Hizbullah, Shi'a militias and regime forces, against both ISIS and the rebels, in tandem with the air strikes. This at first went badly for the regime, but over the next few months considerable gains were made by the pro-regime forces. A great many of the Russian air strikes hit civilians, with hospitals and schools being regular targets. Throughout the autumn of 2015, columns of refugees fled north into Turkey. It was partly the sight of these refugees night after night on *Channel Four News* that had driven me to take more interest in the Syria crisis.

Putin had a number of reasons for his decisive intervention in the war. Alarmed by the rebels' successes in 2015, he felt the need to prevent what he would have seen as a 'US victory' in Syria, had Assad fallen. But he wanted to achieve more than the protection of Assad. His aim was to end the isolation to which Russia had been consigned following its actions in Ukraine and to place it squarely on the international stage as a superpower. Putin was also genuinely alarmed by ISIS and wanted to prevent their seizure of Damascus. He made little distinction between Abu Baghdadi's men and Syria's own radical Islamist rebels; and he was fearful that Islamist successes in Syria might influence Russian Islamists. Many Russian-speakers had gone to Syria to fight and Putin hoped to kill them there, rather than risk letting them return to Russia.

At home the Russian air campaign was a helpful distraction from the hardships suffered by ordinary Russians as the economy contracted under the impact of sanctions. It was popular in some quarters. Some Russian Orthodox churchmen even characterized the campaign as a holy war to assist Syria's Christians.[2]

Putin took trouble to reassure most Middle Eastern states, and particularly Israel, about his intentions in Syria; but the campaign led to a major falling out with Erdogan, who was not informed in advance as to Putin's plans. In November 2015, Turkey shot down a Russian fighter, claiming it had violated Turkey's airspace.

The western response to Russia's entry into the war was a sudden scramble to restart peace talks. Western governments were now more willing to compromise than previously, for a number of reasons. One was the US-led July 2015 nuclear deal with Iran, in which Iran undertook not to obtain a nuclear weapon in exchange for the removal of sanctions. Another was the fear engendered by ISIS's continuing attacks in the west. A third was the arrival of hundreds of thousands of Syrian refugees in Europe. The 'Vienna Process' began in the autumn of 2015, in which a commitment to a negotiated solution was sought from all the states most closely involved in the war. For the first time, Iran was included. Disagreement between the west and Russia over Assad's role in a post-war Syria was played down; and both Britain and the US gave out mixed messages about whether or not Assad's immediate departure was essential to a deal. An International Syria Support Group was formed, including most of the states playing key roles in the war but excluding all Syrians. It called for a Syrian-led political transition based on the 2012 Geneva Communique. Both ISIS and Nusra would be excluded from any talks. Steps were now taken to unite the Syrian opposition into a body that was able to negotiate. Following an opposition conference in Saudi Arabia, a 'Higher Negotations Committee' was formed in December 2015 which included much of the opposition, but excluded Nusra and the PYD. The latter were excluded at the insistence of Turkey, which was now once again in full-scale conflict with the PKK.

Turkey had joined the US-led anti-ISIS coalition in July 2015 after ISIS had begun to launch attacks inside Turkey, but had used its participation as cover for bombing expeditions against the PKK in Iraq – thereby triggering further PKK attacks inside Turkey. This was why Turkey was adamant that the PKK-affiliated PYD could not be part of the talks. This in turn led to the PYD's decision, in October 2015, to form the Syrian Democratic Forces (SDF), a fighting force that included Arab fighters. The PYD were the dominant partners in the SDF but, as an inclusive force, it was able to move into areas of Syria which were not majority-Kurdish.

Importantly, the US felt able to support the SDF and indirectly the PYD.

The SDF had a political counterpart, the Council for Democratic Syria (CDS), which included Kurds and Arabs. Neither the SDF nor CDS were invited to the forthcoming peace talks.

By early 2016, the Syrian regime had made major gains under cover of the Russian air campaign. The Vienna Process led at the beginning of February 2016 to a new round of peace talks known as Geneva III. Although the talks initially collapsed due to the regime and Russia launching a major campaign in Aleppo province, they subsequently resumed, and on 11 February a 'cessation of hostilities' was agreed, which came into force on 27 February. This held reasonably well in many areas and the UN was able to send in limited amounts of aid, including some to people in areas besieged by the regime. The talks resumed in mid-March, against the confusing picture of Russia's announcement that it had achieved its military goals in Syria and would be withdrawing its troops, while simultaneously starting a fresh operation with the regime against ISIS in Palmyra.

When I went to find Hercules the following morning he looked up and grunted his agreement to the information wall. With the help of two young Iraqi Kurdish girls, I spent the next hour taping the various documents to the inside of the plastic awning. Between us, we worked out a good system: I selected the documents, one of the girls cut the Sellotape, fixed it on and held the paper up against the plastic while the other girl, standing on the forecourt, checked that the document was straight. When it was lined up to her satisfaction she would give us a thumbs up with a warm, feisty smile.

A crowd formed in front of the awning as we worked, with people craning their necks to read the small print.

At ten to twelve I thanked the girls and went to find Yasmin, the mother of the boy with the broken glasses. The previous afternoon I'd explained to her about the Skype system and suggested we try to make her Skype call together, during the hour set aside on Wednesdays for speakers of Kurmanji Kurdish. In the absence of a quiet place to sit, we'd have to use the car.

Yasmin's toddler was asleep in her arms. 'I can't leave him in the tent,' she explained. 'If he wakes up and I'm not there, he'll panic.'

'What about the others?'

'They're fine, they're all out playing. Shvan is with them and the neighbours will come and get me if there's a problem.'

We walked the twenty metres to where the car stood parked, half in sun, half in shade. Inside it was suffocatingly hot. Yasmin settled in the passenger seat with the little one on her lap and I wound down the windows. A couple of small boys appeared from the field, wanting to know what we were doing. I told them firmly to go away.

Yasmin's face was tight with anxiety.

'Do you have the passports?' I asked her gently.

'In my bag.'

'Okay,' I said, 'I'll try the call.' I plugged in my earpiece, logged into Skype and tapped the icon for the 'Asylum Service – Kurmanji', which I'd located earlier. On my first attempt there was no response; nor on my second. I was wondering if I'd got the wrong icon when suddenly I heard a bizarre, bubbling engaged tone. I cut the connection, gave the earpiece to Yasmin and tried again.

'The line's busy,' she said a few seconds later. 'Let's wait.'

Again I cut the connection. While we waited I opened the door to let in air, conscious that the small boys were only a few feet away. One of them trotted up, but I looked at him fiercely and shooed him away. Then I shut the door and clicked again on the Kurmanji icon.

Yasmin sucked her teeth. 'The same sound,' she said with a look of bewilderment. 'Why don't they answer?'

I told her what the lawyer had said, about the lack of staff. 'But if we keep trying,' I added, 'they'll answer in the end. We must keep trying.'

For the next forty-five minutes we tried and tried again to make the call, to no avail. When the hour was almost up, I asked Yasmin if she'd be happy to make the call in Arabic. There was a slot for Arabic speakers the following afternoon.

She shook her head. 'My Arabic's not that good. Perhaps Shvan could make the call, he speaks Arabic well, but I don't.' She looked even more worried now than when we had first got into the car. 'I don't know what to do.'

'Let's stop trying now,' I said. 'Let's take a break. You can try again next week . . .' As I spoke I felt a wave of despair. Who was going to help her next week?

That evening, Juwan and I met up again in the restaurant in Efzoni. It had been another hectic day and I was relieved to be somewhere quiet, with the relatively simple brief of listening to Juwan's story.

'I was telling you about my first few days with MSF, wasn't I?' he said as we sat down. He'd spent the day walking in the countryside around the camp and had caught the sun on the bridge of his nose. 'When I arrived, MSF were in the process of setting up and equipping a field hospital in a cave.'

I could smell chips being fried in the restaurant kitchen. 'Hang on Juwan, I'm starving, let's order some food.' The waiter wasn't around, so I went to the counter and asked the older woman who guarded the till to get us two plates of chicken, chips and salad. Then I sat down. 'Tell me about the field hospital.'

Juwan poured us each a glass of water from a jug on the table. 'On my first morning I walked over there with Paul and a couple of others. I'd never walked in mountainous country before and I was amazed how beautiful it was. I remember climbing on an asphalt road. On one side the land fell away into a deep valley, with more and more mountains behind, stretching to the horizon. Then we left the road and walked across an apple orchard. I was just beginning to feel too hot when we came to a large fig tree. Behind it, well hidden, was a stout steel door across the entrance to the cave.'

'A door put on by MSF?'

'No, before the war, the cave had been used by a farmer to store apples. We stepped into a corridor with a low ceiling – so low the Europeans had to duck their heads. The air smelled of damp and there was water running down the walls, which were solid rock. Down a couple of steps was a big open space, where the operating theatre team were installing a surgical tent, with an ex-pat woman surgeon who'd just arrived. One of the technicians was wiring up lights to a generator.'

'What's a surgical tent?'

'For doing operations in sterile conditions. As I was looking round, a British logistician called Dave called me over for a lesson in how to start the generator. It was a completely new thing for me – I'd never had anything mechanical to care for, not even a bicycle. He showed me how to check the oil and the petrol and how to level the generator. From then on it was my responsibility.'

'What was he like, this Dave?'

Juwan hesitated for a moment, as the smell of roast chicken wafted towards us. 'Dave was an outgoing, sociable, funny guy. Always complaining about everything, but I liked him a lot. Over the next few weeks we became good friends.' The door to the kitchen swung open and he glanced up. 'I spent the rest of that day helping in the pharmacy, in an alcove at the back of the cave, labelling medicines in English and Arabic with another translator and the ex-pat woman surgeon. She was lovely.'

'What sort of age?'

Juwan shrugged. 'Forties? At dusk we walked back through the mountains, but this time we stayed in a different place, a little house in a village which MSF had rented for us. From then on we used to cook and eat there in the evenings and the women slept there at night.'

'Where did the men sleep?'

'On the floor of the local mosque.'

'Did you eat well?'

'No.' Juwan grimaced. 'I liked the way we all cooked and ate together – drivers, translators, all the ex-pats – but the food supply was limited, and there wasn't enough of it. Everything had to be brought in from Turkey, so we lived on pasta, tuna, sardines, cornflakes, muesli, cheese and eggs. And bread from a local baker, who we supplied with flour.'

'And what did your work involve?'

'For the first couple of weeks, my main task was translating for Dave and being his helper. He got me building shelves in the warehouse where he was based, to store the medical supplies smuggled in from Turkey. That was a new experience: for my whole life I'd been a student, a book reader, someone who played on a computer; I'd never done anything with tools. But I enjoyed it. After I'd made the shelves, for several days I was opening boxes and organizing stuff. Then one day we went to a militia leader to ask him to help us obtain a supply of petrol for the MSF cars and generators. The militia leaders were local and knew where to get things. I felt a bit funny meeting this guy, because I was almost as much a stranger here in the north-west as Dave was. My family home was hundreds of kilometres away and it must have been obvious that I was a city boy. But the guy was nice. He'd become a militia leader because he was head of his family and had to protect them. It was like that then: most of the militia leaders were civilians who'd started out with hunting rifles.'

'Were some of them Islamists?'

Juwan sucked his teeth. 'I wouldn't say so. Their Islamism was living their everyday life. In the militia they were as Islamic as they were in their normal life.'

The kitchen door swung open again and the old woman walked towards us, carrying two steaming plates of food. A look of delight spread across Juwan's face. 'When you said food, I was thinking that I wasn't hungry. But now I see it, I'm starving!'

When Juwan had emptied his plate he rested his forearms on the table and pulled out the fingers of his left hand one by one. As always, the sound of his knuckles cracking made me feel queasy. He caught my eye and laughed. 'Sorry, you don't like it, I know.' He interlaced his fingers and rested his chin on his thumbs. 'One day, Dave and I went back to the place where I'd spent the week with the refugees. While we were there I saw some FSA men with long beards who I thought were Salafis and I got worried. But Dave said, "No, they're not," and he pointed out that they were smoking. He was right: they were just ordinary local guys who'd grown beards to show they weren't regime supporters.'

'What's the connection?'

'In the Syrian army, there's a strict rule against beards. Every morning, recruits are made to stand in line while an officer wipes their face with a tissue. If he feels any bristle, he sends the man to prison for a day. It's because the regime is so afraid of the Muslim Brotherhood.'

'Sounds like paranoia! What did you do on a typical day at the cave?'

'After breakfast each morning we drove over there. The medical team went in and Dave and I went to the warehouse, a couple of hundred yards across the orchard. The regime was very active in that area, and often we heard helicopters overhead. When you hear one you look up, try to see where it is, decide what you need to do. We could even hear them from inside the cave.

'The helicopters were dropping barrel bombs on the local villages and when there were no big battles going on, our main priority was to help the injured civilians. A helicopter would drop between two and four barrels on each flight. One day a barrel was dropped on the field between the hospital and the warehouse, making a gigantic crater. Thankfully, there were no casualties, just four trees destroyed. But we

were all very frightened by it and the ex-pats saw it as a red
alarm. We closed the hospital early and went to the house.
The next day, the head of the project came from Turkey and
decided to reduce the ex-pat team to just four, but all the
local staff would stay.

'The location of the hospital was really too dangerous
because it could be seen from a regime tower on a distant hill
opposite. Dave left and I was transferred to the medical
team. I started to learn the medical terms, to be able to work
with the doctors.'

'Were you happy about that?' I ate my last chip and pushed
my plate to one side.

'Not really, but it was the kind of situation where you just
do whatever is needed. Most days I was in the cave from
early morning till evening; and sometimes I went back to do
a night shift, when they were short of nurses.'

'You were nursing?'

'At times. Because the staff was so limited, the surgeon
gave us all medical lessons. They recruited several local
women to train as nurses because the ex-pats came and went.
They trained them in how to do blood pressure, give medi-
cation and how to open an IV line. Later they taught them
how to suture and how to keep a wound clean. I was involved
in the first part of the training, but I didn't like medical
work.'

'Was it the blood?'

'It was more the responsibility. I didn't want the doctors
relying on me to take care of a patient. But I did it. At times,
when lots of injured people were being brought in, we
worked round the clock and I was called on to help with all
sorts of tasks: I even helped in the operating theatre, when

one of the doctors got me to pour water during open abdomen surgery. Another time, I helped to wrap up the bodies of dead children.'

I stared at Juwan, thinking what a lot he'd been through. He was only ten years older than my son.

'There were quiet moments, as well as busy ones. When the day's operations were over and the patients were settled in their beds, sometimes we'd make tea and sit outside the cave for twenty minutes. It was always good to get back out into the daylight. We'd smoke and talk and feel relieved that we'd made it through another day.'

'Who exactly did the hospital treat?'

'Anybody in the area who needed it. The core was the operating theatre, but we did outpatient work too. If a pregnant woman needed a C-section we'd do it; but we didn't do non-emergency operations, such as hernias.

'After I'd been working with the doctors for two weeks or so, the militias in the area launched an assault on the regime. There were many militias from different villages and different families, but they launched the assault in mutual cooperation. It lasted for a few days and they gained control of some villages and took a lot of prisoners because the regime army was dissolving in front of them. The foot soldiers, who were mainly Sunni, weren't ready to fight for Bashar. Their morale was low, whereas rebel morale was good.

'Suddenly we started to receive tens of injured people. Eighty per cent of them were from the regime army, young men between twenty and twenty-five, mostly doing their military service. Some had scratches, some had broken legs, some had abdominal injuries. The hospital took care of everyone who was injured, but we wanted to know which side they were on. Personally, I dealt with them according to their medical needs, but I was very alert, observing how they were going to be treated by the militias. I was all eyes and ears.'

Of course, I thought. If Juwan hadn't fled to Turkey when he did, he might have been one of those young men.

'There was an understanding between the head of the militias and the MSF that MSF was not part of the conflict. So the militia men weren't allowed to question prisoners who were patients in the hospital. The militias said, "We'll question the captives after they leave the hospital and deal with them according to the law; in other words we'll ask if they've raped women or killed people." MSF were clear that it was an emergency. Our surgeons worked incredibly hard, sometimes doing up to five complex operations a day. We didn't have enough space in the cave, so we had to keep some patients outside, on stretchers. That was okay because the weather was great, it was September. And we sent patients who didn't need surgery to other hospitals nearby.

'As for me, I was seeing the young militia men close up for the first time. They were very happy about their victory. Some tried to insult the regime prisoners who were outside waiting to be examined. They said things like "You dogs and donkeys, why didn't you defect from the beginning, why weren't you helping us?" Other militia men would wade in and say "Don't say this, perhaps they didn't have any choice." I was relieved to see that the militia guys were quite ordinary people. It made me feel a bit safer, as I realized I wasn't living among criminals. Before that I'd been afraid – all these people with guns and long beards – it was all so new to me.

'The prisoners were very afraid, not knowing what the militia men would do to them. They were ordinary young men, just like me. We'd operate on them and send some on to the other hospital for follow-up. I had conversations with lots of them, I was caring for them, asking if they had pain, did they need the loo, or to be moved, and so on. Another nurse working alongside me was a bearded member of the FSA. Between us we did a good job caring for our patients, and that helped them to feel safer.

'Sometimes, a FSA patient was in the next bed to a regime patient. Once a FSA patient came round from anaesthetic and shouted at the guy next to him, "It was your colonel who did this to you, not us! And you deserved it, you son of a bitch!" I would listen in to the conversation. I had some authority as a hospital staff member to intervene, and I had instructions to do so if the militia men abused the regime men, but I was afraid because I didn't want my loyalty to the rebellion to be doubted. I felt that acutely because I was alone in the area, without family. Some regime patients used to answer the militia men back, but with a small voice, because they felt they were in enemy territory.'

'It sounds incredibly challenging. And you must have worked very hard.'

'We did, for many months. I never got a day off. But that was okay: while I was with the people, working and talking, I felt I was doing something important.

'One of our regime patients was a young Kurd from Afrin. I thought he had a severe head injury because I'd seen part of his brain. He was alive and talking, but his speech was slurred and he wasn't really in control of his body. He'd wake up and ask for water. I'd take it to him, but he couldn't drink, it all went down his front. I'd offer him food – we always had soup and rice ready. He couldn't really eat, the food would fall out of his mouth. I thought he would die soon. The hospital couldn't do brain surgery, it was just a tent inside a cave doing basic operations. If he asked for a cigarette, I'd take him outside and give him one – he could walk, but like a drunk – and he'd smoke some of the cigarette, then say he wanted to sleep. One of the militia men told me the guy had been injured by the army, not by the militias. He was in a car and the army shot him. The militia man said, "Look at the poor boy." Later I asked the Field Coordinator and he said he'd ask the militia leader what he was going to do with him. The militia leader said, "Do what you can for him," since the man couldn't be exchanged for a FSA prisoner. We arranged for an ambulance to take him to the Turkish border, and then to a Turkish hospital.

'After a few days, MSF decided to release all the regime patients who didn't need further hospital care to the militia. We wanted to do follow-up after a week. When the day came, the regime patients who could walk were brought back by the militia, some on crutches, and I saw that good conversations were happening between some of the militia men and the patients. They no longer seemed like enemies. This made me feel more positive.

'The militia assault had liberated new territory and our Field Coordinator started to look for somewhere safer to put the hospital. He found an abandoned chicken farm in the village I'd seen through the trees when I walked to the water tank, the day after my arrival. That village was now liberated and the farm was bigger than the cave, and in a safer place.

'Local labour was hired to clean the farm and slowly we moved in. We decided to keep the upper floor empty as a buffer zone. One part of the building was below ground, which meant it was considered safe. They used a bulldozer to move earth around it to protect it.

'Now we had space for a big emergency room, with up to ten beds. Later we had ten follow-up beds for post–intensive care. Two local towns were liberated and MSF hired new nurses, some fully trained, some students. Local English teachers were hired as translators. The farm was about ten kilometres from the new front line and all the tops of the mountains near it were in rebel control; so it was much safer than the cave.'

I butted in. '*Were* you feeling safer, by this point?'

'I was always thinking about safety. I was integrating with the people, making friendships, but I always had fear. When we moved to the farm it was a different atmosphere. In the previous time of difficulty, in the cave, we staff had all been very close to each other. Now we moved to a different house where actually I felt more exposed and less safe.

'I started to meet men from other militias, and I didn't like all the people I met. I didn't trust them all. Despite the farm being in a safer location, I felt I was more exposed to danger than previously. Also, the atmosphere in the new hospital was different from how it had been in the cave. The staff was now much bigger – it became more than a hundred people, with guards, cleaners, nurses, doctors, translators, dispensers and drivers. There started to be competition between staff members, where previously there had been solidarity. We started to see the ugly side of the people, and the beauty I had seen before was less.

'In the cave we'd never counted the hours we worked, and although we didn't help make the decisions, we were always consulted. Sometimes we worked all day *and* did a night-shift. Now, the new ex-pat medical director started to establish fixed hours and declared that nobody had to do more. I didn't like this at first: I felt pushed away. Previously we'd all been in it together.'

'Is that why you left?' I asked. Juwan had already told me that in 2014 he'd quit MSF and gone back to Turkey.

'That was one of the reasons. The other was that I badly wanted to see my parents and my brothers. By now they'd left Damascus and made their way to Istanbul. I'd saved most of my MSF salary and could afford to get myself smuggled back into Turkey, to meet up with them.'

I knew the rest. When Juwan had reached Istanbul, travelling on forged papers, his parents had urged him to go to Europe. For a time he'd taken a job in a bar; then, in March 2016, as the EU–Turkey Agreement deadline neared, he boarded one of the last dinghies to Lesvos.

Pudding distribution was now an established part of the day at Hara, but we still hadn't worked out a good system for making it a calm and orderly affair. Word had got round that in order to 'qualify' for a pudding, you had to be a child of ten or under. There were grumbles about the fairness of this rule, which I knew were justified; but I didn't dare alter it now.

As we carried the black crates around the camp, arguments frequently broke out between my teenage helpers and the refugees. A child would trot up from nowhere, claiming not to have had his pudding, despite the fact that there were dribbles of the stuff on his T-shirt or around his mouth; a woman would put her head out of a tent and demand four tubs, saying her four small children were asleep behind her. Luckily, my helpers were astute and seemed to know who to challenge and whose word to accept.

One evening I was just setting off from the car with Dilshad and a wiry lad of about fourteen called Muhsin, when Abu Anas appeared, loping towards us from the direction of the mini-supermarket, a lit cigarette smouldering between his fingers. 'I'll help you, T'reza!' he cried. I'd already divided the delivery between eight or ten youngsters, but there was no dissuading him.

'Here, let me take this,' he said, stooping down and removing the crate which Dilshad and I were carrying quite happily between us. As he did so, a long head of ash landed on the lid of one of the tubs. Dilshad shot me a look of annoyance: why was I was letting this man interfere? I tried to explain to Abu Anas that we were fine, we had our system and we didn't really need his help; but the expression on his face told me I was wasting my breath. 'It's no problem, no problem,' he kept saying, drawing on the cigarette before setting off towards the hotel with Muhsin at his side.

I whispered to Dilshad that I was sorry and gave him a packet of spoons. That way he would at least have a small role in the distribution. When we caught up with Abu Anas he was standing by the entrance to an orange tent, still clutching his crate of puddings, arguing with a young father who held a baby in his arms.

Abu Anas' tone was sharp. 'You're lying to me,' I overheard. 'You've only got the one baby. I'm not giving you a second pudding.' He swung round towards me as I walked up.

'These people!' he hissed. 'They're all on the make!' Then he turned to Dilshad. 'Give the man a spoon.' It was an order.

We moved on through the densely packed group of tents where Muhsin was already hard at work, checking numbers by unzipping doors and asking people to point out their children. Abu Anas put the crate on the ground and turned to me in satisfaction. 'That's the way to do it, T'reza. You've got to *see* the kids before you dole out the puddings.' He shook his head. 'There are too many bad people here, T'reza; too many bad people.' He ground the stub of his cigarette into the tarmac, pulled a pack out of his pocket and lit a fresh one.

My view was that people were not so much bad, as ravenously hungry. I knew that if it'd been me with an empty tummy, and perhaps a couple of hungry teenagers, I'd have thought up a scam to get my hands on some pudding. At that moment, a small boy with a dirty face ran up to the crate, grabbed a tub and set off towards the road. Abu Anas's face contorted with rage. 'Hey!' he roared, 'thief!' As he did so, Muhsin darted after the boy. In less than a second he had grabbed him by the arm and was raising his free hand to strike him. I ran towards them, shouting to Muhsin to leave the child be, but it was too late. A howl of pain rang through the air and the furious boy, who looked about four but was perhaps six, set upon Muhsin, pummelling him in the shin with both fists.

It was my last evening at Hara. I'd intended to leave the camp early, but in the end I sat on the verandah till late with

Hasan and Burhan, drinking tea and chatting. Behind us in the bar, many of the male refugees were crowded around a giant TV screen, watching an international football match. Every now and then a roar of delight would burst through the double doors. It was a wonderful, unfamiliar sound, as if the men had momentarily shelved their worries and were having a good time.

When at last I walked across the forecourt in the dark towards the car, several of my teenage helpers and an older man appeared from nowhere with a little iPod speaker, playing a Syrian song about exile and dancing around me. The song was familiar, as if I'd heard it before in Iraqi Kurdistan, with different European countries mentioned in each verse. They said I must listen, they were playing it for me.

When we reached the car, the older man, who was short, wiry and very weather-beaten, and with whom I'd never had a proper conversation, planted himself in front of me. 'On behalf of all the Syrians in the camp,' he said, 'we thank you from the bottom of our hearts for the support you've given us.' Tears ran down my cheeks as I drove away.

In the morning, when I crossed from FYROM into Greece for the last time, I was asked by a stoney-faced Greek border official if I was going to Idomeni. Without thinking I replied breezily, 'No, I'm not, I'm on my way back to London. I'm going to Polykastro, taking a bus to Thessaloniki and a plane to Athens.'

More fool me. A couple of hours later, when I stepped off the bus at the bus station in Thessaloniki, a young woman in skinny jeans and a khaki jacket sidled up to me with a sweet smile.

'Te-re-sa Thornhill?' she murmured. 'I am police.' As she showed me her ID I glimpsed a young man with shoulder-length hair, equally casually dressed, watching me closely from a pace behind her. 'We are not ar-rest-ing you,' the young woman declared in a sing-song voice. 'Just we like you to come with us to central police station, to answer some quest-i-ons.'

I looked at her. There were slits in the knees of her jeans and her long dark hair hung sleekly to her waist. I would never have guessed she was a cop. I smiled. It was the aggression of the secret service men I'd objected to, not the fact that they'd wanted to check us out. I had nothing to hide. I'd been half expecting trouble in the course of my journey home, and had put on lipstick, just in case: I felt I made a more convincing British barrister in lipstick. 'Okay,' I said, 'that's fine; but I have a plane to catch at three this afternoon.'

'No prob-lem, ten minutes, this way please.'

I felt a slight misgiving as I was ushered into the back of another dirty, unmarked car, but in less than five minutes we pulled up at a large concrete building clearly marked as police headquarters. I was taken to an office on the top floor, where a middle-aged man in jeans standing behind a large desk nodded in a friendly manner.

'What's in the bag?' he asked, pointing at my rucksack.

'My clothes,' I replied. 'Do take a look.' But the man sucked his teeth and took out a file.

'You were ar-rested a few days ago,' he said in broken English, flicking through a wad of notes typed in Greek.

'That's right,' I replied. 'They were very aggressive with us.' The man's attitude was so calm and pleasant that I felt cautiously optimistic about catching my plane. I was seated on a sofa on the far side of the desk from him, peering at the file upside down and wishing I read Greek.

'The reason you were ar-rested', he went on, 'is because you were seen telling a group of refugees, in Arabic, to go to the border fence and break it down.'

My mouth fell open in astonishment. 'That's absolute rubbish! Do you seriously believe that a middle-aged woman like me, a British lawyer, is going to do a thing like that?' I glanced round at the long-haired girl, who was sitting beside me, still smiling sweetly.

To my relief, the man laughed. 'Not really, no I don't!' he replied. 'But we need you to make a statement.'

'Fine, I'm happy to do so, but not in Greek. I'll write you one in English.'

The man's face fell. 'It has to be in Greek.'

There followed a long discussion in which I insisted that I wasn't signing anything in Greek and he protested that he couldn't use a statement in English. Reluctantly, as I knew it would cause delay, I said I'd need to consult a lawyer. He said that was fine; meanwhile he would send for an interpreter, to help with the statement. He got on the phone, I got on mine, people came and went and an hour went by. There was no interpreter available, and an atmosphere of chaos pervaded the room. I was beginning to worry about the time, when quite suddenly the man came off the phone and stood up. 'It's okay,' he smiled. 'I spoke to the prosecutor. We don't need a statement from you, after all: you're free to go.'

I returned his smile as I picked up my rucksack. 'It must be very difficult for Greece, having to deal with so many refugees.'

'It's a nightmare. We're in a crisis of our own and we don't have the resources.'

'And the EU? Is it helping?'

'Ahhh, the EU! We asked Frontex to send us 400 trained immigration officers, and all they've sent is sixty. We're drowning!' He pulled out a packet of cigarettes and offered me one, which I declined. 'Would you like a lift to the airport?'

Part II
Austria, August 2016

On 24 May 2016, the Greek authorities began to dismantle the camp at Idomeni. They bussed those refugees who were willing to go to army-run camps in different parts of Greece, some in very remote areas. The dismantling of Hara followed on 14 June. Many Hara refugees were taken to camps in and around Thessaloniki.

15
Refugees Are Welcome Here

On a warm English summer's evening in late July I decided, on a whim, to attend a refugee support meeting in my local Gloucestershire town.

I parked outside the church hall and took a seat at the back of the room. In front of me, no less than thirty mostly grey heads were turned towards a big man dressed in jeans and a T-shirt. He was a priest and a leading light in Refugees are Welcome Here, the group that had called the meeting.

'Hello everyone,' the man began. 'Good to see so many of you. I'm going to give you a little update on the Syrian Resettlement Scheme, and then I'll hand over to Mike from the furniture bank.' He cleared his throat. 'You may know that we've already welcomed two Syrian families in the last couple of months. I can't tell you exactly where they're living, for obvious reasons, but I'm happy to say they've both been given an extremely good welcome, thanks to all of your efforts . . .'

A murmur of agreement went round the room.

'. . . and a third family is expected shortly.'

An expansion of the Syrian Vulnerable Person Resettlement Scheme (SVPRS) had been David Cameron's response to the public outcry about Aylan Kurdi, the drowned Syrian child washed up on a Turkish beach in September 2015. At that point, just 216 Syrians had been resettled in the UK under the scheme, in four years.[1] Cameron now promised to resettle a further 20,000 Syrians by 2020 – an average of four thousand a year.[2] He was adamant that the UK's policy was to concentrate its efforts on assisting Syrians to remain 'in the region' and he frequently cited the sums of UK money that had already been spent helping Turkey, Lebanon and other countries with their refugee burden.[3] The SVPRS did not take refugees who'd already made it to Greece or elsewhere in Europe; its intended beneficiaries were people living in camps in Turkey, Lebanon, Iraq, Egypt and Jordan and who were deemed to be exceptionally 'vulnerable'. This was initially defined as those who needed urgent medical care or had been subjected to torture or sexual violence; but later redefined as those whom UNHCR considered vulnerable. On arrival, they'd be given five years' 'humanitarian protection', housed and entitled to work or claim benefits. The cost of the scheme was to come out of the Overseas Development Assistance budget.

In autumn 2015, as the media began to cover the refugee crisis on a daily basis, many British people had gone to their MPs and local councillors saying they were willing to take a refugee or even a whole family into their homes, if the government would let them into the country. Such acts of generosity were officially rejected. Local authorities participating in the SVPRS were not allowed to place refugees with families wanting to host them; rather, they had to identify suitable housing from the private rented sector. When and if housing and school places were available, families would be flown to the UK, one by one. As a result, there were delays in implementation of the scheme and by December 2016, only approximately 5,000 Syrians had been resettled in the UK under it.

The priest had finished speaking and the man from the furniture bank got to his feet. 'We've been overwhelmed with donations,' he began. 'You've all been incredibly generous. Some days I don't know where to send our lorry first, there are so many items of furniture to collect . . . We managed to fully kit out the two homes for the families who arrived in June. And the patchwork quilts are very popular indeed!'

I'd seen on Facebook a quilt made by a bunch of local women. All winter and spring, various groups had been working on different aspects of what they thought the refugees would need. There was an education group, preparing to teach English; a social group, planning an 'international café'; and an employment group. The town was brimming with good will, far more than would be needed by just three refugee families.

I drove home in the summer dusk, feeling angry about Cameron's determination to keep meaningful numbers of Syrians out of the UK. It wasn't just the absence of compassion that upset me; it was also the sheer stupidity, from the point of view of British self-interest, of leaving so many people to suffer.

Successive governments have been understandably concerned about so-called 'radicalization', the name used for the process by which small numbers of usually young Muslim men and women adopt jihadi values and some go on to launch attacks against human targets. Whether or not they are coherent and effective, there are strategies in place to address radicalization occurring within the UK. What recent British governments do not seem to comprehend is the risk of radicalization occurring in the camps in Greece, Turkey, Lebanon and Jordan as a result of young Syrians being condemned to grow up in terrible conditions and with minimal or no education.

I'd just unlocked the door to my house when I heard a WhatsApp message arrive on my phone. It was from Sintra. *'Hi T, guess what? Juwan's in Austria! He walked.'* #

16

A Long Walk in the Mountains

A month later I flew to Vienna, having managed to contact Juwan via Facebook. He was keen to meet up and promised to tell me about his walk across FYROM.

At the railway station I bought a British newspaper and read the latest news from Syria while I waited for my train. ISIS had killed fifty people at a wedding in Gaziantep in Turkey at the weekend. On 24 August, claiming it was partly in response, Turkey had sent tanks and warplanes into northern Syria. A photo showed tanks rolling south across the border through cultivated fields. Turkey called its offensive 'Operation Euphrates Shield' and claimed that the objective was to dislodge ISIS from the Syrian town of Jarablus, on the Euphrates. A second confessed goal was to 'contain' the expansion of the Syrian Kurdish militias and block their presence west of the Euphrates.

My heart sank as I read: I was in no doubt that in reality Turkey's main goal was the destruction of the Kurdish fighters who were young, female as well as male, and ill-equipped to repel airstrikes.

The air was warm when I came up the steps of the railway station, an hour later, in the town where Juwan was lodging. I looked up and down the quiet residential street, wondering which direction he'd appear from. It was going to be strange meeting in a different environment from Hara, and I felt a bit uncertain. On the phone he'd said the town was full of cafés. 'We won't have any trouble finding a quiet place to talk,' he'd added, 'it's not like Hara!'

I was slapping sun cream on my bare arms when a bicycle whizzed to a halt in front of me. A clean-shaven man in jeans and a black and gold check shirt swung his leg over the cross bar. 'So sorry I'm late,' Juwan said, as we grinned awkwardly at each other. 'The place I stay is far from here and I had to borrow my friend's bike.' I wanted to give him a hug but thought he might be embarrassed, so I smiled, squeezed his hand and stood back to study his face. He looked less haggard than when I'd last seen him at Hara. His hair now almost touched his shoulders and the scar above his left eyebrow was fading.

After a ten-minute walk through leafy streets with Juwan wheeling the bike, we settled at a café table in a concrete shopping centre.

'You look really well,' I told him as we sat down.

'Really? I don't get much sleep in the place I'm staying!'

'What's it like?'

'A big hall with little areas separated by screens, five or six beds in each one. At one end, it's all Africans playing really loud music. At the other end, it's Indians. Their music's quieter, but they never turn it off. Then there's us Kurds,

Arabs and Afghans in the middle, and you know how loudly we talk . . .' He grinned.

'But this is Austria! Aren't there rules against making noise at night?'

'No music after ten o'clock, but nobody takes any notice. It's a nightmare . . . I'm hoping they'll give me a place of my own . . .'

'Why, have they given you asylum already?' I was surprised by Juwan's confidence.

'Not yet. I'm waiting to make the second interview.'

We ordered coffee and chatted about friends and other characters from Hara. Then I leant across the table. 'Tell me about your walk!'

'Sure, but . . . where to begin?' He poured two packets of sugar into his espresso.

'When I left Hara in April, you were talking about going to Athens to look for a job.'

'But I didn't go.' He pulled a packet of cigarettes out of his pocket. 'Actually, after you left, I worked with the other volunteers at Hara. I liked them, and it was better to be occupied.'

'And you started smoking?'

'I wasn't smoking when we met at Hara? I started again before I left for Macedonia.'

Hardly surprising, I told myself, given the stress he was under.

'Everyone at Hara was trying to figure out what to do. Lots of people were trying to get to Macedonia on foot, some with smugglers, some alone.' Juwan stirred his coffee. 'One day a group of people I knew asked me to walk with them. Ziad was one – I think you met him – from Aleppo, curly hair, always cracking jokes?'

'I don't remember.'

'And Ali: early twenties, short, bit of a belly. His parents were already in Belgium. The other two were Basil, the guy I shared my tent with at Hara, and a young one called Ramsi.'

I remembered Basil, a handsome, energetic man, who'd often come up to speak with Juwan when I was with him at Hara.

'They were thinking of setting off in a couple of weeks.'

'How young was the young one?'

'Seventeen, but I thought he was older.'

'Did you all know each other well?' Behind Juwan, a man in his sixties sat perched on a bar stool. As I glanced at him, his gaze shifted from Juwan to a TV screen on the wall behind our table, which was showing the Olympics.

'*Yani*, I met them all at Hara, so no, I didn't know them well. When they asked me to go with them, I said, "We need a leader. It can be any of us, but that person must take responsibility." They agreed, and they wanted me to lead. I was happy, because I wouldn't have trusted any of them with my safety! They were good guys, but they were all younger than me, and I knew it was going to be difficult and dangerous.'

'What happened with the seventeen-year-old?'

'Ramsi. He was at Hara with his mum, his little brother and his aunt. His mum was keen for him to walk with me, but she didn't tell me his age. If I'd known, I would have refused to take him.' Juwan sighed. 'He was trouble. A few days before we set off, he fell over playing basketball and cut his hand badly. I told him it was risky to come as we'd be in a dirty environment and his hand might get infected, but he didn't listen.'

'So did you make a detailed plan?'

'Yes and no!' Juwan raised his eyebrows and smiled and the scar shifted towards his hairline. 'I had connections in NGOs and through them I obtained food, boots and backpacks.'

I remembered seeing a pile of walkers' backpacks in the Czech store in Polykastro and wondering what use they'd be put to.

'Sleeping bags, a tent and a compass. We had to have these things.'

It sounded like a kit list for a walking trip in the Alps. 'Did you take a camping stove?'

'No stove, and we never made a fire. The smoke would have been visible in the daytime, and the flame at night.'

'No hot meals?'

'It wasn't a problem.' Juwan held a cigarette between his fingers.

'What was your plan?'

'To walk the whole length of Macedonia, south to north, and cross into Serbia.'

'With a smuggler?'

'No smuggler.'

'Wow, I didn't realize you did it alone!' I'd felt really proud of Juwan when I got Sintra's message. Now I was even more impressed.

'I had almost no money. I needed the little I had to pay a smuggler to get me from Serbia into Hungary, because that bit's impossible without one. And I didn't trust the smugglers I met at Hara.'

I shook my head and stared at him. 'You're amazing.' I'd done many long distance walks in the French Pyrenees, but I couldn't imagine going for days on end without a hot meal.

A glimmer of delight shone in Juwan's eyes. However hard the walk had been, I could tell he'd enjoyed it.

'I got a basic first aid kit, water purifying tablets, two solar power banks and a spare battery for the phone,' he went on.

'Did you have a proper map?' The eyes of the man on the stool kept flicking between Juwan and the screen, making me uncomfortable.

'I had a compass and I used Google Earth. And someone got me a Macedonian sim card with a data plan, so that I could pick up internet once we got across the border.'

I shook my head in astonishment.

'And I got emergency numbers for the Macedonian police, in case we were attacked by mafia.'

'*Mafia?* From where?'

'Macedonia. Every night at Hara I was talking with people who'd set off on foot but been forced to give up. Some had met mafia with guns. They steal everything: phones, money, documents. Because of that I decided to leave my papers in Greece. I made photocopies and gave the originals to a friend, and after I arrived, she posted them.'

I glanced again at the man on the stool. This time I was in no doubt: he was staring directly at Juwan, listening to his every word. I slid my cup noisily across the table and said in Arabic that we should find somewhere more private to talk.

But by now it was lunchtime, the sun was high in the sky and all the cafés in the town centre were crowded. After a lot of walking, we reached a park where we found a spot under trees beside a small river. The ground was marshy, covered in wild garlic and ivy. I spread out my jacket and settled with my back against a tree. A couple of feet away, Juwan perched astride a log. It was uncomfortable, with lots of flies, but we were in the shade and nobody could listen.

I watched Juwan as he lit a cigarette. He seemed remarkably at ease, as if he'd been in Austria for years. But he'd also given the impression of being very much at ease at Hara: perhaps that was just the way he was, an infinitely adaptable person. Or perhaps that was the essence of refugee survival: being able to be yourself, wherever you ended up. 'Tell me,' I said. 'Had you ever walked in mountains in Syria?'

Juwan sucked his teeth. 'I'd been on a few walks and picnics outside Damascus. And one time with MSF, I did four or five kilometres on a mountain road.'

'After all those weeks at Hara, you can't have been very fit – any of you?'

Juwan shifted position on his log, bent back the fingers of one hand and cracked his knuckles.

'We weren't fit, at the beginning . . .'

'Did you worry you might not make it?'

'No. I was confident I could do it.'

'How did you work out the route?'

'I talked with other refugees who'd tried to get through but hadn't made it. There'd been cases of Macedonian border guards breaking people's arms and hitting them round the head causing injuries that needed stitches. I asked the exact locations where that had happened. I asked about landmines, too, but people said there weren't any.

'In the end I decided to take a completely different route, going far, far in a different direction from the one most people took. There were no mafia in the area I chose. I spent hours looking at Google Earth, trying to see the location of the forests, the rivers and the villages.'

I was puzzled. 'Do you mean those aerial photographs? But they don't have contour lines.'

'No contours. Look.' He took out his phone and summoned a photograph in which I could just make out a mass of dark green forest and a meandering blue water course. There was no way to tell if the terrain was mountainous or flat.

Juwan stubbed his cigarette on the underside of the log and pulled another one from the packet. 'I didn't want to make too detailed a plan. I knew that once we started walking, it might seem completely different on the ground.

'Before we left, we shaved and tidied ourselves up, so if anybody saw us they wouldn't immediately think we were refugees. I took one pair of very clean trousers, which I kept back for once we were in Serbia; a change of underwear, a warm pullover and a jacket. And of course we all had water bottles.

'We divided the food and the rest of the stuff into five equal shares so that nobody was carrying more weight than anybody else – well, except for Basil.' Juwan chuckled. 'Basil really likes his clothes. I told him he should leave them behind, but he insisted on bringing everything, so he had two bags instead of one. A backpack on his back and another small one on his chest. He would have rather died than leave his clothes behind.'

I smiled. 'Did people at Hara know you were going?'

'When people asked about our plans, we'd be as vague as possible, saying, 'Oh, we won't be leaving for a while yet, we're not ready.' And in fact when we were ready, it started to rain, so we had to wait a few more days for the ground to dry out.

'I'd arranged through one of the Hara smugglers for us to be picked up by car, very early in the morning. It was still dark when the guy arrived. He drove us to the place where I wanted to start walking, in the foothills of the mountains. It was just getting light when we got out of the car.

'Our backpacks felt incredibly heavy with all the food and water. We started to climb on a dirt track, but I was very jumpy, thinking a tractor was going to come along at any minute. So I led the guys off the track into the undergrowth. We took off the packs and sat down and I told them they had to be really quiet while I tried to get my bearings with the GPS and Google Earth. I let them smoke, but I told them not to move: each time they shifted their backsides on the ground, you could hear twigs cracking and leaves rustling. And before we left I made them bury their cigarette butts. I was planning to head straight for the border, cross country.'

'What sort of terrain was it?'

'Forest, and when we got higher up, dry grass, rock and little thorn trees.'

'Beautiful?'

'To begin with, no, and I was so afraid I wasn't thinking about beauty. But later, yes, in some places it was very beautiful. Especially in the early morning, and at dusk.' He drew on his cigarette. 'That first morning, we climbed a lot. Ali and Ramsi really struggled with the weight, so we kept having to wait for them.'

'Were *you* okay with the weight?'

Juwan wrinkled up his nose. 'It was hard, I'm not saying it was easy, but I was so worried about meeting a border patrol, or foresters or the army, that I didn't think about the weight. I tried to pick a route which kept us hidden under trees as much as possible. I told the others not to damage any branches, so as not to leave a trail. But nobody had walked in that place for a very long time: I didn't see any footprints.

'After a couple of hours we stopped to eat breakfast.'

'What did you have?'

'Bread, cheese, nuts, water. Ramsi kept rubbing his shoulders, saying the backpack was uncomfortable, so I adjusted the straps for him. Ali was talking about his mum, who was already in Belgium with his dad, and about the *mahaashi taht iddam*[1] that she was going to cook for him when he got there. Basil took his boots off and lay down in the grass, but I told him no, we have to keep moving.

'We set off again, on a little animal path with black, shiny droppings scattered in little piles.'

'Sheep shit?'

'Maybe. We were walking north by the compass and now we went steeply down, through patches of forest. After several hours, at the bottom of a deep valley, we came to a small river. I kept urging the guys to be silent, because I felt sure the army was waiting for us.

'We filled the water bottles from the river, ate a bit and crossed over on some rocks. Then we started up the far bank. By now I believed we were in Macedonia. It was very steep and with the weight and the heat we had to stop every few minutes to catch our breath. I was at the front, but I had to keep turning round to make sure the others were following me. Basil was struggling with his two bags and the other three kept wanting to drink.'

'Was it very hot?'

Juwan shook his right hand from the wrist. 'It was end of May: maybe thirty degrees. All the time we were walking, sweat was dripping down our faces and into our eyes.' He paused, trying to regain his thread. 'I began to feel annoyed because the others didn't seem to get it that this border area was the most dangerous part of the whole walk, and we had to cross it as quickly as possible.'

'It sounds terrifying.'

He stood up and stretched his arms above his head. 'Actually, I was *really* scared that first day. I felt sure we'd be caught.' He pulled his pack of cigarettes out of his pocket and sat down again. 'We went on and on up the mountain-side until the others said that was it, they couldn't go any further. It was two hours before sunset and I still hadn't picked up a Macedonian signal on my phone, but we were all exhausted, so I agreed to camp. We found a patch of grass among trees, and I left Basil, Ali and Ramsi to put up the tent while I walked on a bit with Ziad to see if I could get a signal. At last I got one, very weak, but it made me feel better. When we got back, the others were sitting in the tent, eating cheese and nuts and muesli. As soon as I took my boots off and squeezed in beside them, they started to complain.'

'About what?' I felt indignant on Juwan's behalf.

He rolled his eyes as he lit his cigarette. 'It was all too difficult. They wanted to go back to Hara. They wished they'd gone with a smuggler. There had to be an easier way to get to Serbia. Why weren't we walking along the railway line from Idomeni to Skopje, on the flat, like some people had done a couple of months earlier?

'I made a big effort not to lose my temper. I explained that I'd rejected the railway line idea because by now the army and border guards were catching people on that route and pushing them back. "Look," I said, "for me, there's no easy solution. If you don't want to carry on, you're free to leave, but I wouldn't advise going back the way we've come. Give it a couple of days, at least."

'Before we got into our sleeping bags I told them we had to take turns to keep guard, in case we were attacked by mafia or border guards or wild animals. They didn't like it, but I insisted. I divided the night into five shifts and everybody had to take a turn.'

I raised my eyebrows. 'And did they?'

Juwan laughed. 'Basil did, Ali did, but Ziad and Ramsi slept right through! Nothing happened, we weren't attacked.

'My plan was to wake at first light and start walking in the very early morning. But we didn't leave as early as I wanted. To start with we walked in silence, Ramsi and Ali asleep on their feet, Ziad, Basil and I smoking. We were high up, on a plateau, following a dirt track. After an hour, Basil spotted a communications antenna with a winking red light and some buildings on the top of a mountain ahead of us. He and I were immediately petrified that we were being watched. It would be so easy to see us from up there, especially with the bright colours of our backpacks: mine was blue, Ziad's was red . . .

'I decided to take a big detour to avoid that mountain. It meant scrambling down into a deep valley, crossing a stream and going up the far side, through scrub and rock. On the way down, on a tiny path, Ziad tripped over the jaw bone of an animal. We picked it up and looked at it. From the teeth, Basil decided it belonged to a carnivore.'

'How big was it?'

'Like this.' Juwan held his hands a foot apart. 'There were wild boar in the area, we saw their droppings everywhere, but this thing was too big to belong to a boar.'

'So what was it?'

'No idea, but it scared us witless.'

I hesitated. 'Had you checked about wild animals, before you left Hara?'

Juwan sucked his teeth. 'I assumed there were animals that could attack us and we shouldn't camp near water, in case they came to drink at night.'

A couple of days earlier, before leaving home, I'd googled 'fauna of Macedonia'. Several respectable-looking articles claimed there are wild bears and lynx in the mountains of western Macedonia, while wolves roam the entire country.

'There were turtles everywhere, as big as a melon. I kept picking them up and moving them because I didn't want the guys to tread on them.'

I found this quite touching. 'You'd bend down and pick them up?'

'Most of the time the others were struggling so much to walk that they didn't even notice them . . . Or they were too busy cursing. If one of them pushed a branch out of the way and it swung back and hit the person behind him, there'd be a fuss.'

'You were going down into the steep valley.'

'Before we got to the bottom, we came to an area of dense, spiky bushes. I was in front and my arms were getting badly scratched, so I put on my thick jacket. It was better to be hot than cut to pieces. Ali said I went through those bushes like a bulldozer! He was behind me and the knee of his trousers got ripped right out.

'At last we came to a stream and filled the water bottles. I told the others to sit and wait while I went ahead to look for a path.'

'Didn't you get them to help you?'

'Not really. They seemed happy to leave it all to me, and I preferred it that way: at least we weren't in conflict. I was always going on ahead to check things out. If I found a way through I went back to fetch them, and if I didn't find a way through, I still went back. In the end we came up with a whistling system: One short whistle meant "Come" and a series of whistles meant "Don't come, wait." I tried to whistle like a bird.

'We were getting into wild country now, as we skirted round the antenna mountain. At times the undergrowth was so thick that we had to crawl through it, getting underneath the branches. We followed dried-up water courses and boar tracks. Sometimes when we came to the top of a ridge and looked down into the valley below, the drop was almost vertical. I'd follow the ridge till I found a safe way down.'

'Did the walking get easier as you all got fitter?'

'It did, after a few days we were all coping better, but we got very tired. For me it was the constant tension, being on hyper alert in case we met a border patrol or foresters. And always having to charge my solar banks and check Google Earth and work out the route.'

'And not much sleep and not enough to eat?'

'Not much sleep. The food was okay, although it was the same thing, meal after meal. I wasn't ever left hungry.'

'Did you pray?'

'No, but Basil did, and Ziad, each time we took a break. One night at dusk we heard bells, and on a distant hill opposite, we made out the shapes of cattle. In Syria, cows are kept for milk and where there are cows, there's a cowherd, so I felt worried. I made everyone take turns to keep watch that night, and in the morning we set off early.

'Coming down into the valley at the base of the cow hill, we found a fast-flowing stream. I was still worried about meeting a cowherd, so we filled the bottles and started to climb. We were very close to the antenna mountain, probably being watched.

'By mid-morning, we were in a place thick with bushes and rocks and the sun was beating down on our heads. We were walking in a line, not speaking, and at the front Ziad and I picked up the sound of a big herd moving in our direction. As we came out from behind a patch of boulders, we saw them a couple of hundred metres below us, all different colours, black, white and brown. I ducked and signalled to the others to do the same, expecting to see a cowherd any minute. But the cattle were moving down the hill, away from us, and nobody was with them. They were going down to drink from the stream we'd drunk from earlier.

'Now we tried to find a way through the bushes, keeping low so as not to be visible to the antenna. I was still wearing my jacket, but the others were in T-shirts, getting badly scratched with every step. Flies buzzed around our faces and the sun burned our skin. It was so bad that in the end we gave up and took another route, exposed to the antenna, walking very fast. In half an hour there was a hill between us and it, blocking the view of anybody trying to watch us.

'That night we looked back to the south and saw the red light winking in the darkness behind us.'

'That must have been a relief!'

'It was. We all began to feel good, as we were making progress.' Juwan peeled a piece of bark off the log, exposing the pale wood beneath. 'On the afternoon of the fourth day, I knew from Google Earth we were near a village. We were on a track and came to a group of graves, one of which was freshly dug. The names were in Turkish, with some words from the Koran.' Juwan tore at another strip of bark. 'Finding those graves made me feel better, too.'

'Why?'

'I thought that if by accident we stumbled into a Turkish village, the people might be friendly. They must be a minority group in Macedonia, so they might understand our situation . . . Later, far below us through the trees, we saw houses and the minaret of a mosque. An old man was working in a field with a scythe. I gestured to the others to stop talking: if the man looked up he might not see us, because we were high above him under trees, but he might hear us talking. We stayed on the path till we reached a dry water course. Red and white rings were painted on the trunks of the trees.'

'Foresters' markings?'

'I think so.'

'So there were people around?'

'Definitely. Early the following day, we were on another track and I noticed marks from the tyres of a tractor, but I thought perhaps they were old. We could hear noises in the distance and Basil was convinced it was someone using a chainsaw. I kept looking at the tyre marks, and now I decided they were fresh. Ali spotted a shady place above the track where we could be hidden by trees, so we scrambled up there to eat our breakfast. But as we sat down on a carpet of dead leaves, a tractor came along the track towards us, pulling a trailer. We lay down flat. I could just see the driver and two men sitting with him. For a moment the tractor stopped and we heard a pinging sound as if something had broken; then the engine started up again and on it went. I was so unnerved that I stayed lying down for another twenty minutes, in case it came back.'

I was beginning to wonder how Juwan had handled so much pressure. 'Did you ever feel you'd taken on more than you could cope with?'

Juwan crossed his legs underneath him on the log. 'I had confidence I could do it, but when we left Hara I didn't understand what a lot of difficulties I was going to face.' He took out another cigarette and twisted it between his fingers. 'A couple of times, we almost ran out of water. I kept telling the others not to empty their bottles, they must warn me when their supplies were getting low, but they didn't take any notice. One day we'd wasted a lot of time waiting for a big herd of cows to move from across our path and I said we had to keep walking into the evening, to make up the lost time. The others were annoyed, of course. Quite late, around midnight, Basil told me he'd just drunk his last drop of water. Then Ramsi said the same, and Ali told me he'd got just a quarter of a bottle. So there we were, in the pitch dark – we couldn't use torches – and we had to find a water supply. Everybody got very bad tempered.'

'And did you find water?'

'We did, by chance. And I let Basil put his torch on just long enough to see that it was full of black particles, so then I had to work out a way to filter it.'

'How?'

'I got my spare vest, and two plastic bowls, and I poured it from bowl to bowl through the vest. It took ages and the water still tasted funny, but we survived.' Juwan lit the cigarette.

'It sounds like the four of them were a bit hopeless . . . like they left everything to you.' I was uncomfortable, so I shifted onto my knees and stood up.

'They did. But I was the oldest by five years.'

In the distance, I picked up the dull roar of traffic. Ten feet away, the river continued on its sluggish course through the park. Cigarette smoke mingled with the smell of muddy water. 'Did you walk all night?' Now I squatted with my back against the tree.

'No, after we'd filtered the water I agreed to camp. Everyone was worn out. Once we were in our sleeping bags, Ramsi asked to use my internet connection to contact his mum via Facebook. He asked me every night and because he was young I always let him. But this particular night he couldn't reach her and he got very upset and started to cry. I told him not to worry, his mum was a strong woman and she had family with her at Hara; but I couldn't console him. I think he was awake most of the night.

'I didn't sleep well either. In the early hours I was lying awake and I heard a loud, deep, throaty sound, far away. I thought it was a bear picking up the scent of humans and I was terrified, but I didn't want to wake the guys because I knew they'd panic and that would make it worse. Also I thought, "If a bear attacks us, what the hell can we do?" So I just lay there, wide awake, listening hard.

'When I woke the others it must have been very early, because it was extremely cold. We walked for a couple of hours through a forest till we came to a place where sweet-tasting water trickled out of a stone wall. By now the sun was up and we washed our faces and filled our bottles.

'While we were eating breakfast, I remembered the bear and decided it would be a good idea to cut a stick. Ali wanted one, too, so I found a sapling and cut two sticks with my penknife, which took quite a while. But when we set off I couldn't carry my stick because I had the compass in one hand and my phone in the other, so I asked Ali to carry both sticks. Ali was the youngest in the group after Ramsi and even after five days of tough walking, he still had a belly like a middle-aged man.

'The rest of that morning went badly. I spent two hours trying to fight through some dense undergrowth to a path I'd seen on Google Earth. My GPS played up, giving me the wrong location, and I became more and more pissed off. There was no shade and the heat was intolerable. In the end I said we should take a break under a tree.

'I lay down on the ground and shut my eyes. Half an hour later, I stood up and saw a way through the bushes to the path I was looking for. By now Ali was complaining about having to carry the two sticks, so I said he could throw the weaker one away. But when we stopped for a drink, a bit later, I discovered he'd thrown away the strong one. I was furious and I shouted at him. Ziad and Basil took the piss out of him for tossing away the good stick, and suddenly Ali lost his temper and stormed off.

'I called to him to come back, but he just kept going and Ziad and I decided we had to go after him. We went back up the path, shouting "Ali, Ali!", but he'd vanished. After half an hour we went back to where we'd left Basil and Ramsi, only to find Ali standing a few feet away from them, clearly still upset. When he saw me he said he was sorry.

'At that point I gave the whole group a talking to. I said if anyone else stormed off on their own, I wasn't going after them. Nobody replied and we started walking down the valley. After a bit we came to a big stream with clear, cold water and Ali threw me a pleading look. I knew what he wanted so I said, "Ok, have a bath, but be quick." I thought it might help to de-stress him. The four of them stripped off, bathed and washed their hair. I didn't, because I was too worried about the time. While I was waiting for them I picked some wild mint growing by the stream.

'From there we climbed on a big track which took us out of the valley and into open country, with a village perched on a hilltop over to the west. As the ground dipped down, the village disappeared, but an hour later we saw it again. Just before dusk we came to another stream. We found a grassy spot hidden by trees, put up the tent and ate our supper.

'After we'd finished eating, Basil and Ziad asked to use the internet. Now we got a shock. On Facebook there were pictures of the refugee camp at Idomeni being dismantled by the Greek authorities. It was unsettling news. Then Basil got a message from a friend that Hara would be next and that a smuggler was taking people to Serbia, by truck, for less than 300 euros each. The guy had already got through safely with his first one hundred people.

'When Ramsi heard all this, he panicked, thinking his family might have gone with the smuggler. I gave him my phone to contact his mum, but like the night before he wasn't able to reach her. He tried his dad, too, who was somewhere in Holland, but got no reply.

'By now Basil and Ziad were openly discussing whether to pack in the walk. They thought that if they handed themselves in to the Macedonian police, they'd be driven straight back to Hara and could then take a comfortable ride all the way to Serbia in the smuggler's truck. It sounded so easy: no more slogging up thorny mountainsides in the hot sun, no more rough nights in the tent, and only a couple of hundred euros to pay.

'There was a long discussion, at the end of which Basil and Ziad decided to go to the police in the hilltop village. Ramsi was uncertain, but I pushed him to go with them, because I felt he was too vulnerable to carry on walking. Ali was the only one who wanted to continue. He was dubious about the smuggler and, like me, he felt we should keep going for as long as we could. Before we went to sleep, we agreed that in the morning we'd divide up the food, Ali and I would set off as usual and the other three would wait a few hours before walking to the village.'

I was astonished. 'My God, I wasn't expecting them to abandon you! How did you feel?'

'Actually, I didn't have any bad feelings towards Basil and Ziad. Just, I hoped they would get back to Hara safely. And with Ramsi, I was relieved to no longer be responsible.'

'Did they get back safely?'

'They all got back, but by then Hara was being dismantled. The smuggler was no longer taking people to Serbia, so Basil and Ziad went to a government camp.'

'And Ramsi?'

Juwan's face fell. 'Ah, Ramsi's story is a sad one. He was right about his mother and little brother, they *had* gone with the smuggler and were already in Serbia. When the Greek authorities came to Hara, they took Ramsi to a children's detention centre, because he was legally still a child. He was there at least a couple of months. He's eligible for Family

Reunification, so one day he'll be sent to join his mother, but it's going to take a long time.'

'Poor kid.' I'd heard bad things about the Greek detention centres for unaccompanied children. 'Are you in touch with him?'

'No. I heard about him from Basil.'

I was getting hungry. I suggested to Juwan we should walk back into town, to get some lunch. Wheeling the bicycle back across the park and through the leafy streets, he told me about the last few days of the walk.

After parting company with Basil, Ziad and Ramsi, Juwan had made a serious error of judgement. In order to avoid passing an agricultural building, he'd decided to go down into a deep, wooded valley. 'Ali warned me it was dangerous, but I didn't pay attention. Down we went, skidding and sliding with our heavy packs, grabbing at the trunks of young trees for support. It was only when we were eating our breakfast beside the stream at the bottom that I studied the far bank and realized that it was going to be almost impossible to climb it. The lower part was vertical rock and the next part was covered in wet moss. I started to panic as I walked along the stream, looking for an easier way up. The bank was vertical. Most of the overhanging trees were dead so you couldn't ask them to take your weight. But just before a waterfall, I decided to try.'

The men's backpacks were heavier than usual because they were now carrying most of the food and the tent, which had previously been shared between five.

I felt sick as Juwan described the point where, twenty feet above the stream, clinging to the protruding root of a tree, he'd felt he was at the limit of his physical and psychological endurance. His heart was thumping and he was desperately out of breath. He was convinced he was going to fall, and reached the point where he was ready to abandon himself to fate. But somehow, instead of letting go, he spotted a thorn bush and used it to pull himself up, not caring about the pain as the thorns pierced his palms. Above him he could see that the ground was starting to level out, with lots of young, healthy trees, so he wedged his pack behind one of them and went back to help Ali.

When the pair of them finally reached the top they collapsed on the ground, deeply shaken by their close brush with disaster. They were still feeling shaky when they heard sheep bells.

'We hid in the trees as the bells came closer and closer. Suddenly we heard a shocking, drawn-out bellow, like a genie yelling in a fantasy movie. It was a terrifying sound, but we were so exhausted that we shook with hysterical laughter. Then it came again: it must have been the shepherd calling to his animals. We stayed where we were for a long time after that, talking in whispers and smoking.'

The following day, Ali started to complain. If they tried to walk all the way to Serbia, he said, it would take them two months. Instead, he wanted to walk into a village and find a taxi to drive them close to the border. Privately, Juwan began to wonder whether he had a point. 'After our bad experience climbing out of the valley, I felt I had to accept that I wasn't superhuman. I still had a little bit of strength left, but within a few days I would be completely exhausted. We were only getting a couple of hours' sleep each night, we hadn't had a hot meal in a week and I was constantly on edge. But I didn't share these thoughts with Ali. Instead, I said that in the tiny villages we were walking past there wouldn't be a taxi driver. If we showed our faces, someone would turn us into the police.

'Late that afternoon we were walking on a wide, rocky track, eating wild strawberries that grew on the verges, and I was thinking over Ali's idea. One voice in my mind said that I'd been walking for seven days now, and wasn't that enough, why was I was making it so hard for myself? The other voice said, "You still have some strength, you must continue."

'Without knowing what was going on in my mind, Ali spoke more about his idea. "We'll take a bath in a river and put on our clean clothes. Neither of us looks typically Middle Eastern, we'll tell the taxi driver we're Spanish or Portuguese, and your Turkish will help."'

In the end Juwan walked into a village, went to the mosque and presented himself as a Turkish tourist. A driver was found, and for a modest sum of money he agreed to drive the pair to a village near Kriva Palanka, just twenty or thirty kilometres from the Serbian border.

By now we'd found a quiet-looking café in a side street off the town centre. Juwan propped the bike against a lamp post while I ordered food. While we waited, he described the very difficult couple of days he'd spent with Ali trying to cross the densely populated area between Kriva Palanka and the border. The landscape was dotted with villages and the fields bustled with fruit pickers and goatherds, so that walking at night was the only option. On the second night, going down into a valley in the pitch dark – there was no moon and no stars – they'd heard a strange and terrifying animal sound. The creature, whatever it was, hissed like a cat then growled like a dog. Panicked, they beat a retreat back up the side of the valley. I wondered if they'd had a brush with a lynx.

The following night the pair were only five kilometres short of the border when the weather broke and they were caught in a torrential rain storm. Juwan leaned across the table to describe it to me.

'It was around seven in the evening and the wind was blowing so hard that we had great difficulty getting the tent up. By the time we finally crawled inside, we were soaked to the skin. Water seeped in through the groundsheet and dripped through the roof. I was shaking with cold, squatting over my backpack to keep it dry, because the solar banks were inside. The groundsheet was soon so wet that we couldn't lie down. Then we heard an engine and saw lights and I thought, "That's it, we're finished." But the vehicle passed five metres away from us and didn't stop.

'That night was the worst one of the whole walk. For a while I crouched over my pack and prayed, as the rain drummed on the roof of the tent. But I was too exhausted to sit up all night. In the end Ali and I both lay down on the wet floor, back to back, and got a bit of warmth from each other. We were too exhausted to think of getting out our sleeping bags. I lay awake listening to the roaring of the wind and thinking I could hear an animal outside. I must have fallen asleep, because I had a nightmare. I woke up thinking somebody was calling us.

'At dawn, afraid that the vehicle we'd heard might come back, we decided to move. The rain had stopped, but we were both trembling with fatigue and cold. We followed the track for a couple of kilometres, passing some parked construction vehicles and a bulldozer. Finally, in the middle of a tangled forest, the track ended about one kilometre from the river which marks the border.

'With great difficulty, we found a way down through the undergrowth. As we got lower we could hear the river. When at last we came out of the trees, there it was, the biggest body of water we'd seen in ten days of walking, wide, shallow and full of rocks. We were mad with happiness. The rocks were too slippery to stand on, so we took off our boots and waded around them in water that came to just below our knees. It was dirty, dark green and incredibly, freezing cold. When we reached the far bank we knelt and prayed.

'After that we sat down under a big oak tree, wondering what to do, but we were too tired to think. Behind us in Macedonia we could hear foresters at work and in front of us we could hear the sounds of a Serbian village.'

In the early evening Ali and Juwan changed into their clean clothes and set off again. This time, as soon as they reached a main road, they attempted to hitch-hike. A pair of women picked them up and by eight o'clock they were in a big village with a bus station, buying tickets for the night bus to Belgrade. They reached the city at six a.m. the following morning.

'We walked about in a daze, feeling unbelievably happy. We stumbled into a bakery and bought pastries. Then I contacted some Serbs I'd been told about at Hara. They sent me to a park where volunteers were giving out free tea, information and free clothes. One of them took us to a hostel.

'For the next few days we rested and collected information on how to continue our journey. A smuggler told us to take a public bus to a certain town in northern Serbia. When we arrived, taxis were waiting to take us and many others to the departure point. We were about forty people trying to cross into Hungary that night.

'From where the taxi dropped us, we walked for about an hour to the border fence.[2] The smuggler had already cut a hole for us to go through, but on the Hungarian side we could see police cars. Each time someone tried to climb through the hole, a car came. Finally, there were no cars and I went through, followed by Ali and some others. But immediately a police car zoomed towards us and we started to run.

'The police got out of the car to chase us and one officer got really worked up, shouting and threatening us. We evaded him a couple of times, but now a helicopter flew very low above our heads. I decided it was better to give ourselves up. So I walked towards the policeman with my hands raised, and Ali and some of the others did the same. I knew we'd be fingerprinted and that it might cause us problems, but I decided it was a risk worth taking.

'The policeman calmed down when he saw we were giving ourselves up. We were put in a van and taken to a police station in the city of Szeged, where they took our fingerprints, strip-searched us and searched our bags. Then we were told we had to either claim asylum in Hungary or be sent back to Serbia. But if we chose Serbia, they said, it was likely Serbia would refuse to accept us, in which case we'd be detained in Hungary for six months or more. So we claimed asylum in Hungary.

'We spent that night crammed together with lots of other refugees in the police station. The following day we were taken to an open refugee camp close to the Austrian border. After a couple of days I told the camp authorities I had relatives in Budapest and obtained permission to go there for a visit.

'Again, I made use of the contacts I'd been given at Hara. Within a couple of days I'd found a smuggler to take me and Ali to Austria, in a taxi with some other refugees. Hungary and Austria are in Schengen, so there's no effective border control: the taxi drove us straight to Vienna. I went to the police and made my claim for asylum.'

'And what happened to Ali?'

'He carried on to Belgium.'

'And made it?'

Juwan smiled. 'Sure, he's with his family there.'

Part III
Greece, January 2017

17

Freezing to Death on Europe's Doorstep

In January 2017 I returned to Greece to investigate how things had moved on – or not – for the Syrians I'd met at Hara. Many had already left for Germany and elsewhere, but some were still in camps around Thessaloniki. I'd arranged to base myself at one of those.

As I stepped from the plane into the dark of a January Sunday evening, the icy wind hit my cheeks like the lash of a whip. I was warmly dressed, but nothing could have prepared me for this sudden drop in temperature. In London it was eight degrees; in Thessaloniki, minus seven.

Waiting in the queue for passport control I fell into conversation with a white-haired academic from the University of Thessaloniki. He told me that Pakistanis, Afghans and a trickle of Syrians were continuing to arrive by boat in Lesvos, Chios, Samos and Kos where, under the terms of the EU–Turkey Agreement, they were detained in outdoor tent camps. 'I don't know how they'll survive this weather,' he added. 'The islands have already had a fall of snow.'

'Is this a normal Greek winter?'

'No. We often get one or two days of snow; but it hasn't been cold for this long in forty years. In some places, it's minus fourteen!'

Happily for me, the Airbnb I'd booked near the university was in a fifth-floor apartment with ferocious heating. Alexi, my hostess, explained that the heating would be on all night: she daren't turn it off, as so many of her neighbours had faulty boilers or frozen pipes.

Outside, the temperature was still dropping. At nine p.m. I left the apartment dressed like Michelin woman in warm trousers, three long wool jumpers, a fake sheepskin coat and a wool scarf wound several times round my head and neck. Even like this it wasn't pleasant to be out for more than a few minutes and I soon took refuge in a neighbourhood taverna. The lights were dim, the windows decorated with fake snow-flakes and the plump, middle-aged manager brought me a mug of what he called 'our tea, mountain tea' which was warming and delicious.

I glanced round at the rows of empty tables, the courting couple in the corner and the curly-haired chef who was pack-ing the day's leftovers into a giant fridge. It felt good to be back in Greece, but I was plagued by thoughts of the people lying on the ground in tents: how would they possibly keep warm?

Over the previous few weeks I'd been similarly plagued by the TV footage of traumatized and injured refugees from the Russian- and Iranian-backed regime assault on Aleppo, as they arrived in Idlib in heavy snow.

Rebel-held eastern Aleppo had been under siege by the regime since the previous summer. In October 2016, Russia's only aircraft carrier had sailed to the eastern Mediterranean via the English channel, accompanied by seven warships and unimpeded by the European states through whose waters it passed, in an eloquent display of military capacity. Russia had cleverly timed its airstrikes to coincide with the US presidential election. Apparently concerned about the possibility of Clinton winning, given her relatively confrontational attitude to Russian policy in Syria, Putin had decided to create 'facts on the ground' by crippling the opposition while the western media's attention was focused on Washington. Nevertheless, the pounding of civilians in eastern Aleppo by Russian and Syrian jets had shocked the world, the more so since each and every hospital was hit. The return of the city to regime control represented a huge victory for Assad and Putin, and a major blow for the rebels.

On 30 December, as the evacuation of the surviving civilians drew to a close, Russia and Turkey declared a ceasefire. Russia now claimed that its military objectives in Syria had largely been achieved, and that henceforth it would play the role of 'mediator' between the warring parties, some of whom were to be invited to talks in Astana, Kazakhstan, in late January. Russia had made similar declarations before, only to resume military involvement.

In the morning the weather was no warmer. I waited forty-five minutes in the wind at a bus stop outside a bakery in a crowd of frozen-looking men in drab black jackets and beanies, and old women in heavy overcoats. Everyone kept glancing from the electronic 'buses coming' board to the slowly grinding three lanes of traffic proceeding towards us from the university. I took shelter in the doorway of a pharmacy with a law student who told me she lived near the camp I was going to and would show me where to get off the bus.

'The refugees are a big problem for us,' she said. 'The older people remember the Albanians who arrived in the 1990s, after the break-up of Yugoslavia. They were prepared to work for very low wages and took our jobs. And many never went home.'

Eventually, I was so cold that I took a different bus to the end of the line. I would take a second bus from there. On the first bus a young male dental student from Cyprus with a kind, open face told me that people were very unhappy about the refugee presence, 'because the refugees steal'. Half an hour later, when I was shivering at a deserted bus depot on the outskirts of town, in a spot as bleak as it was depressing, a tourism student dismissed his views as nonsensical. 'The refugees don't steal,' she scoffed, 'it's the media who say this! Okay, possibly there was the odd case of theft, but Greeks steal, too!' She raised her dark eyebrows expressively, digging her hands further into the pockets of her coat and stamping her feet. 'The real problem is the economic situation. People feel the government does more for the refugees than it does for us . . . But they would do well to remember that in the 1960s many Greeks went to Germany as refugees.'

I think she was referring to the Greek communists who went into exile in Germany after the colonels took power in April 1967.

The camp was in a large disused factory. In collaboration with the Ministry of Migration, a NGO was in the process of converting it to house refugee families in individual rooms, around thirty of which were already occupied. I'd read that, compared with other camps in Greece, it was something of a 'model' institution. There was a shared kitchen where the refugees made their own meals, using raw materials supplied to them daily; showers, toilets, areas for socializing and a couple of classrooms where children aged four to seventeen were offered three hours of education each morning.

When I walked in, the temperature in the common parts of the building was little higher than that outside. The water pipes were frozen and a couple of volunteers in jackets, hats and gloves were trying to siphon bottled drinking water into buckets for use in the bathrooms and toilets.

After a tour of the building, I was asked to help sort through items of donated clothing to be distributed through a 'free shop' the following day. I worked alongside a German volunteer, opening cardboard boxes, checking the contents and arranging them according to gender and size. After an hour, my fingers and knees were aching with cold and I had a strange sensation in my head, as if my brain itself were starting to freeze. I found my bag, dragged myself into the toilet and put on long johns under my trousers.

When I came back, a couple of Syrians were looking at children's shoes in the 'shop', although it wasn't officially open. The taller of the two was a large, weary-looking woman with a pale cotton headscarf tied tightly under her chin. She glanced at me, I glanced back and to my delight I recognized her as the woman who used to sit cooking on a log in the warm April sunshine at the entrance to Hara, in the company of the very old woman who'd reminded me of my mum.

We kissed on each cheek. 'How are you?' I asked.

'*Alhamdulillah*. And you?' Her smile was warm.

'I'm fine thanks, just cold! How's your mother?' I dreaded the reply.

'Om Abdullah? She's my mother-in-law, not my mother. She's okay. '

I felt a wave of relief. 'Is she here?'

'She's upstairs, in our room. She's eighty-eight now.'

'That's wonderful! Did you come here straight from Hara?'

'We were in another camp most of the summer, living in a tent.' She gazed at me steadily. She wasn't beyond her mid-thirties, but her eyes and skin had a care-worn look. 'They moved us here a couple of months ago, when the weather got cold.'

'Well thank goodness for that! You wouldn't want to be in a tent in this weather.'

The woman smiled again. 'We're in room 519, drop in for a cup of tea? If you forget the number, ask for Shireen.'

When at last the rails of the shop were groaning with winter jackets, jeans and sweatshirts, it was time for a break. I made my way to the volunteers' kitchen, where half a dozen people wrapped in coats sat huddled round an electric stove, drinking coffee from plastic cups. I soon got talking to a Swiss woman and her mother, who seemed to flip easily from English to German to Italian and back to English. They told me that, in November, Greece had made it obligatory for all refugee children between the ages of six and sixteen to attend school. The government bussed the children from this camp to a school in Thessaloniki every afternoon, after the Greek children had finished. The kids loved to go, the Swiss woman said, and the parents were relieved to get a few hours to themselves.

While we were talking, a striking Syrian woman appeared in the doorway. She was dressed in jeans, a khaki men's jacket and a red wool headscarf. Several people turned to greet her and the Swiss woman introduced me.

'This is Rima,' she said, 'our resident Arabic teacher.'

I got up, greeted Rima in Arabic and asked which age group she taught. 'The seven- to eleven-year-olds,' she replied in a slightly husky voice, regarding me with friendly, intelligent eyes. 'Every morning at ten o'clock. Where are you from?'

'England.' I explained I'd been at Hara in the spring.

'Can you write Arabic?'

'A little, why?'

'Come to my class!'

'I'd love to. So long as the buses are running better tomorrow!' There was something deeply attractive about this woman. She had fine, delicate cheekbones and the expression in her large eyes communicated both strength and an ability to see the funny side of things.

By now it was early evening. The Swiss women were driving into Thessaloniki and gave me a lift to Aristotelous Square, from where I could walk home along Egnatia, the main shopping street. Most of the shops were already closed, as if in preparation for the desperately cold night ahead. The few people on the streets cut hunched, miserable figures, bundled up in dark jackets with hoods. After passing a long line of shoe shops – all advertising dramatic price reductions – I came to a place where the pavement was covered in an inch of ice. Icicles a metre long hung in rigid streaks from a wrought iron balcony above. A pipe must have burst on an upper floor and the icicles had formed as the leaking water froze.

After retrieving my laptop and an extra pair of socks from the apartment, I went to the taverna of the night before. I felt exhausted from battling the cold all day, as if I'd just walked fifteen miles on a mountain ridge and I was ravenously hungry. Seeing how cold I looked, the manager ushered me to a glass counter displaying the dishes of the day, where I chose a dish of potatoes in a thick meaty sauce, followed by kalamari. Then I found a table beside a radiator and settled down, intending to write my journal; but I was too hungry to think.

When the food arrived I warmed up, but even more than the day before I was tormented by the thought of the refugees who were battling to survive under canvas. It must be particularly dangerous for small children, I thought, who are extra vulnerable to hypothermia. As I ate, I searched Google for more information.

Officially, around 62,000 refugees and migrants were still in Greece, of whom roughly 16,000[1] were living in dangerously overcrowded tent camps on the islands. On Lesvos, for example, Moria, an army camp with a capacity of 1,500 people, now held approximately 4,000. On Samos, a centre with a capacity of 700–800 now held 1,400.[2] There had been violent protests, including a case of self-immolation, and nasty accidents, such as one in which an adult and child had died in a fire caused by a cooking gas canister.

The majority of the detainees were people who'd arrived after the 20 March deadline. The EU–Turkey Agreement provided for them to be detained for a maximum of twenty-five days while their cases were 'fast-tracked', but in practice there were huge bottlenecks in the asylum process and the average period of detention was now eight months.[3]

People were still arriving at an average rate of forty-three per day. I found appalling pictures of small, lightweight tents close to collapse under heavy weights of snow. A US paediatrician was treating residents of Moria for frostbite.[4] In late December, the *Guardian* had quoted the head of MSF in Greece expressing 'outrage' at claims by both UNHCR and ECHO[5] that the winterization programme, for which both had received substantial funding, had been a success. He described the claims as 'disconnected with reality', pointing out that winterization of the island camps hadn't even started.[6]

By the end of January there would be at least one death in Moria from hypothermia and two from inhalation of plastic fumes, burned for warmth by desperate people.[7]

If the 62,000 figure was correct, that left 46,000 refugees on the mainland.[8] They were spread across the country in an undisclosed number of camps run mainly by the Greek army, and some unofficial squats in Athens.[9] I couldn't establish how many mainland refugees were still in tents. What was clear was that there had been massive delays in 'winterizing' all the outdoor camps, despite the provision of generous funding by the EU for this purpose. When snow had first fallen in northern Greece at the start of December, fifteen camps had still been waiting to be adapted for winter.[10]

Charly had told me in our WhatsApp conversations in November and December that refugees north of Thessaloniki were waiting to be moved into disused hotels. The move was delayed until just before Christmas, even for women with newborn babies.

As I chewed my last ring of kalamari, I reflected that the camp where I was based was indeed a 'model' camp, Spartan though it was. I would have to visit some others.

Early the next morning I hurried to the bus stop at Kamara, an ancient stone archway which stood incongruously in the midst of bakeries and mobile phone shops near the university. I was lucky with the buses and reached the camp before ten. After climbing a filthy marble staircase I found Rima in the classroom on the top floor of the camp, warming her hands on an electric stove and complaining that her youngest child had kept the whole family awake coughing.

'You must be so tired.' I studied her face, thinking she looked amazing even without much sleep. 'How many of you are there?'

'I have four girls and three boys.' Rima raised one eyebrow. 'But my oldest daughter's in Sweden with my husband. I haven't seen her for over a year!' She winced. 'It's so hard to be apart. And you? D'you have kids?'

'Only one,' I replied, feeling rather inadequate. 'A boy of sixteen. He's with his dad while I'm here.' I was always afraid people would assume I'd left my beloved boy to fend for himself.

'Just one! Didn't you want more?'

I considered for a moment. 'Not really.' I was about to elaborate when I saw, through the giant industrial windows, that snow was starting to fall in swirls of small white flakes, coating the fir trees on the side of the hill. We watched in silence for a moment, but soon the classroom door burst open. Four children tumbled in, greeted Rima and ran to the window.

Five minutes later, when Rima called the class to order, I counted seven pupils, all in winter coats, mainly boys. Given the size of the camp there ought to have been more, but many children slept all morning prior to attending Greek school in the afternoon.

Rima began by teaching the letter 'sheen'. Using coloured pens, she demonstrated how sheen is written at the beginning of a word, in the middle and at the end. Then she wrote a couple of sentences on the whiteboard, and asked who could insert the correct *harakat* (the accents that add vowel sounds to the letters). While the boys sank their chins to their chests, looking uncertain, a girl in a quilted jacket went to the board and inserted all the *harakat* in precisely the right places. Then she turned to her classmates, folded her hands with an air of triumph and recited a ditty which explained the function of each *haraka*. Rima congratulated her warmly and started to write another sentence on the board.

At this point, I and some of the less studious children became distracted, because outside the window the snow-flakes were growing larger and falling faster and the vehicles in the car park below the window were vanishing under a coating of white. Two of the boys rushed to the window. For a few moments Rima herself gazed out at the snow with a dreamy look. Then she flashed me a smile, called the class to attention and told the children to copy down the sentence she'd written on the board, a description of children playing in snow.

After Arabic, the children had English and maths, taught by a pair of British volunteer teachers. I left the classroom with Rima, crossed the icy wasteland of the corridor and accepted her offer of a cup of tea. We passed the kitchen where several women were already hard at work and opened Rima's door, removing our shoes in a narrow passageway where crockery, cooking pots and a small fridge were arranged against the wall. It led into a spacious room bathed in a snowy white light from giant windows. Four sets of bunk beds stood against the walls and in the middle of the floor, three small children slept cuddled up together under grey UN blankets on a pair of mattresses, their dark hair a wild tangle on the pillows.

It was reasonably warm in the room, although the only source of heat was a small electric heater. Rima gestured to me to relax on a pair of mattresses arranged at right angles in a corner, while she fetched glasses, tea and sugar. Between the two mattresses, a hand-knitted patchwork blanket was spread on the floor to serve as a rug. Good old British knitters, I thought to myself. I bet they never imagined where their work would end up.

I sat down cross-legged and took the cushion Rima offered me to lean against. I was wondering where the older children were, when two young girls in headscarves entered the room and greeted us. One was carrying a kettle, the other a stack of flatbread wrapped in plastic. They were tall, slim, leggy girls in skinny jeans and both exuded a feisty intelligence. A few moments later there was a groan from a top bunk, and a length of luxuriant, dark brown hair cascaded over the side, followed by the emergence of a large brown foot from under a blanket. 'My big sister,' one of the girls told me with a smirk. 'She never gets up before midday.'

Rima filled our glasses with boiling water and sat down beside me. On the mattresses a few feet from us, a small boy flung an arm out from under the covers and opened an eye.

'Your children are gorgeous,' I remarked with a smile.

Rima glowed. 'I love to have children around me,' she exclaimed. 'But I miss my girl who's in Sweden so-o much!'

'I bet you do! How long till you go and join her?'

'It won't be soon. We've been in Greece almost a year, but I only had the first interview three months ago. It'll be at least another three months before we get our papers.' She stirred her tea.

'So your husband and daughter went on ahead?'

'My husband was an officer in the army. Once he deserted, he had to get out of Syria as quickly as possible: it was terribly dangerous.'

I'd read about the difficulties faced by deserters. They not only had to find the right moment to slip away, but they had to get to a 'liberated' area without being stopped at a regime checkpoint. 'We decided he should take my oldest girl with him,' Rima went on, 'because she has a heart problem and she needed hospital treatment.' Her eyes welled up. 'Poor creature, she had to have an operation without me there to support her.'

I found Rima's pain infectious and my eyes started to sting. 'Is she okay?'

'Yes, thank God, she is, yes.' She breathed in sharply and forced herself to smile.

Rima was from Aleppo. After her husband had decided to desert, she and the six younger children had left the city and travelled to the east of the country, to one of the 'liberated' areas. Initially, Rima's father had travelled with her because it was very difficult for a lone woman with young children to be a stranger in a new area.

'What was it like in the east?' I asked.

'Very different from Aleppo. Very, very hot in summer . . .'

'Did you rent a place to live?'

'We were in a rural area where some of the houses had been abandoned, so at first we lived in one of those, a simple place, built of mud and wood. Just two rooms.' She smiled. 'It was a very different life from the one we'd lived in Aleppo, as the family of an officer . . .'

'Was it frightening?'

'At times. One night, in summer, we were sitting in the house, and a snake got in, a really big, poisonous snake, like this' – she held out her arms, demonstrating that it was more than a metre long. 'And fat like this.' She put her thumbs and fingers together to make a ring some ten centimetres across. 'The younger children were asleep and I was sitting drinking tea with my father. Luckily, he saw the snake as it was slithering across the floor. He grabbed it by the tail and pulled it out of the house. It reared up this high' – she demonstrated waist height – 'but he managed to kill it before it bit him.'

I was mesmerized. '*How?*'

'Shot it.'

I shuddered.

'We didn't stay in that house very long. The fighting kept getting closer, so we had to keep moving.'

'Who was fighting who?

'Mainly it was Daesh fighting with the FSA. One night, Daesh arrived in the area where we were, and went from house to house, breaking down doors and dragging out the people they wanted. We were living in a little row of houses and ours was the end one.

'My father had gone back to Aleppo by then, so I was alone with the children. I felt completely terrified. We could hear Daesh smashing doors just metres away from us. I had no idea what to do, so I just sat in the doorway of the room where my children were sleeping, waiting for the fighters to burst in. I thought we were finished. But suddenly it all went quiet. I heard vehicle doors slamming and engines starting up and then nothing at all. For some reason, and I'll never know what it was, the last house they broke into was the one *before* ours.'

I took a swig of hot, sweet tea. 'What did you do?'

'We moved on, of course, the very next day. We couldn't stay there.'

'Where to?'

'To another remote area in the countryside. Another house of mud and timber.'

One of the small boys had crawled out of bed and fetched an exercise book and a pencil. He was sitting a couple of feet away on the mattress, watching me with unabashed curiosity.

'Zain, honey,' Rima spoke to him. 'Show Teresa how you write your name in English.' The boy shook his hair out of his eyes and stared at me for a long moment, until he could no longer suppress a smile. Slowly he opened the book and began to write, in capitals, Z-A-I-N.

'Fantastic!' I exclaimed, 'Clever you! Look, I'll write my name for you.' I wrote TE-RE-SA in my best Arabic script and he read it back to me.

Then he grinned with a slightly wicked expression. 'I can write 'Zain' in Greek, too, do you want to see?'

'In Greek! Yes please!' I'd been trying to figure out the Greek alphabet as I looked out the window on every bus ride, and was miffed that this six-year-old had got there before me. I glanced at Rima. 'He's clever, your lad.' I watched as he bent over the exercise book and carefully formed the Greek letters.

But I wanted to hear more of Rima's story. 'What else happened while you were in the east?'

She leaned back against the cushions. 'All kinds of things, it was one drama after another . . . The worst experience I had was one day when I sent my girls to buy bread. There was a bakery half a kilometre from our home, in a little village nearby. The area was controlled by the FSA and it was perfectly safe to walk around, because there wasn't any fighting, there was nothing.

'I gave Betoul some money and sent the girls off down the hill. After half an hour they weren't back, and I began to wonder where they'd got to. I went to the door, but I couldn't see them coming. It was a hot, dry morning and all seemed calm, so I went back indoors and gave the little ones their breakfast. Another half hour went by, still no girls, and I began to feel worried. Then, all of a sudden, I heard shooting coming from the village. At that point I really panicked, because we were only an hour's drive from territory controlled by Daesh. For all I knew they were carrying out a raid.

'I had to think very fast what to do, and without panicking the little ones. I put on a black abaya and a black hijab, the sort where only your eyes are left showing. If Daesh fighters see a woman dressed in anything less, they beat her up. Then I told the little ones I was going to the outdoor toilet and they must stay in the house until I came back. I wedged a big piece of wood against the door.

'I was shaking as I ran down the hill. Opposite the bakery was a half collapsed building, hit by a mortar a few weeks earlier. As I drew level with it, I caught sight of something moving inside. The shooting was still going on and there was smoke coming out of the back of the bakery, and I heard men shouting. I thought that any minute I would be shot at, but I had to find my girls. The only thing I could think to do was to walk right into the bakery. While I stood outside, hesitating, my eye was drawn again to the half-collapsed building. I could just make out the profile of a young girl in a headscarf, and a small hand gesturing, trying to attract my attention. It was Betoul. I didn't dare go to her, because for all I knew there was a sniper watching me from one of the rooftops. But somehow I managed to blink in such a way that Betoul got the message that I'd seen her.

'At that moment a bunch of FSA fighters burst out of the bakery and ran up the street, shooting in the air as they went. I stepped back against the wall. By now I was pretty sure that the guys inside were Daesh. I had to distract them for long enough so they wouldn't find my girls in the broken building opposite. Okay, I thought, I'll go into the bakery and pretend I want to buy bread. So I pushed open the door. There wasn't time to feel afraid, all I could think of was that my girls were in danger.

'It was dark inside and the smell of fresh bread was mixed with the smell of gunfire. The air was full of flour dust, and a pool of dark liquid lay on the floor in front of the counter. For a second I thought the place was deserted, but then my eyes landed on a pair of limp bodies in black fatigues, lying against the wall. I clapped my hand over my mouth and shot back out the door. I was across the street and into the half-collapsed building in less than a second. My girls were crouched on the floor by a broken wall. "Come, now!" I hissed at them. I took the hand of the youngest and dragged her out into the street, dazed and terrified, with the other two following. We ran all the way to the house.'

When I spoke, my voice came out very softly. 'Then what?'

'We left, of course, later that day. We couldn't stay in an area where Daesh was active! I paid one of the locals to drive us to another village in his car, a couple of hours away.

I spent the afternoon helping out in the free shop. By the time I was ready to leave, at six p.m., the snow was several inches deep and the buses had stopped running. Somewhat dubiously, I accepted a lift from a group of British volunteers in a tiny hired Panda, and we set off slowly on the untreated road outside the camp. As we were grinding up a slope towards the main highway, our path was blocked by stationary vehicles with hazard lights flashing. A lorry was jackknifed across the road in front of us, leaving only the narrowest of channels to get round it. The driver thought she could get through, but I had doubts about going any further without chains. So I apologized profusely and said I'd make my own way into the city.

I started to walk back towards the camp. I hadn't gone far when a kind Greek couple in a large vehicle with chains on the front tyres opened their window and insisted I get in. Half an hour later, they dropped me on the outskirts of Thessaloniki and from there I walked the five kilometres into town. The snow-laden streets were almost deserted and the snow was fresh and deep and beautiful. I sang as I walked and when I slipped and landed on my bum, I was immediately rescued by a kind middle-aged Greek who walked beside me and offered me his arm each time we had to cross a slippery side road.

When I rolled up my shutters late the following morning, nothing was moving in the street below my window and snow continued to fall. I knew it would be hopeless to try to reach the camp, so I got up slowly, made tea and wrote notes. In the kitchen I found Alexi, keen to chat. She told me she'd worked for the railways all her life. When, in 2010, the salaries of public servants had been cut by 45 per cent, she'd packed it in, turning her four-room apartment into a tiny hostel and sleeping in the box room.

In the early afternoon I ventured out. The building was on a narrow, steep side street and the snow was virtually pristine. I walked slowly uphill, enjoying the biting cold on my cheeks and the thought that I could retreat at any moment into the well-heated apartment. On the bigger road at the top, young men raced along the main street, oblivious to the snow and ice. I stuck my head round the door of a cheap dining room, crammed with noisy students eating in groups. Through the crowd at the counter I glimpsed trays of moussaka, stuffed peppers and other oily delights. But I wasn't hungry. Instead I pushed open the door of a tiny café, bought a mint tea and perched on a stool in the window.

The snow had stopped falling and cars were gliding slowly down the street. On a long wall opposite, somebody had scrawled 'NO FUTURE', followed by something in Greek.

A couple of men and a woman stood three feet from me on the far side of the glass, smoking cigarettes and stamping their feet. What did they think, I wondered, about the refugees in tents? Did they know? I'd been astonished to discover that the amount of money made available by the EU for the Greek refugees amounted to over £4,000 per head, per year.[11] Why, then, were so many living in dire conditions?

The reasons seemed to be multiple and complex. The $803 million that had come into Greece for refugees since 2015 made this the most expensive humanitarian response in history, but much of the money – up to 70 per cent according to one source – had been squandered.[12] As far as I could tell, the squandering was due to both mismanagement by the Greek government and a lack of political will, both in Greece and Brussels. Greece had refused to set up the management authority and produce the strategic plan required by the EU prior to the release of much of the money, with the result that desperately needed funds had had to be sent via less well-audited contingency funds. Too many agencies had become involved, with UNHCR and a number of international NGOs working alongside first one, then two Greek ministries as well as the Greek army and police, with no clear chain of command. The result was buck-passing from one agency to another, and nobody taking responsibility for the numerous problems that arose. The failure to monitor how such huge EU sums were being spent, and to hold their recipients to account, was hard to fathom.

The backdrop, of course, was the government-debt crisis which rocked Greece from 2009 and the resentment felt by Greek politicians towards the EU for imposing a bail-out underpinned by strict austerity. That resentment may have influenced how Greece handled the money with which it was entrusted for the refugees.

Some critics say that the mess in Greece was allowed to develop deliberately, in the hope that the resulting suffering would deter future refugees from seeking to enter Europe. Having made so much money available, the EU could claim to have discharged its moral responsibility, while turning a blind eye to the wasting of its funds. Another theory is that some Greek politicians may have intended the dire conditions to serve Greek interests, by making it harder for other EU countries to return asylum seekers there under the Dublin Regulations. These regulations require states to return refugees to the first 'safe country' they come to. In 2011, the European Court of Human Rights had excepted Greece from the scope of the regulations, due to the degrading conditions there. In December 2016, however, the European Commission said that European countries could resume returning refused asylum seekers to Greece from mid-March 2017.

18
Sunlight on Snow

On Thursday morning I woke to sunshine so dazzling that I needed dark glasses on my walk to the bus stop at Kamara. The snow remained, but the main roads had been gritted and the buses were running.

When I reached the camp, an Australian volunteer asked me to translate for her as she went from room to room, checking who wanted curtains, which she was making out of spare UN blankets. At one point I went downstairs to fetch a tape measure. As I came back up, a strangely familiar face appeared above me, framed by a pale blue headscarf.

'Yasmin!' I cried out. She was the person I'd most wanted to see when I was planning my return trip to Greece, but Charly had thought she was already in Germany. 'How come you're here?' I ran up the last few steps and embraced her.

'T'reza! How come *you*'re here? Shvan's still using the spectacles you got him . . . We talk about you often. Come and visit us, we'd all love to hear your news! Room 566.'

When I knocked on Yasmin's door an hour later she embraced me again. 'We loved you so much when we met you at Hara! I can't believe you're here with us again . . .'

Warm air enveloped me as I stepped through the door. Despite her six children Yasmin had a small, L-shaped room, much easier to heat than the large ones. Shvan jumped up to greet me while Shiro, who was now a sturdy two-year-old, clung to his mother's legs, regarding me with a look of arch suspicion. I unwound my scarf and asked Shvan why his brother was so dubious about me.

'Don't take it personally,' Shvan laughed. 'He does it with everyone. Even with my dad, when he came to visit us from Germany!'

'Your dad came? From Hamburg?'

'Just for five days. Shiro hadn't seen him since he was six weeks old, so he didn't know who he was.'

'Oh dear! But was it great to see your dad?'

'Of course.' Shvan smiled with a quiet confidence.

'But he's not well,' Yasmin added unhappily. 'He has a rare blood disorder. Really quite unwell.'

'Is he seeing a doctor in Germany?'

'He is, but I wish the Greeks would sort out our papers so we could go and join him.'

'You still don't have papers?' I remembered the suffocatingly hot day in April when Yasmin, Shiro and I had sat in the tiny hire car, trying to Skype the Greek Asylum Service.

'We do, the Family Reunification was granted, but we can't buy our air tickets till *both* the German authorities *and* the Greek ones send our details to the airport; and they're taking forever.'

I shook my head in disgust. 'Bureaucracy, that's what it is. How ridiculous. But I'm thrilled to hear you got your papers.' According to Greek Asylum Service figures, by the beginning of November 2016, only 283 people had been reunited with their families under the Family Reunification procedure; and at least 5,600 refugees were waiting.[1]

After Hara was dismantled, Yasmin and the kids had spent the summer at Lagadikia, a camp run by the military in the countryside outside Thessaloniki. It was good there, Shvan said, and he'd made a lot of friends. 'He still goes there now,' Yasmin added, 'on the bus, to visit.'

As we talked, I realized that this was a different Shvan from the tongue-tied adolescent I'd driven to the optician's in April. Still only fifteen, Shvan was now a young man. I'd noticed back then how much Yasmin relied on him, asking his opinion when she had to make a decision and glancing at him whenever something worried her.

'Were you in a tent in Lagadikia?' I asked as Yasmin set out cups for coffee.

'All summer we were in a tent. It was bigger than the one we had at Hara, but still . . . When the weather got colder, the camp authorities kept saying they were going to bring "boxes", but they didn't.'

'Did it snow while you were there?'

Yasmin nodded. 'And we all got sick. We were sleeping on the ground, with just a blanket under us . . .'

'But right after the snow melted, we came here,' Shvan added. 'And now the whole of Lagadikia is boxes.'

'Boxes?'

'Like shipping containers, but with heating.'

Yasmin poured coffee into my cup. 'D'you want to go there?' she asked. 'It's only an hour on the bus. Shvan can take you.'

The following day Shvan and I sat side by side on a half-empty bus, looking out through filthy windows at snow-bound fields. Shvan was shy at first, answering my questions but not initiating conversation. When I asked him how he saw the future, once the family were established in Germany, he said he'd like to study medicine or possibly engineering.

'I can see you becoming a doctor,' I responded. I'd been struck by the way he handled little Shiro the day before, picking him up and talking to him with tenderness.

'But first I have to learn German,' Shvan replied. 'And finish school!'

We passed a frozen lake, where snow lay in swirls on top of the ice. After an hour the bus dropped us in a village, in a street with several bars. The way to the camp lay down a snow-bound lane lined with short squat trees. Dry orange leaves shaped like stars clung to the lower branches.

There was no security at the entrance to the camp and the main artery was almost deserted. Here the snow was packed down hard. Shvan pointed out communal washing areas, a kitchen and several ranks of toilets and showers, stopping briefly to greet the very few people who were out and about. Behind the facilities, neat rows of white metal containers filled an area the size of a commercial campsite, their doors and windows tightly closed. Alleyways had been left between the rows, and tall pine trees marked the perimeter of the site.

Shvan turned to me. 'Before, when we were here, it was tents, just rows and rows of tents.'

I nodded. 'But where is everyone?' There were about 700 refugees at Lagadikia.

'Inside. It's too cold to come out!' He led me down an alley and knocked on a door. 'This is where my friend Jalal lives.'

The door was opened by a short young man with thick, spiky hair. 'Shvan!' he cried, beaming at us both. 'Come on in!' Shvan explained who I was and a moment later we were seated on a divan in a tiny room. Here Jalal introduced me to his friend Serwan, who had a ginger beard and was equally welcoming. The pair were Syrian Kurds and had spent some time at Hara.

It was so warm in the room that I took off my gloves and loosened my scarf. A third man, tall and slim, stuck his head round the door to greet us.

Jalal seemed thrilled to have a foreign visitor. 'Tea, Teresa?' he asked with a mischievous smile, bending down to plug in an electric kettle.

'This is wonderful!' I exclaimed. 'So warm! Yes please.'

'Oh we're very happy in our box, very happy!' Jalal replied. His eyes sparkled as he spoke.

'How many of you?' I noticed with astonishment that there was mesh on the inside of the window, and above it a Venetian blind.

'Four. Two in here, two across the passage.' He gestured towards the door.

'And you have a kitchen?'

'*Yani*, we have a sink, and a kettle. For our food they provide us with ready meals in boxes. And for the bathroom, we must walk to the communal area.' He lined up four plastic cups on the floor at his feet. 'Except that the pipes are frozen, so the toilets and the showers are out of use . . . But, hey, it's better than a tent! Ha! We're lucky people!' He grinned at me and turned to Shvan. 'How are things? How's your mum? Little Shiro?'

While Shvan was giving Jalal the family's news, I asked Serwan how long they were expecting to be at Lagadikia.

'We've no idea,' he replied. 'We've not even had our first interview. None of us have family in Europe, so it's Relocation or nothing.'

'Do you mind where you go?'

'I'll accept any European country they offer me!' He looked anxious. 'We're all worried they'll send us back to Turkey.'

'That's not likely, is it?'

'Who knows, who knows? We've been sitting here month after month, not knowing what the hell's going on. We're very worried.'

I was aware that the Relocation scheme had largely failed, not due to any fault of the overloaded Greek Asylum Service, but because the majority of the states which had agreed to participate had failed to deliver. Greece could only relocate eligible people when the receiving countries indicated readiness to take them. One hundred and sixty thousand places had been pledged by European states in September 2015, for the relocation of refugees from Greece and Italy, but by early February 2017, only 5 per cent of that number would be delivered.[2] By the end of the month, Finland and Malta alone would take the numbers they'd pledged to take.[3] Participating states were supposed to process requests for places on the scheme within ten days, but in practice it was taking up to six months.[4]

From the men's worry about their future, the conversation moved on to the plight of the Syrian Kurds, and the war which the PYD was now fighting on three fronts, against ISIS, the regime and Turkey. As we stood up to leave, I glanced at what I'd thought was a rumpled blanket on the second divan. 'Latif,' Jalal said with a grin. 'He'll be sorry he missed you.' Looking again, I made out the shape of a head, a long back, and a pair of legs under a grey UN blanket.

We parted firm friends, promising to stay in touch. Shvan and I walked slowly back to the village. After we'd spent half an hour on the bus, our bus driver pulled into a lay-by and switched off the engine. We watched as he got out, screwdriver in hand, and walked to the back of the vehicle. Here he opened a panel and poked about inside grunting with annoyance. Happily the repair was successful, for twenty minutes later the bus dropped us at the entrance to the camp, where a brilliant sun bounced off the snow, filling the surrounding slopes with light.

Hungry now, we climbed the filthy marble stairs to Yasmin's room. She'd made me promise to eat with her, and now she produced the best meal I'd had in weeks: potatoes, chunks of chicken breast, aubergine, carrot, onion and garlic, cooked in a single pot under a thick layer of rice.

I spent an hour cleaning out the volunteers' toilets. Then I scoured my hands with anti-bacterial gel and went to knock on the door of room 519, hoping to catch Shireen. A small girl opened it a few centimetres, turned round and called for her mother.

A moment later I heard Shireen's voice calling me in, so I stepped through the door and removed my boots. It was a bright, spacious room and pleasantly warm. Three small children played on the floor, but my eye fell immediately on Om Abdullah, who lay on a tall metal bedstead set against a wall. She was gazing at the ceiling with a duvet tucked up under her chin, and her cheekbones were as sharp and fine as ever.

As I approached the bed, Shireen reminded Om Abdullah that I'd been at Hara. The old lady turned her pale blue eyes in my direction. I thought she looked remarkably good, but Shireen explained that a couple of hours ago they'd thought of calling an ambulance because Om Abdullah wasn't feeling well.

'I'm a bit better now!' The old lady piped up, in a thin but feisty voice. 'The doctor gave me two pills, and they're helping.'

I told her how clearly I remembered her from Hara, and how pleased I was to see her. Then Shireen called me to the table, where she was spooning sugar into glasses. Her husband, Abdullah, sat a few feet away on the edge of a bed. He had a lined, thoughtful face and his hair was flecked with white. We reminisced about Hara while Shireen served the tea, and then I asked about their situation.

'Our sixteen-year-old's in Germany,' Abdullah replied. 'He made it there by himself, so we're entitled to Family Reunification.' He wrapped his fingers round his tea glass. 'We're just waiting for our papers to come through. In a couple more months, we'll be off!'

'That's brilliant.' Perhaps not so great for the old lady, I mused, but they could hardly leave her here.

I told them about my trip to Lagadikia, and how warm it had been in the boxes.

'You should go to Softex,' Abdullah replied. 'Then you'll really see how bad it's been for some people.'

Softex camp, which took its name from the disused toilet paper factory where it was based, was notorious. 'I'd like to go,' I replied, 'but will they let me in?'

Abdullah stood up. 'I'll ask my neighbour to go with you. He was there for eight months; his youngest child was born there.' He placed his glass on the table and looked at me hard. 'You'll be shocked by what you see there. It's grim.'

Every day the marble stairs grew more filthy, and each time I went up or down I swore I would fetch a broom and sweep them, but the moment never came. The sun was out today and I stood at the huge metal window in the corridor, enjoying the light on the snow-covered outskirts of the city and thinking how sunlight could make even an industrial wasteland look interesting. Behind me, small children charged about, desperate for exercise and a change from the confinement of their rooms. I was waiting for Abdullah's neighbour, who'd agreed to accompany me to Softex.

Tarek was a big, reserved man in his thirties, the father of three children. As we waited at the bus stop, he told me that conditions at Softex had got a lot better recently: what I'd see today would be nothing compared to how it had been before he left, in December.

After a long ride across the centre of Thessaloniki, the bus dropped us in a desolate area of squalid single-storey housing, barking dogs, chicken runs and sheds. A ribbon of litter decorated the side of the road, interspersed with odd abandoned shoes. As we approached the camp on a narrow lane, Tarek pointed out an oil refinery and several industrial chimneys belching out clouds of toxic-looking smoke. A month earlier, he said, Softex's 1,900 residents had been in tents, mostly on the waste ground beside the chimneys. Last summer, when his wife had come out of hospital after delivering their baby daughter by caesarian, she'd had to walk for half an hour across the waste ground, to reach the toilet.

In December, after the first snow, more than a thousand Softex residents had been moved to indoor accommodation in other parts of Greece. The remaining 700 were given 'caravanettes'.

To avoid security we entered the camp through an open panel in a wire fence, emerging in a gravel yard where patches of snow and grey puddles separated two rows of ancient-looking mobile homes.

Tarek's eyes darted up and down the yard. 'Take photos, if you want, I can't see any guards.' The caravenettes were old, he said, and many had been delivered without doors, but doors had since been provided. A grizzled-looking man in his fifties called to Tarek as we walked past, inviting us to join him on a verandah he'd constructed beside his caravan-ette out of scaffolding and plastic sheeting. Tarek introduced me and I was ushered to an upturned box beside a home-made chimenea, on which the man was burning scrap wood. Several younger men milled about, smoking cigarettes and warming their hands on the fire.

'This is a great little stove,' I remarked. The smoke was channelled into a tumble dryer exhaust, but half of it blew back into the enclosed verandah area.

Tarek explained to his friend that I was a writer, and had come to Softex to see the conditions there.

'Great!' the man cried. 'Write about it all, every detail! And take photos! We want the world to know how we're forced to live, here in Europe.' So I took out my phone and snapped away, capturing the washing hanging on the fence opposite, the two-foot-high pile of mud in the middle of the yard a short distance from the verandah and the dangerous stove. The place reminded me of refugee camps I'd visited in Gaza in the 1980s.

When I sat down, Tarek's friend told me he and his family were still waiting for their first interview with the Greek Asylum Service, after nearly a year in Greece. Relocation was their only option, as they had no relatives in Europe. He'd complained about the delay, but been given no explanation. As he spoke he became very angry, railing against European governments for condemning Syrians to more suffering, and in the coldest winter for forty years. 'We've been through horrors in Syria,' the man exclaimed. 'Then we risked our lives on the sea to get to Europe; we didn't think when we got here we'd be treated like this!'

I felt moved to apologize, explaining that I was ashamed of my government, who had flatly refused to participate in the Relocation scheme.

The man grunted politely and offered me a cigarette. 'The worst problem we've had in this place', he went on, 'is the fighting. Every night, *every single* night – until recently – the young guys used to fight each other, in groups.' He rested his elbows on his knees and leaned towards me. 'Not the Syrians,' he hastened to add, 'and not men with families. The worst were the young Algerians. They used to bring cannabis into the camp, smoke and then go round having fights and harassing women.' Before the size of the camp had been reduced, he said, things were so bad that many parents had been afraid to send their daughters to the camp school, for fear of what might happen to them.

I'd heard about this from Yasmin. She'd mentioned a lone Kurdish woman she knew, who'd been terrified, alone in her tent night after night, in case men came in and molested her.

But I'd also heard that security at Softex was strict. 'Don't the police intervene?' I enquired.

The man sucked his teeth. 'The police', he said in a tone of disgust, 'used to cross their arms and watch, or go inside their caravan and shut the door. Nobody was ever arrested.'

Now it was my turn to get angry. 'But *why not?*' I thought out loud. Why did Greece want people who behave like that on the loose?

The man raised his eyebrows and his hands in a gesture of incomprehension and despair.

Tarek had wandered off to visit friends. Now he came back and put his head under the plastic awning. So I said my good-byes, wished the man luck and promised to write about what he'd told me. We walked away past a line of outdoor wash basins and portaloos to a vast concrete warehouse, open at the sides.

'This is the old factory,' Tarek explained as I followed him in.

Much of the floor space was occupied by grey-green tents and I felt as if we'd entered Hades. Everything, even the light, was grey-green, the colour of mould. It would be impossible, I thought, to spend more than a couple of nights in that space without becoming depressed. Soon we bumped into another friend of Tarek's, a lean good-looking man called Mounif, who wore a bulky jacket over his sagging black trousers. He had a neat, stylish beard and a smile so warm that the gloom seemed to clear instantly. Mounif and Tarek embraced, I was introduced and we were invited to drink coffee. We followed Mounif under a blanket suspended from a washing line to his family's tent, where he gestured to us to sit on plastic chairs. A moment later he produced a jar of Nescafe, a jar of sugar, some cups and a camping gas stove. As we were spooning the coffee into the cups, a slim young woman in a black robe carrying a little boy appeared from another tent and Mounif introduced her as his wife. The child, she told me, had been born just three days after they arrived in Samos, by dinghy, from Turkey.

Mounif butted in. 'Imagine, if he'd come while we were still at sea! But thank God, he didn't.' He seized his son from his wife, kissed him on the cheek and jiggled him up and down, making the boy giggle.

'He was born by caesarian,' the mother went on.

'In a hospital in Samos?' I asked. 'What was it like?'

'The hospital was very good, the Greek staff were lovely.'

'Did they speak Arabic?'

'No, and there was no translator, but we managed!'

For the fiftieth time that week I doffed an imaginary hat to the extraordinary resilience of the Syrian woman.

On the morning of my last day in Thessaloniki I made it to the camp in time for the Arabic class. I found Rima standing by the whiteboard with her shoulders hunched and her arms wrapped tightly round her torso. One of the kids was ill, she said, chesty, waiting to see the doctor.

After the class she insisted that I go to her room again for tea. 'You have to see my handiwork! I stayed up till four a.m. cleaning and tidying, the chaos was getting me down.'

Other volunteers had told me that many of the refugees were in the habit of staying up very late. Personally, I found it unfathomable why anyone would want to stay up late in a cold building on long, dark winter nights; but the nocturnal regime was a pattern which had been established from the days at Hara and Idomeni and it was now entrenched.

As I followed Rima through her doorway, I saw the children's clothes and bedding stowed neatly against the walls and a new knitted patchwork blanket spread on the floor. One wall was filled with drawings and artwork and sun was streaming through the windows.

'Bravo!' I cried, 'it looks great!' Haitham, Zain and Yasser were climbing up the frame of the bunks under the window, looking out at the thawing snow.

'Sit down, Teresa, make yourself at home!' Rima stooped to fold a blanket. 'These kids! The moment I get the room tidy, they mess it up again!'

As she spoke, Haitham, who was standing on the windowsill, began to cough with a rasping, ugly sound.

'See?' Rima turned to me. 'Doesn't he sound terrible?'

He did. I asked how old he was.

Rima had the kettle in her hand and was filling glasses with hot water. 'He must be three. Next month it'll be a year since we arrived in Greece, and he was two then.' She looked at me wearily. 'I'm losing track of time.'

Behind her, Zain punched Yasser on the top bunk and Yasser retaliated. Haitham had stopped coughing and lay flopped across the pillow. I watched Rima's face as she settled down beside me on the mattress. 'Sometimes I feel *so-o* tired,' she confided.

'I'm not surprised! Look at what you're coping with!' Although I barely knew Rima, I felt as if she were an old friend. 'You're doing an amazing job, I added.'

'Do you know,' she went on, 'I've lost twelve kilos since we left Damascus. And I feel at least ten years older than I am.' She gazed at me uneasily, as if waiting for me to confirm her doubts about herself.

'That's because of everything you've been through! Give it a year or two in Sweden and you'll feel young again.' I hoped I was right. Privately I feared that a lot of the refugees would experience intense disappointment when they finally reached northern Europe. 'How old are you, Rima?'

'Thirty-six. I look a lot more, don't I?'

'No you don't, you look fantastic! I thought you were thirty-two.'

'See how I used to look, before the war.' She picked up her phone and scrolled through photos. 'Look, this is me, in Damascus in 2010.' The photo showed a well-dressed and carefully made-up woman in a pale grey headscarf, surrounded by small children. The face was much fuller than the one I'd taken such a liking to; if I hadn't known, I would never have guessed it was Rima.

'But you're *more* beautiful now, not less!' I insisted.

She shot me a grateful look. 'Really?'

As we drank our tea, she showed me other photos from her previous life: her parents at a party, the weddings of her sisters, her cousins eating in a restaurant, their husbands, their babies.

It was time for breakfast. Rima got to her feet, cut open a black bin liner to make a tablecloth and spread it on the floor, sending Betoul and her sisters to the kitchen with a frying pan, tomatoes and a box of eggs.

Meanwhile, on the top bunk Zain had won the fight, leaving Yasser whimpering beside Haitham. Rima paid them no attention, and after a few minutes Zain threw himself off the bunk, landed with a thud, rummaged for his notebook and settled beside me on the mattress. Soon he was drawing a grid for noughts and crosses.

Epilogue:
And the War Goes On

After its success in driving the rebels out of eastern Aleppo in December 2016, Russia announced that its military goals in Syria had been largely accomplished. From now on, Russia would play the role of mediator between the remaining warring factions. To this end, in January 2017, Putin initiated a series of meetings in Astana, Kazakhstan, hosted jointly with Turkey and Iran. Initially the US was excluded from the talks, and some observers saw them as a calculated attempt to steal the initiative from the UN-led Geneva process. One of Russia's goals has been the establishment of so-called de-escalation or deconfliction zones in certain areas of Syria, primarily Idlib, Homs, the eastern Ghouta, Latakia, Aleppo and Hama.

Shortly after his arrival in the White House, in April 2017 Donald Trump surprised the world by launching a missile attack on al-Shayrat airbase near Homs. This was presented as his response to convincing evidence that the regime had killed ninety-two civilians, including thirty children and babies, in the village of Khan Sheikhoun by the use of a nerve agent.[1] Trump, the isolationist who had previously opposed US intervention in Syria and boasted of his admiration for Putin, went on television to protest against the murder of 'beautiful babies' by the regime.

The intervention was popular among Syrian refugees, who had long been angered by US and European inaction. During a brief moment of optimism, some wondered whether Trump would turn out to be the western leader who would confront Bashar al-Assad and his supporters. But, five months later, in September 2017, there is little to suggest that Trump has a clear policy on Syria. Broadly speaking, his administration has followed Obama's approach, prioritizing the elimination of ISIS and doing little to help the Syrian opposition, much less the beleaguered Syrian people, most of whom remain banned from entering the US as refugees. Despite occasional claims by administration spokespersons that regime change is a US goal, in practice US strategy is based on the proposition that while ISIS remains a threat, Bashar al-Assad must remain in power.

There have been moments when the US-led campaign against ISIS has risked escalating into a full-scale confrontation with Russia and Iran, notably after the US shot down a Syrian warplane in June, shortly after destroying an Iranian-built armed drone. Despite this, the battle against ISIS progressed throughout the summer of 2017, with their defeat in Mosul in July, near defeat in Deir Ezzor in September and substantial progress made against them in Raqqa. Many civilians as well as combatants lost their lives in the course of the operations against ISIS, and many surviving civilians became refugees. In Mosul, 900,000 former residents fled the city, while in Raqqa governorate 190,000 had been displaced by early July.[2]

While the western world's attention was focused on the gradual defeat of ISIS in Iraq and Syria, Syrian opposition forces were undergoing realignment.

In January 2017 Jabhat Fateh al-Sham (formerly Nusra) merged with four smaller groups, this time under the title Hayat Tahrir ash-Sham (HTS) (Movement for the Freedom of Syria). After inflicting some startling damage on the regime in Homs in February and destroying the slightly more moderate opposition militia Ahrar al-Sham, HTS concentrated its efforts around Idlib. With a force of around 30,000 experienced fighters, and linked to al-Qaeda, HTS is now the most powerful opposition formation after ISIS. Once the latter is defeated, HTS will fully dominate the opposition. Given its jihadist ideology and al-Qaeda connection, it seems possible that both Russia and the US will turn on HTS once the task of destroying ISIS has been accomplished.

Major uncertainty hangs over the fate of the Syrian Kurds. Will the US abandon its erstwhile Kurdish allies, once it no longer requires their services to combat ISIS, for the sake of improved relations with Turkey? If it does, there is a real danger that Turkey will invade north-eastern Syria, rather than tolerate the continued existence of an autonomous Kurdish entity on its southern border.

Syrian and Iraqi refugees continue to arrive on the Greek islands. Less than 1,000 per month arrived in the first few months of 2017, but in August the number rose to 3,700, possibly due to people fleeing from the newly liberated areas formerly held by ISIS.[3] Conditions in the camps remain very difficult, particularly on the islands, where overcrowding is a serious problem. There are reports of sexual and physical assaults on children and young women in the camps, most commonly unaccompanied minors; there are incidents of self-harm and fights between different groups. Some of the big NGOs have pulled out, leaving the refugees dependent on the support provided by the smaller volunteer-run groups. Many school-age children living in camps on the islands still don't go to school, despite Greek law requiring their attendance.

When I left Greece in January 2017, Rima was expecting to join her husband in Sweden within a few months. Saying goodbye, I told her that if she was still there in April, I would try to come and visit. But when April came around I was starting a new job and wasn't free to travel, so I sent an apologetic WhatsApp message. A few hectic weeks went by and then, one evening in July, I called her, feeling pretty sure that by now the family would be reunited.

'How are you T'reza?' Rima's voice was even huskier than I remembered, and faint, as if she'd just woken up. 'What's your news? How's your son?'

'We're fine,' I replied. 'How are *you*? Did I wake you?'

'No, no, I'm sitting here with the kids.' I realized now that what I was hearing wasn't a sleepy voice: it was a tone of deep exhaustion.

'In Sweden?'

'No, no, we're still in Greece!'

'What, after all this time?'

'They closed the camp, and put us in a little house, on the outskirts of Thessaloniki.'

I struggled to take this in. 'But why? It was a good camp!'

The weary voice came again, every word an effort. 'Nobody told us why. Just, we had to go.'

'And in the new place, are you with other refugee families?'

I heard Rima sigh. 'Everyone got a place to live, but we're all spread out.' Rima explained that she knew nobody in the local area, and felt completely isolated. Life had been better in the camp, where she'd had Syrian neighbours, a supply of free food and access to a doctor. Now she was obliged to fend for herself and without a source of income. I asked what was happening about Sweden.

'I really don't know. Every time I ask the lawyer, he tells me to wait.'

'Still? It's been so long!'

'Yes, he says we still have to wait. Last time I saw him, he said it could be as much as ten months till our papers come through.'

I was horrified. 'But you've been in Greece for ages. What's gone wrong?'

'We've been here one year and a half. Sweden is very slow now processing cases.'

I wished there was something I could do to help. 'Are you okay? How're you coping?'

There was a second's silence. Then the husky voice again: 'I'm tired, T'reza, I'm very, very tired.'

September 2017

Acknowledgements

I would like to thank the following people for the support I have received in the writing of this book:

A great many Syrians, whom I cannot name for security reasons; and Sintra Burgess, Alice Doherty, Leo Hollis, Claudia Lank, Rachel Lathan, John McHugo, Ian Morse, Lara Pawson, Christopher Phillips, Chris Pilditch, Karen Raney, Gabriel Reiser Craven, John Saddler, Leila al-Shami, Alan Thornhill, Marina van Vessem, Charly Vestli, Rosie Warren, Sarah Westcott, Philip Walker, Robin Yassin-Kassab and Samar Yazbek.

The names of most of the Syrians referred to in this book have been changed, in order to protect their privacy and security. In some cases other identifying details have also been changed. Place names and personal names have been transliterated in accordance with accepted rules.

Readers who wish to learn more about the conflict might want to read *Burning Country: Syrians in Revolution and War* by Robin Yassin-Kassab and Leila al-Shami, *A Woman in the Crossfire: Diaries of the Syrian Revolution* by Samar Yazbek, and *The Battle for Syria: International Rivalry in the New Middle East* by Christopher Phillips.

Notes

Chapter 2   'We didn't risk our lives for this'

1   The PKK was designated a 'Foreign Terrorist Organization' by the US in 1997.

2   PYD is the acronym for the Democratic Union Party, the most radical of the various Syrian Kurdish political parties and the one which pursues a separatist agenda. It has a highly organized armed wing and its ethos and modus operandi are very similar to those of the PKK; some say it is an offshoot of the PKK in all but name. Today the PKK and PYD are engaged in delivering the most effective military opposition to ISIS in northern and north-eastern Syria, with the support of air power from the US, France and the UK. This alliance is one of the many ironies of the current situation.

3   Robin Yassin-Kassab and Leila al-Shami, *Burning Country: Syrians in Revolution and War*, London: Pluto Press, 2016, p. 38.

4   Ibid., p. 49.

5   Human Rights Watch, 'Syria: Rampant Torture of Protesters', 15 April 2011.

6   *Burning Country*, p. 49.

7   See for example Samar Yazbek's *A Woman in the Crossfire: Diaries of the Syrian Revolution* (Haus Publishing, 2012), in which she documents her own and other people's experiences in detention.

Chapter 3   The Assad Dynasty

1 The Sunnis are numerically the largest sect within Islam, the Shi'a constituting between 10 and 15 per cent. Of the countries close to Syria, those which have sizeable Shi'a Muslim populations are Lebanon and Iraq, which are both Arab states (although Iraq has a large population of Kurds), and Iran, which is not Arab and is made up of a number of different ethnic groups.

2 The split within Islam between the Sunnis and the Shi'a dates back to a seventh-century dispute as to how the leadership of the faith should be decided following the death of the Prophet Mohammed. The Shi'a wanted the leadership to go to those with family ties to the Prophet, whereas the Sunnis said the elders of the community should make the choice.

3 Syria: International Religious Freedom Report 2005. US State Department, available at: state.gov/j/drl/rls/irf/2005/51610.htm. Retrieved 15 September 2015.

4 Lebanon achieved independence from France in 1943; Iraq achieved independence from Britain in 1932, Jordan in 1946 and Egypt in 1953.

5 Sayyid Qutb was a leading member of the Egyptian branch of the radical Islamic group the Muslim Brotherhood. He was executed by Nasser in the 1960s.

6 John McHugo, *Syria: A Recent History*, Saqi Books, 2015, p. 207.

7 Ibid., pp. 216–17.

Chapter 5   A Young Helper

1 Syrian refugees in Turkey were eventually given the right to work, in January 2016.

2 *Burning Country*, p. 58.

3 Amnesty International, 'It Breaks the Human: Torture, Disease and Death in Syria's Prisons', London: Amnesty International, 2016. The report states that 17,723 died in Syria's prisons between March 2011 and August 2016.

4 Salafism is a highly puritanical school within Sunni Islam which was developed in Saudi Arabia.

5 Jonathan Littell, *Syrian Notebooks: Inside the Homs Uprising*, Verso Books, 2015, p. 7.

6 Phil Sands, Justin Vela and Suha Maayeh, 'Assad Regime Set Free Extremists from Prison to Fire up Trouble during Peaceful Uprising', *The*

National, 21 January 2014; *Syrian Notebooks*, p. 7; and Christopher Phillips, *The Battle for Syria: International Rivalry in the New Middle East*, Yale University Press, 2016, pp. 131, 200.

7 Sands et al., 'Assad Regime Set Free Extremists'.

8 *The Battle for Syria*, p. 131.

9 Emile Hokayem, *Syria's Uprising and the Fracturing of the Levant*, Routledge, 2013, p. 69.

Chapter 6   Children's Corner and a Smuggler

1 In Turkey, many school-age boys were obliged to work illegally to support their families.

Chapter 7   A Burning Summer

1 In October 2011, those Syrian Kurds who were not supporters of the allegedly PKK-affiliated PYD formed the Kurdish National Council (KNC), which later refused to join the SNC, partly because it was hosted by and had close relations with Turkey. The PYD, for its part, could not join the SNC because Turkey would not allow it to; but at this stage, in any event, the PYD was regarded with suspicion by most of the opposition, who thought that Assad's decision to withdraw his troops from some Kurdish areas in July 2012 indicated that he had a secret alliance with the PYD – something the PYD hotly denied.

2 *Syria's Uprising*, p. 81.

3 This issue is dealt with movingly by Yassin-Kassab and al-Shami in the inspiring account of the revolution from the perspective of activists on the ground, *Burning Country*.

4 *Syria's Uprising*, pp. 86–7.

5 The PKK are very big in Diyarbakir and the city's Kurdish population are constantly subjected to surveillance by the Turkish security services.

Chapter 8   Turkey, Saudi Arabia, Qatar and Iran

1 Jason Burke, *The New Threat from Islamic Militancy*, Bodley Head, 2015, p. 71.

2 *The Battle for Syria*, p. 31.

3 Ibid., p. 137.

4 *Syria's Uprising*, p. 125.
5 *The Battle for Syria*, pp. 143–4.

Chapter 9   'Here, have my boots!'

1 The World Food Programme is the UN agency tasked with feeding people in emergencies.

Chapter 10   Rice Pudding

1 *The Battle for Syria*, pp. 63–4.
2 Ibid., p. 76.
3 Ibid., p. 78.
4 Ibid., p. 95.
5 Ibid., pp. 95–6.
6 Ibid., p. 81.
7 Ibid., p. 91.
8 'Arabization' was a series of policies implemented by the Assad dynasty with the aim of diminishing any sense of national identity on the part of the Syrian Kurds.

Chapter 11   'Why won't the UK let us in?'

1 *The Battle for Syria*, p. 131.
2 *Burning Country*, p. 109.
3 Ibid., p. 192.
4 See ibid., pp. 123–4.
5 Nusra was renamed in July 2016 as Jabhat Fateh al-Sham (Front for the Conquest of Syria). In January 2017 it merged with other militias to form Tahrir al-Sham.
6 The Paris attacks in which 130 died took place on 13 November 2015. The Brussels attacks in which thirty-five died occurred on 22 March 2016. ISIS claimed responsibility for both attacks.
7 By late 2016, ISIS required women to cover their eyes too, using a film of black cloth that covers the entire head.
8 *Burning Country*, p. 132.
9 Patrick Cockburn, *The Rise of Islamic State: ISIS and the New Sunni Revolution*, Verso Books, 2015, p. 44.

10 Moazzam Begg, 'I was in Guantanamo. Donald Trump can take it from me that torture doesn't work', *Guardian*, 27 January 2017.
11 *The Rise of Islamic State*, p. 11.
12 *Burning Country*, p. 195; *Syrian Notebooks*, pp. 7–8.
13 *The Battle for Syria*, p. 131.
14 *Burning Country*, p. 136.

Chapter 13   Rain and an Encounter with the Greek Secret Service

1 *The Battle for Syria*, p. 185
2 Ibid.
3 Ibid., p. 186.
4 France joined the anti-ISIS coalition a year later, on 27 September 2015.
5 *Burning Country*, p. 196.
6 *The Battle for Syria*, p. 209.
7 Reuters in Idomeni, 'Hundreds hurt in police clashes at Greece–Macedonia border', *Guardian*, 10 April 2016.
8 Ibid.

Chapter 14   Farewell to Hara

1 *The Battle for Syria*, p. 218.
2 Ibid., p. 221.

Chapter 15   Refugees Are Welcome Here

1 Gov.UK, 4 September 2015, gov.uk/government/news/syria-refugees-uk-government-response (accessed on 6 September 2017).
2 This was in addition to the small number of Syrians who made it to the UK independently and succeeded in claiming asylum via the usual channels – approximately 5,000 between 2011 and 2015 (ibid).
3 A sum of £1.12bn between 2012 and 2015 (ibid).

Chapter 16   A Long Walk in the Mountains

1 Stuffed vegetables cooked with meat bones, a Syrian dish.
2 Approximately 400,000 refugees passed through Hungary in 2015. Although few of them sought to remain in Hungary, in August of that year the right-wing government of Viktor Orban erected a four-metre-high razor-wire fence along its southern border. Between January and August 2016, only 18,000 refugees passed through Hungary. Despite that, in August 2016, Orban announced his intention to build a second border fence to run parallel to the first one. This was partly motivated by a fear that the EU–Turkey Agreement of March 2016 would break down, resulting in a new influx of refugees on the Balkan route.

Chapter 17   Freezing to Death on Europe's Doorstep

1 Figure given by the Red Cross to the *Guardian*, quoted in article by Nadia Khomami, 'European countries mistreating refugees in cold weather, says UN', 13 January 2017.
2 Rachel Banning-Lover, 'Greek refugee camps remain dangerous and inadequate, say aid workers', *Guardian*, 10 February 2017.
3 Ibid.
4 Khomami, 'European countries mistreating refugees in cold weather, says UN'.
5 ECHO's full name is the European Civil Protection and Humanitarian Aid Operation. It has a 'global network of field offices' and describes itself as the 'European mechanism for disaster response both inside and outside the EU'. (From ECHO website, 29 March 2017.)
6 Patrick Kingsley, 'Thousands of refugees left in cold, as UN and EU accused of mismanagement', *Guardian*, 22 December 2016.
7 'Concern over spate of deaths in Greek refugee camp', *Al Jazeera*, 30 January 2017; Daniel Howden and Apostolis Fotiadis, 'Where did the money go? How Greece fumbled the refugee crisis', *Guardian*, 9 March 2017.
8 The figure was open to doubt since the Greek authorities, wanting to conceal the weakness of their border control from the EC, refused to discount the considerable numbers of refugees who had left the country with smugglers.
9 In Athens, in the absence of proper provision for their care and support, unaccompanied child refugees were working as prostitutes and drug dealers in a city park.

10 Kingsley, 'Thousands of refugees left in cold, as UN and EU accused of mismanagement'.

11 Banning-Lover, 'Greek refugee camps remain dangerous and inadequate, say aid workers'.

12 Dollar figure calculated by the online media project Refugees Deeply and cited in Daniel Howden and Apostolis Fotiadis, 'Where did the money go? How Greece fumbled the refugee crisis', *Guardian*, 9 March 2017, which is also the source for the propotion of money squandered.

Chapter 18   Sunlight on Snow

1 European website on Integration, 'Living Separately: The challenges of family reunification and resettlement programmes for refugees arriving in Greece' , https://ec.europa.eu/migrant-integration/librarydoc/living-separately-the-challenges-of-family-reunification-and-resettlement-programmes-for-refugees-arriving-in-greece (accessed 7 September 2017).

2 Rachel Banning-Lover, 'Greek refugee camps remain dangerous and inadequate, say aid workers', *Guardian*, 10 February 2017.

3 David Boffey, 'European countries have carried out 8% of promised refugee relocations', *Guardian*, 2 March 2017.

4 Data from the Ministry of Migration website, 7 February 2017, http://asylo.gov.gr/en/wp-content/uploads/2017/02/Press-Release-Relocation-Insights-08-02-2017.pdf.

Epilogue: And the War Goes On

1 'Death by Chemicals: The Syrian Government's Widespread and Systematic use of Chemical Weapons', Human Rights Watch, 1 May 2017.

2 The United Nations High Commissioner for Refugees (UNHCR) collects public donations to help families returning home to Mosul. To donate, search 'UNHCR + Mosul emergency appeal'. UNHCR staff, 'Syrians risk all to flee Raqqa, as new aid route offers hope', UNHCR.org, 11 July 2017.

3 'Refugee Surge on Greek Islands', Deutsche Welle, 16 September 2017, dw.com.